MARRIAGE
AND
FAMILY
AMONG NEGROES

JESSIE BERNARD is Research Professor, Honoris Causa, The Pennsylvania State University. Dr. Bernard, a former vice president of the American Sociological Association, also has been president of the Eastern Sociological Society; Society for Study of Social Problems; and the District Sociological Society. She received her Ph.D. at Washington University. Dr. Bernard is the author of numerous books, some of which are: *American Family Behavior*, *Social Problems at Midcentury*, and *Remarriage*. Her most recent book, *Academic Women*, won The Pennsylvania State University Press award for Best Book, 1965.

MARRIAGE
AND
FAMILY
AMONG NEGROES

JESSIE BERNARD

PRENTICE-HALL, INC.  *Englewood Cliffs, New Jersey*

A SPECTRUM BOOK

© 1966 by
PRENTICE-HALL, INC.,
Englewood Cliffs, New Jersey.

A SPECTRUM BOOK

Current printing (last number):
10 9 8 7 6 5 4 3 2

*Library of Congress
Catalog Card Number 66-16338*

Printed in the United States of America—C
P55905, C55906

The author wishes to thank the following publishers
for permission to reprint their material in this volume:
The Free Press, a division of The Macmillan Company,
for extracts from *Black Bourgeoisie* by E. Franklin
Frazier (copyright © 1957 by The Free Press, a corpo-
ration, a division of the Macmillan Company) and
The Macmillan Company for extracts from *The Negro
in the United States* by E. Franklin Frazier (copyright
© 1949 by The Macmillan Company).

PREFACE

This book is not about race relations, although it will be interesting and may be useful to anyone concerned about them. Negroes and whites are now locked in a vise forged out of a long series of errors and misunderstanding. There is enough blame for everyone, but this book is not on that theme.

This book is about a major segment of our population, a group with a unique history. Perhaps a knowledge of that history will help to give new meaning to the current scene. Our emphasis is on the twenty-odd million citizens who constitute something more than 10 per cent of our population—a segment important enough to deserve study in and of itself, quite apart from its relation to the rest of the population.

Indeed, our deliberate and purposive exclusion of control data on the white population is based on the assumption that such comparisons usually turn out to be studies of the white population with emphasis on Negro or nonwhite data as representing deviance from a white norm.

Many readers, for example, will be surprised to learn that the "typical" (in the sense of *commonest*) type of family among Negroes is one in which both husband and wife are living together in their first marriage.[1] It is surprising only because such families are relatively rarer among Negroes than among whites. The ap-

[1] In 1960, 76.1 per cent of all ever married Negro men fourteen years of age and older were living with their wives; 58.5 per cent, with their first wives. For the women, the corresponding figures were: 61.0 per cent and 48.5 per cent (U.S. Bureau of the Census, *Nonwhite Population by Race* [1960], Table 9, p. 9). Three fifths (61 per cent) of all Negro households in 1960 were headed by a man with his wife present (U.S. Bureau of the Census, *Families* [1960], Table 1, (p. 1). This image is in contrast to the common "image" of the Negro family as one of a woman with a succession of—often clandestine—paramours and a brood of children, each, usually, of a different father. Actually, only 1.3 per cent of all nonwhite families were certainly of this type in 1960; as many as 11.6 per cent or more may have been. The first figure was arrived at by dividing the total number of *single* women heads of families with children under eighteen by the total

proach here is based on the conviction that data on Negro families should not be viewed as deviance from a white norm.

The terms *disorganization, anomie,* and *alienation* are also absent from this book. They have become clichés, almost void of meaning, in part because they have been stretched to mean almost anything. *Alienation,* introduced by Marx to refer to the severing of the worker from his tools, is now used to describe any malaise of modern man. So far as *anomie* is concerned, there does seem to be one period in American history when this term could adequately serve: the tragic Reconstruction Era.[2] This was, indeed, a period of normlessness. Hundreds of thousands of freedmen became, in effect, displaced persons or refugees. There really were no norms; no one seemed really to know what to do.[3] But if the word serves accurately for that period, how can it serve equally well for other times and places when the situation is one of a plethora of too rigid, too unyielding norms? The viewpoint here is that one form of organization succeeds another, some forms last longer than others, and some forms perform more functions than others.

In this connection, it may be added, that in attempting to delineate marriage and family among Negroes it is important to bear in mind how kaleidoscopic the changes have been and still are. These changes are taking place throughout the Western world, and Negro families are reacting to them as other families do. In addition, they react to forces operating on them in a unique and peculiar way.

---

number of families; the second, by dividing the total number of *all* female-headed families with children under eighteen, regardless of marital status of head, by the total number of families (U.S. Bureau of the Census, *Families* [1960], Table 6, p. 55).

[2] It is my personal conviction that the terms *alienation, anomie,* and *lonely crowd* owe their continuing popularity to their alliterative and evocative beauty. *Anomie* has the same sound as Poe's *Annabelle Lee;* and the *lonely crowd* sounds much like Wordsworth's *lonely cloud.* The awkward and unlovely term, *normlessness,* is not nearly so popular as *anomie.*

[3] For example: "People left Augusta in droves. About a thousand would all meet and walk going to hunt work and new homes. Some of them died. I had a sister and brother lost that way. . . . People died in piles. I don't know till yet what was the matter. They said it was the change of living. I have seen five or six wooden, painted coffins piled up on wagons pass by our house. Loads passed every day like you see cotton pass here. Some said it was cholera and some took consumption. Lots of the colored people nearly starved" (B. A. Botkin, *Lay My Burden Down* [Chicago: University of Chicago Press, 1945], pp. 241-42).

The major contribution of the present book may be its greatest defect: the data for most of the chapters are extremely thin. There are serious gaps in our knowledge of marriage and family among Negroes, and it is hoped that—by focusing attention on these gaps—this book will encourage researchers to fill them.

If there are not enough data, it may well be asked, why write the book at all? The answer is that the great classic studies of marriage and family among Negroes in the United States—those by Frazier, Davis, Dollard, Johnson, Warner, Reid, Sutherland, and Drake and Cayton—are now at least a generation old. No one can afford to reject or even to ignore them, but they do not reflect current situations; they do not take account of the second, or self-emancipation. Quite aside from this, the Negro population—or "social generation"—today is different in crucial ways from that of, let us say, the 1930s.[4]

In 1930, for example, about four fifths of all Negro families still lived in the South; in 1960, less than three fifths did. In 1930, about 44 per cent of the Negro population was urban; in 1960, almost three fourths (73.2 per cent) were. In 1930, the average number years of schooling was less than 6; in 1960, it was 7.9. In 1930, 2.5 per cent of Negro workers were in professional occupations; in 1960, about 11 per cent were. In 1930, Negro earnings averaged a third to two fifths those of white workers; in 1960, over half.

The commonest Negro family in 1930 was rural; in 1960, the rural farm family constituted only 6.4 per cent of all Negro families, and 40.5 per cent was now urban. The Negro population of 1960, in brief, was not the same as the Negro population of 1930. It was no longer rural; it had had more years of schooling, jobs, and more income. More to the point, although not revealed in the statistics, it had a new image of itself. These facts seem to justify a new look.

My indebtednesses should be obvious from my citations. First and foremost, of course, is the indebtedness to E. Franklin Frazier, a leading scholar in the sociology of race. He was a fellow graduate student at the University of Chicago in the late 1920s while he was first thinking through many of the ideas that were later embodied

---

[4] See Leonard Broom and Norval Glenn, *Transformation of the Negro American* (New York: Harper & Row, Publishers, 1965).

in his great classic study of the Negro family. They were as exciting then as they are now. The great series sponsored by the American Council on Education has also contributed greatly to the thinking in this book. Hylan Lewis has taught me for many years, both through his research and through personal discussion. Elliot Liebow, field worker for the Child-rearing Project, directed by Hylan Lewis, gave me many insights from his dissertation on "streetcorner" Negro men. Much of the material on out-of-wedlock births came from an unpublished study by the Children's Bureau under the direction of Elizabeth Herzog. The interpretations here presented do not necessarily reflect those of the Children's Bureau. I found B. A. Botkin's anthology of slave memories especially valuable. The contrast between these memories and white reports on the same events was a chastening lesson in historiography. Catherine Chilman, U.S. Department of Health, Education, and Welfare, has been a patient discussant, who always listened appreciatively and tactfully indicated where the defects lay. In addition, Franklin Edwards has always lent me his ear, much to my profit. He also "lent" me the Sociology Club at Howard University, as Sophie McDowell did her sociology students, to serve as informants and subjects for my own studies. My awareness of Herbert Blumer's appreciation has always been supportive. To all these people, my thanks. None, it hardly need be added, is responsible for the book's defects.

This book is dedicated to Negro women, one of the most remarkable phenomena in American history. With a minimum of preparation, against all but insuperable odds, these women have borne the major burden of pulling up the Negro population by its bootstraps. They have been spirited and independent, as well as self-sacrificing. As wives, they have not taken advantage of their—"unnatural"—superiority; as mothers, they have worn out countless washboards earning money to educate their children. They deserve a place alongside the women who pioneered the West with their husbands, for these women have pioneered another frontier—one fraught with no less danger than the West, against odds no less formidable, and, it is hoped, with equal, if delayed, success.

JESSIE BERNARD

CONTENTS

Chapter 1

THE MARRIAGE TRAJECTORY, 1

Introduction, 1
Overview, 1
The Third Phase: Reversal of Trend, 6
The Institutionalization of Marriage among Freedmen and Their
    Children, 9
Third Phase of the Marriage Trajectory: Retreating Husbands
    and Fathers, 13

Chapter 2

THE TWO CULTURES, 27

Introduction, 27
Two Distinctive Styles of Adaptation, 27
The Reshaped Culture, 35
The Culturally White, 41
Cases in Point, 50
The Great Divide, 58

Chapter 3

PEOPLE, 67

Introduction, 67
Women and Men, 67
Mate Selection, 77
Wives and Husbands, 89
Mothers and Fathers, 103

Chapter 4

SOCIALIZATION, 117

Introduction, 117
Circumstantial Socialization: Families and Homes, 118
Masks, Roles, and the Hawthorne Effect, 144

Index, 153

MARRIAGE
AND
FAMILY
AMONG NEGROES

Chapter 1

The Marriage Trajectory

Introduction

The norms of monogamic marriage as institutionalized in our society make two basic demands upon men and women: one, that they shall bear no children until they have made a life-long public commitment to one another and, the other, that they shall support and protect until maturity all children borne in the union. To the extent that men and women conform to these demands—whether through inward conviction or outward pressure—marriage may be said to be institutionalized. Conformity to these norms is, therefore, taken here as an index of the institutionalization of monogamic marriage among Negroes in the United States.

Overview

THREE TRENDS

There was a time when marriage was so uncommon among Negroes that almost every Negro infant in the United States was borne out of wedlock. For few masters encouraged even unofficial marriages among their slaves.[1] Thus most of the children of slaves—and probably a considerable proportion of those of the relatively few free Negroes—were borne out of wedlock.

If or when the relations between the sexes became subject to institutional controls, however, the proportion of infants borne out of wedlock could be expected to decline and, conversely, the proportion of those borne in wedlock could be expected to increase. The proportion of infants borne *in* wedlock can, therefore, be used as a rough measure of the process by which at least the first norm of monogamic marriage became institutionalized among freedmen.[2]

---

[1] Henderson H. Donald, *The Negro Freedman* (New York: Abelard-Schuman, Limited, 1952), p. 56.

[2] Another measure is used as an index of the institutionalization of other aspects of marriage and family relations; see p. 13: the proportion of female-headed families.

It is, of course, a far from perfect index. The most eminent student of marriage and family among Negroes was of the opinion that it is "impossible to draw any conclusions from available statistics concerning either the volume or the trend" of out-of-wedlock births among Negroes.[3] Exact figures for out-of-wedlock Negro births in the early years of freedom do not exist. But if we begin with a rough estimate that by, let us say, 1880, a third of all Negro infants were borne in wedlock, and extrapolate to 1917 (when data for the birth registration area began to include legitimacy status), we get the curve shown in Fig. 1-1 for the proportion of Negro infants borne in wedlock.[4] At least there was a parental relationship permanent enough to convince the registrar that some form of marriage—consensual, perhaps—existed. This curve might be called *the marriage trajectory,* the curve describing the process by which marriage became institutionalized among Negroes in the United States.

There seem to be three phases in this process: a rising phase (up until 1917), an uncertain middle phase (1917-50), and a declining phase (since 1950). In order to magnify the trends, the data from Fig. 1-1 since 1917 are presented on a larger scale in Figs. 1-2 and 1-3. For another perspective, data for the last two and a half decades are shown in Fig. 1-4.

The First Phase: Institutionalization.   The trajectory indicates that the proportion of Negro infants borne in wedlock increased in the latter part of the nineteenth century and the early part of the twentieth. Propulsive forces were at work to institutionalize the unions of men and women, increasing the proportion of infants borne in wedlock. The rate at which institutional controls were imposed on the freedmen and their children, and its fluctuations in different times and places, cannot be traced with any precision.[5] Its general direction was doubtless upward, as shown in

[3] E. Franklin Frazier, *The Negro Family in the United States,* rev. ed. (New York: Holt, Rinehart & Winston, Inc., 1948), p. 8.

[4] Since 1934, all nonwhite births are included; the data refer to nonwhite rather than specifically to Negro births. Nearly all nonwhite data, however, refer to Negroes. The justification for selecting 1880—rather than, let us say, 1865—lies in the unusual situation following the Civil War. To use any year of that period would exaggerate the slant of the first segment of the trajectory. It is conceivable that the proportion of infants borne in some form of stable union was probably as high a decade or two earlier. But in the immediate postwar years there was such an upheaval, such a vast milling about, that perhaps the stability, as well as the informal sanctions, of hundreds of thousands of relationships was destroyed. The proportion *a third* is only a guess. It was reported of Maryland in 1887 that half the Negro births in one county were in-wedlock births (Donald, *op. cit.,* p. 61). The assumption made here is that the proportion in Maryland would be higher than in the Deep South.

[5] Frazier has summarized some of these differences. In some rural areas in the 1930s (Kentucky, Maryland), the proportion of infants borne in wedlock was fairly high (90 per cent and about 85 per cent, respectively); but in others, such as St. Helena Island, it was low (70 per cent). In some counties of North Carolina, 1923-27, the proportion was 92 per cent; in the state as a whole, 83-87 per cent (Frazier, *op. cit.,* p. 90). In the

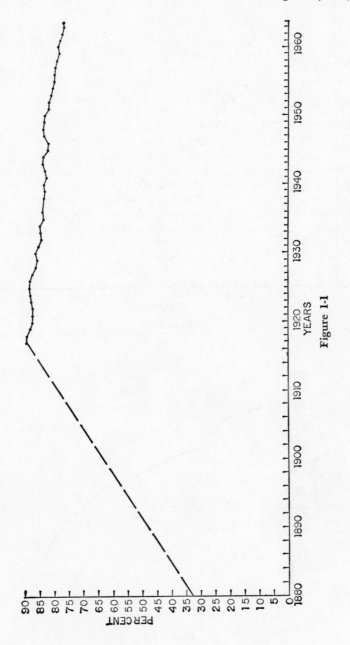

Figure 1-1

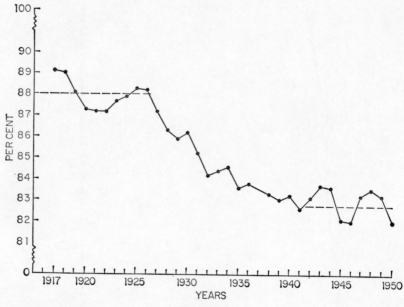

Figure 1-2

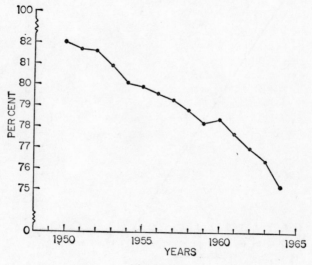

Figure 1-3

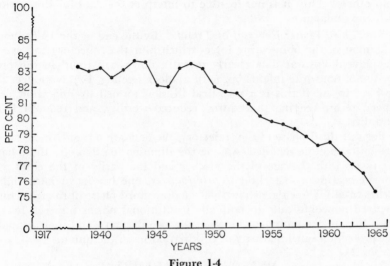

Figure 1-4

Fig. 1-1. Though the diffusion of this change was almost certainly uneven, by the second decade of the twentieth century, marriage had become so widespread among Negroes that the proportion of infants borne in wedlock—or of a stable relationship—rose to about 89 per cent. A host of forces (see pp. 10-13) had succeeded in the task of imposing institutional norms on most Negro unions.

The Second Phase: Reversal of Trend? Artifact? Some time after 1917 the forces toward institutionalization declined, or were counteracted by other trends. The proportion of Negro infants borne in wedlock seemed to decline (with two probable "pause" periods: 1922-26 and 1940-49).

But little is made here of the trend in the 1920s, 1930s, and 1940s. Some of the differences over time undoubtedly resulted from the increased registration of out-of-wedlock births as women from rural areas moved to the cities, where record-keeping was more thorough, and also from improved record-keeping procedures in the rural areas as well. Some of the differences unquestionably resulted from such demographic factors as decreased sterility and declining rates of fetal and neonatal deaths, both of which affected the women most vulnerable to out-of-wedlock births more

District of Columbia, there was an upward trend between 1910 and 1929; then it began to decline, slowly at first and then, after World War II, rapidly. In-wedlock births in Baltimore increased from about 74 per cent to about 80 per cent from the beginning of the century until 1929. In some cities fluctuations were marked; in others, the trends were up until some time in the 1920s or 1930s, and down thereafter.

than others.[6] Thus it is not feasible to interpret the data for this period with any confidence.

The Third Phase: Reversal of Trend. By the end of the 1940s, however, most of the obfuscating forces which blur the trajectory had spent themselves.[7] Postwar data clearly reveal a downward trend in the proportion of nonwhite infants borne in wedlock (see Fig. 1-2). No longer do we have to ask if this is a statistical illusion formed by migration, improved record-keeping procedures, reduced sterility, and reduced fetal mortality.

For this third phase of the trajectory, the data are not only more accurate but also more detailed. Among the illuminating data are those having to do with the age of the mother and the parity of the child. (A woman bearing a first child is *primiparous;* one bearing a later child, *multiparous.*) These data show that the downward phase of the trajectory involved nonconformity to both the institutional norms imposed by society: life-long commitment between the two partners, and their support and protection until maturity of children borne in the union.

YOUNG WOMEN: FIRST BABIES

The "classic" kind of out-of-wedlock birth involves the young unmarried woman who has a first child.[8] Although it is possible for the mother of a first out-of-wedlock child to be a divorcée or a widow, such probabilities are not great. First births out of wedlock, especially to young women, may therefore be taken as indicating nonconformity to the first of the institutional norms: the bearing of children before marriage. The mari-

---

[6] Between a fifth and a fourth of all nonwhite fetal deaths in the 1950s occurred among illegitimate infants (22.5 per cent in 1955; 24.2 per cent in 1959). These figures were slightly higher than the corresponding proportions of live births (18.3 per cent anl 21.8 per cent, respectively) which occurred among illegitimate infants in those years.

[7] In 1940 almost one fourth (24.2 per cent) of all births among the rural half (52.1 per cent) of the nonwhite population escaped registration and it is likely that an even larger proportion of the out-of-wedlock births went unreported. In 1950, this proportion of "hidden" or unreported rural cases was reduced by more than half; by then only 11.3 per cent of the rural (now only) two fifths of the population were not "visible," that is, in the records. The changes in the urban nonwhite population were even more drastic, though relatively less sizable. In 1940, 11.6 per cent missed being recorded; in 1950, only 3.5 per cent (Dorothy D. Tuthill, "Completeness of Birth Registration in Urban and Rural Areas; United States and Each State, December 1, 1939, to March 31, 1940," *Special Report*, Vol. 23, No. 6 (Washington, D.C.: National Office of Vital Statistics, June 30, 1949), p. 102, Table C; and Sam Shapiro and Joseph Schachter, "Birth Registration Completeness in the United States and Geographic Areas, 1950," *Special Report*, Vol. 39, No. 2 (Washington, D.C.: National Office of Vital Statistics, September 1954), Table B, p. 46.

[8] In 1955, about two thirds (65.6 per cent) of white out-of-wedlock births were first births (Joseph Schachter and Mary McCarthy, *Illegitimate Births: United States, 1938-57* (Washington, D.C.: National Office of Vital Statistics, September 30, 1960), Table H.

tal status of older multiparous mothers is less clear-cut; they may have been married at some time or other, although not necessarily to the father of the out-of-wedlock child.

Did the upward trend in the proportion of children borne out of wedlock indicate a growth in promiscuity among the young? It is true that the number of such births to teen-age mothers increased by 79.4 per cent between 1947 and 1962 (see Table 1-1),[9] and that the number of out-of-wedlock first births also increased by 57 per cent (see Table 1-2), but the increases among older women and higher parities were considerably greater.

OLDER WOMEN: LATER BABIES

The increases in the number of out-of-wedlock births between 1947 and 1962 were very great among the older women: 172.3 per cent among those in their early thirties, and 150 per cent among those in their late thirties (see Table 1-1). The increases in parities beyond the first were also

Table 1-1.

**Estimated Number of Nonwhite Out-of-Wedlock Births
by Age of Mother, 1947, 1955, and 1962***

Year	Age of Mother						
	Under 20	20-24	25-29	30-34	35-39	40+	All ages
1947	33,500	20,800	9,000	4,700	2,800	800	71,500
1955	48,300	34,700	18,900	10,700	5,300	1,400	119,200
1962	60,100	44,000	21,800	12,700	7,000	1,800	147,500
Percentage increase, 1947-62	79.4	111.5	142.2	172.3	150.0	125.0	106.3

* *Sources:* Data for 1947 and 1955 are from Joseph Schachter and Mary McCarthy, *Illegitimate Births: United States, 1938-57* (Washington, D.C.: National Office of Vital Statistics, September 30, 1960), Table D. Data for 1962 are from Public Health Service, *Natality Statistics Analysis: United States, 1962* (Washington, D.C.: October 1964), Tables 1-23. The years 1947 and 1955 are used to make the data comparable with parity data, which are also available for those years in Schachter and McCarthy, *op. cit.*

great. Between 1947 and 1962, the total number of out-of-wedlock births increased by 106.3 per cent. But first births increased by only 57 per cent while second and higher-order birth increased by 160.5 per cent. Fifth and higher-parity births increased by 444.6 per cent (see Table 1-2). Fur-

[9] The increase in number among white teen-age girls was 31.1 per cent.

Table 1-2.

Estimated Number of Nonwhite Out-of-Wedlock Births by Parity, 1947, 1955, and 1962*

Year	Parity					
	1	2+	2	3	4	5+
1947	37,200	(34,200)	15,600	7,400	4,100	7,100
1955	49,500	(69,000)	25,000	15,100	10.000	19,500
1962	58,410	(89,000)	27,875	17,405	12,242	31,565
Percentage increase, 1947-62	57.0	(160.5)	78.7	135.1	198.6	444.6

* *Sources:* Data for 1947 and 1955 are from Joseph Schachter and Mary McCarthy, *Illegitimate Births: United States, 1938-57* (Washington, D.C.: National Office of Vital Statistics, September 30, 1960), Table D. Data for 1962 are from Public Health Service, *Natality Statistics Analysis: United States, 1962* (Washington, D.C.: October 1964), Tables 1-23. The years 1947 and 1955 are used to make the data comparable with parity data, which are also available for those years in Schachter and McCarthy, *op. cit.*

thermore, the proportion of all out-of-wedlock births which were first births declined from 52 per cent in 1947 to 39.6 per cent in 1962; conversely, the proportion which were fifth or higher-parity births more than doubled: 9.9 per cent in 1947, 21.1 per cent in 1962 (see Table 1-3).

It appears clear, then, that a great deal more was involved in the down-

Table 1-3.

Parity of Nonwhite Out-of-Wedlock Births, 1947, 1955, 1962*

Year	Percentage Distribution					
	1	2	3	4	5+	
1947	52.0	21.8	10.3	5.7	9.9	100.0
1955	41.5	21.0	12.7	8.4	16.4	100.0
1962	39.6	18.9	11.8	8.3	21.1	100.0

* *Sources:* Data for 1947 and 1955 are from Joseph Schachter and Mary McCarthy, *Illegitimate Births: United States, 1938-57* (Washington, D.C.: National Office of Vital Statistics, September 30, 1960), Table D. Data for 1962 are from Public Health Service, *Natality Statistics Analysis: United States, 1962* (Washington, D.C.: October 1964), p. 50.

ward trend in the marriage trajectory than nonconformity to the first institutional norm resulting in premarital births to young women. Something was apparently happening to the second norm also, resulting in higher-parity births to older women. A new type of family seemed to be emerging, a type which the census labels "female-headed families."

The Institutionalization of Marriage among Freedmen and Their Children

THE MIRROR IMAGE

In 1945, one of the most famous textbooks on marriage and the family was prefaced by this statement:

. . . the family in historical times has been, and at present is, in transition from an institution to a companionship. In the past the important factors unifying the family have been external, formal, and authoritarian, as the law, the mores, public opinion, tradition, the authority of the family head, rigid discipline, and elaborate ritual. At present, in the new emerging form of the companionship family, its unity inheres less and less in community pressures and more and more in such interpersonal relations as the mutual affection, the sympathetic understanding, and the comradeship of its members.[10]

The story of marriage and family relations among Negroes in the United States from emancipation until the 1920s was just the reverse of this trend. During these years, the effect of "external, formal, and authoritarian" (that is, institutional) factors was increasing among Negroes.

"MARRIAGE" UNDER SLAVERY

The idea of marriage was not, of course, completely unknown among slaves. To be sure, some masters had bred slaves as they did livestock, and even some kindly masters insisted on supervising the mating of their slaves.[11] But some masters celebrated slave marriages with a ritual:

All Old Master's niggers was married by the white preacher, but he had a neighbor who would marry his niggers hisself. He would say to the man: "Do you want this woman?" and to the girl, "Do you want this boy?" Then he would call the Old Mistress to fetch the broom, and Old Master would hold one end and Old Mistress the other and tell the boy and girl to jump this broom, and he would say: "That's your wife." They called marrying like that jumping the broom.[12]

And some even solemnized it with a religious ceremony of sorts:

[10] E. W. Burgess and H. J. Locke, Jr., *The Family: From Institution to Companionship* (New York: American Book Company, 1945), p. 7.
[11] B. A. Botkin, *Lay My Burden Down* (Chicago: The University of Chicago Press, 1945), p. 159.
[12] *Ibid.*, p. 65.

When two of the slaves wanted to get married, they'd dress up nice as they could and go up to the big house, and the master would marry them. They'd stand up before him, and he'd read out of a book called *The Discipline* and say, "Thou shalt love the Lord thy God with all thy heart, all thy strength, with all thy might and thy neighbor as thyself." Then he'd say they were man and wife and tell them to live right and be honest and kind to each other.[13]

In no case, however, was a vow of life-long commitment required and, for most slaves, "marriage" was probably a fragile bond that depended on the way the partners felt toward one another. The master's regulations were, in effect, a kind of substitute for institutional regulations. Although he probably could not enforce strict sex codes—and may not have wanted to—he represented a measure of "external, formal, and authoritarian" control which disappeared after emancipation.   .

Accounts of marriage among the freedmen in the first years after emancipation vary. Some observers reported great sexual laxity; others, the reverse. Unions were based on mutual attraction. Love was important, and it was usually faithful—as long as it lasted.[14]

But however satisfactory the "companionship" pattern may have been for the men and women involved, it left children and old people unprotected, and so it was not long before action was taken to change this situation—to make Negro marriage conform as much as possible to the prevailing marriage system.[15]

MARRIAGE AFTER EMANCIPATION

Experience in recent decades with so-called underdeveloped parts of the world has provided vivid lessons on the difficulties involved in attempts to bring about social change. The same difficulties arose after the emancipation of the slaves. After the Civil War, there were hundreds of thousands of freedmen milling about in great uncertainty, many with equivocal family status. The task of imposing order on this fluid, almost undifferentiated mass was an enormous one and necessarily shared by institutional agencies of all kinds.

LEGISLATIVE APPROACHES

One legislative approach involved a simple declaration that existing relationships formed under slavery were to be binding. But this law left many freedmen open to penalties for desertion, bigamy, and adultery, for as slaves they might have had more than one mate. Thus, in many states, the law was changed to legalize marriages dating from the passage of the

[13] *Ibid.*, p. 147.

[14] ". . . among the newly freed Negroes, each party to a marital union was usually satisfied with one partner, and seldom was it heard that the one or the other had a lover on the side" (Donald, *op. cit.*, p. 57).

[15] *Ibid.*, p. 57.

Reconstruction Acts. Georgia legalized relationships existing in March 1866; any former slave who had more than one partner had to select only one of them. In Florida, those living together were given nine months to decide with which partner they wanted to remain. South Carolina gave the freedmen until April 1, 1866, to decide which mate was to be the legal spouse; thereafter the state considered the children of such a union legitimate.

Efforts were made to facilitate the registration of marriages before any state, county, or municipal officer; and failure to comply with the new laws rendered offenders liable to penalties for adultery. But concessions were usually made to common-law marriages.

There was a widespread belief that the freedmen would not take advantage of the right to enter official marriage. And, indeed, why should they? The sanctions provided by law were not often imposed. The whites were so accustomed to polygamous relationships among slaves that they ignored violations of the norms and refused to consider any complaints worthy of investigation.[16] But in many cases the idea of marriage dignified by a minister appealed to the newly freed Negroes, for it implied equality with whites. Official marriage became a status symbol, and weddings became occasions of great gaiety.[17]

MILITARY MEASURES

The military authorities also lent a hand in the great institutionalizing effort. They called attention to cases of men and women who indulged in marital relations without contracting marital obligations, and advised responsible authorities to instruct such persons in their duties, "especially their duty to support and educate their offspring." They informed such men and women that "the laws of God as well as the laws of their country forbade their living together as man and wife without the solemnization of marriage." They insisted that no unnecessary formalities be required, but that all marriages be registered and certificates issued. Unnecessary expenses should be discouraged: fees should be charged but remitted.[18]

THE FREEDMEN'S BUREAU, THE CHURCH, AND THE SCHOOLS

The Freedmen's Bureau contributed to the effort by issuing an order which clarified the rules relating to marriage among Negroes. Ministers and civil officials were authorized to solemnize marriages and to send the certificates to the Bureau. Religious organizations were also given the power to dissolve marriages. The duties of men to "former wives," and to wives and children were clearly outlined.[19]

[16] *Ibid.*, p. 63.
[17] *Ibid.*, pp. 59, 62.
[18] *Ibid.*, p. 58.
[19] *Ibid.*

The contribution of the church to the process of institutionalization was not inconsiderable. Frazier presented the case of one family that helped to establish a church and commented that "the reference to the founding of the church in their old home shows the close relationships between the beginnings of the family on an institutional basis and the building up of the church or the institution which expresses more than any other the autonomous and collective life of the Negroes after emancipation." [20]

Schools, especially those manned by New England missionaries and others trained by them, also lent their weight to the institutionalizing effort, as did the mass media, opened to those whom the schools taught to read.

Thus, the outside world came increasingly to impinge on the Negro world. With the advent of child-welfare programs and public-health activities, all kinds of documentary proofs of relationships came to be required, and the old, casual patterns became anachronistic. People had to prove that they had been borne, had married, had borne children, had died. The intrusive hand of the official recorder appeared even in the backwoods, and once-spontaneous—even impulsive—human interrelationships were forced to take on the stern permanence of a written form.

Demands of this kind, along with the faithful efforts of the churches and the schools, slowly—almost imperceptibly—imposed institutional patterns on the primary-group pattern of marriage among an increasing proportion of Negro men and women. Little by little, the institutional imperative that reproduction was the exclusive function of a duly constituted union began to gain at least overt acceptance, and this was evidenced by the upward thrust of the marriage trajectory.

DIFFERING LEVELS OF CONFORMITY

For some Negroes, conformity to the institutional norms of monogamic marriage was only superficial. Because they lacked the traditional preparation for such a union, the duty-responsibility-commitment complex which constitutes monogamic marriage remained foreign to them. They remained "innocently unconscious . . . that both had entered into a mutual pledge to be faithful to the vows that they had pronounced." [21] Love, affection, jealousy, resentment—all the spontaneous reactions characteristic of primary groups—still dominated the marital relationship. The fact that their union had been solemnized did not always mean that they understood the significance of marriage. To some, official mar-

---

[20] Frazier, *op. cit.*, p. 133. Frazier also noted that "sometimes nothing short of force could get the former slaves to abandon their old promiscuous sexual relations," and he quotes a white woman's account of "old Nat's boy" who refused to marry in the church even when "Old Nat," "Old Ben," and "Uncle Sam" pitched into him. He finally surrendered "and was married before a whole church full of people" (p. 82).

[21] Donald, *op. cit.*, p. 62.

riage implied little more than the slavehood rite of jumping over the broom; certainly, it was not a binding and life-long commitment.

But some Negroes gladly accepted the institutional norms. Many of those who had been freed before the Civil War had already accepted these norms: for them, official marriage was more than a mere status symbol or a mark of respectability; it was a form of self-discipline and, as such, evidence of emancipation. Many freedmen also assimilated the institutional pattern. Indeed, their behavior reflected more than the mere imposition of "external, formal, and authoritarian" controls; it reflected acculturation, inner acceptance.

Whatever the level of conformity, institutionalization progressed to such an extent that the proportion of Negro infants borne in wedlock rose markedly—so markedly, in fact, that such births became the "normal" or "expected" thing. (The fact that a rise in the proportion of illegitimate births should occasion widespread concern is itself a measure of the success of the processes which institutionalized monogamic marriage among freedmen and their offspring.)

Third Phase of the Marriage Trajectory: Retreating Husbands and Fathers

ABSENT HUSBANDS AND FATHERS

The index of institutionalization of marriage used in the marriage trajectory—the proportion of all births that were in-wedlock births—indicates only that there was a father present when the child was born. The institution of marriage in the West, however, demands not only that the father be present at the time of the child's birth but also that he remain committed to the child until maturity, and to its mother "until death do them part." Data pertinent to this index are fragmentary, but they are available for the third phase of the marriage trajectory. This index, like the proportion of infants borne in wedlock, reveals a marked change in marriage and family among Negroes since World War II and especially in the 1950s and 1960s.

FAMILIES AND HOUSEHOLDS HEADED BY WOMEN[22]

Some of the changes in the family structure in the period 1940-60 are summarized in Table 1-4. The increase in the proportion of female-

[22] Some of the census data refer to "households"; some, to "families." *Family* is defined by the U.S. Bureau of the Census as "two or more persons in the same household who are related to each other by blood, marriage, or adoption; all persons living together in one household who are related to each other are regarded as one family." Thus, a household may contain more than a single family, or it many contain none. Some of the census data combine all nonwhite races; some are broken down into separate racial categories. Negro heads of families in 1960 included 95.5 per cent of all

Table 1-4.

Women Heads

Year	As Percentage of All Nonwhite Heads of Households	As Percentage of All Nonwhite Heads of Primary Families*	As Percentage of All Negro Heads of Household	As Percentage of All Negro Heads of Families
1940	22.6	17.8	23.7	—
1960	25.4	20.9	27.1	21.7

* As distinguished from primary individuals in households.

Sources: Data in first two columns are from U.S. Bureau of the Census, *Families* (1960), Table 2, pp. 11, 12; data in third column are from Table 1, pp. 1 and 2; data for fourth column are from U.S. Bureau of the Census, *Nonwhite Population by Race* (1960), Table 14, p. 25.

headed families among nonwhites was especially great in the younger age brackets; the number of female heads of family who were under forty-five increased 85.9 per cent; that of those forty-five and over, 63.1 per cent.[23] Between 1950 and 1960, although there was a great increase in nonwhite female-headed families in cities (see Table 1-5), there was a decline in the number of such families in rural farm areas.

Table 1-5.

Changes in Frequency of Specified Nonwhite Female-Headed Families, 1950–60

Age of Female Heads	Total	Urban	Rural Nonfarm	Rural Farm
Under 35	62	70	47	−57
35-44	54	67	40	−50
45-64	34	43	51	−44
65 and over	34	53	36	−43
Total	46	58	44	−48

Source: John C. Beresford and Alice M. Rivlin, "Characteristics of 'Other' Families." Unpublished paper presented before Population Association of America, April 1963.

The marital statuses of the women who headed these households and families varied. The proportion of those who were widowed declined between 1950 and 1960, reflecting not only a declining death rate for men

---

nonwhite heads of families. For most analyses, *nonwhite* is about the equivalent of Negro, except in the Pacific Coast region.

[23] U.S. Bureau of the Census, *Families* (1960), Table 2, pp. 11, 12.

but also a change in the age composition of the population (see Table 1-6). If the age distribution of the women had been the same in 1960 as in 1950, almost half of the women (instead of only 40 per cent) would have been widowed (see Table 1-6), and the change in proportion of these female heads of families who were single or separated from their husbands would have been considerably smaller, while the change in the proportion of those widowed or divorced would have been greater (Table 1-7).

Table 1-6.

Marital Status, By Age, of Nonwhite Women Heads
of Families, 1950 and 1960

	Percentage Distribution		
Marital Status	*1950*	*1960 (actual)*	*1960 (estimated*)*
Widowed	52	40	49
Divorced	8	12	9
Married, spouse absent	32	37	33
Separated	27	30	28
Other	5	7	5
Single	8	11	9
	100	100	100

* Estimate arrived at by applying 1950 age-specific rates to 1960 data.
Source: John C. Beresford and Alice M. Rivlin, "Characteristics of 'Other' Families." Unpublished paper presented before Population Association of America, April 1963.

Table 1-7.

Changes in Number of Nonwhite Women Heads
of Families in Specified Marital Status, 1950–60

	Percentage Increase	
Marital Status	*1950-60 (actual)*	*1950-60 (estimated*)*
Widowed	15	40
Divorced	52	55
Separated	70	58
Spouse absent	100	52
Single	92	61

* Estimate arrived at by applying 1950 age-specific rates to 1960 data.
Source: John C. Beresford and Alice M. Rivlin, "Characteristics of 'Other' Families." Unpublished paper presented before Population Association of America, April 1963.

In 1960, more than half of these families (55.6 per cent) had children under eighteen in them, and some had as many as four or more (see Table 1-8). The proportion of female-headed households with children under eighteen increased slightly, from 45.4 per cent in 1940 to 47.2 per cent in 1960.

Table 1-8.

**Proportion of Nonwhite Women Family Heads
with Specified Number of Children
Under Eighteen, By Age, 1960**

Age	*Percentage, by Number of Own Children under 18*				
	None	*One*	*Two*	*Three*	*Four or more*
Total Families with Women Heads	44	17	13	9	17
Under 35	8	21	22	18	31
35-44	26	22	16	12	24
45-64	67	16	8	4	5
65 and over	96	3	1	—	—

Source: John C. Beresford and Alice M. Rivlin, "Characteristics of 'Other' Families." Unpublished paper presented before Population Association of America, April 1963.

One segment of these households is of special interest: those in which the mothers were under forty-five and there were children under eighteen. These young households constituted about 5.8 per cent of all Negro households in 1940, and 8.6 per cent in 1960.[24] The marital status of the mothers in these households changed markedly between these years, as shown in Table 1-9. Especially noteworthy was the increase in the proportion of such mothers who were unmarried, which confirms the marriage trajectory based on the proportion of in-wedlock births.[25] The picture is rounded out by Table 1-10, which shows the proportion of female-headed households with children under eighteen in 1940 and 1960.

[24] *Ibid.*, Table 1, pp. 1, 2.

[25] The unmarried head of a family with children under eighteen tended to be somewhat younger than heads in other marital statuses, averaging 29.4 years as compared with 36.5. She was otherwise little different. Both were urban (84.1 per cent and 82.8 per cent, respectively). About half were in the South (49.7 per cent and 53.3 per cent, respectively). The average number of children was about the same (2.6 and 2.9, respectively) but the younger women were more likely to have only one child (33.8 per cent and 29.9 per cent, respectively), and less likely to have four or more (22.7 per cent and 30.6 per cent, respectively). *Ibid.*, Table 6, p. 45.

Table 1-9.

Marital Status of Women under Forty-five Who Are Heads of Households and Have Own Children Under Eighteen, 1940–60

Marital Status	1940		1960		Percentage Increase	
	Number	Per cent	Number	Per cent	Numbers	Proportion
Married, husband absent	77,560	40.8	222,867	54.5	187.4	36
Widowed	81,720	43.0	67,785	16.6	—17.5	—61
Divorced	12,820	6.7	60,310	14.8	370.4	12
Single	18,200	9.6	56,045	13.8	207.9	43
Total	190,300	100.0	409,007	100.0	113.9	—

Source: U.S. Bureau of the Census, *Families* (1960), Table 3, p. 18.

It is of interest that whereas only 28.2 per cent of the young unmarried women who headed households had children under eighteen in 1940, about half did by 1960. This, too, corroborates the marriage trajectory based on proportion of in-wedlock births.

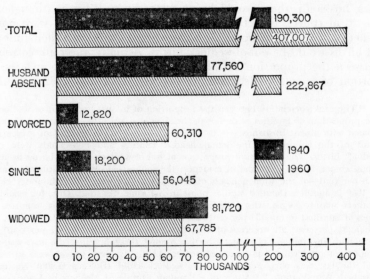

Figure 1-5

Table 1-10.

Nonwhite Households Headed
by Women under Forty-five Which
Included Own Children
under Eighteen, 1940–60

Marital Status	Percentage	
	1940	*1960*
Married, husband absent	58.9	68.7
Divorced	49.8	65.1
Widowed	59.2	70.9
Single	28.2	49.6
Total	52.9	68.7

Source: U.S. Bureau of the Census,
Families (1962), Table 3, p. 18.

RELATIONSHIP BETWEEN THE MEASURES

Such corroboration should not, of course, be surprising. It is fairly obvious that there is a relationship between the proportion of women who are unmarried or separated from their husbands and the proportion of infants borne out of wedlock. If all fertile women were living with their husbands, there would be no out-of-wedlock births (though some might, of course, be actually illegitimate if the husband were not the father). Conversely, if no fertile women were living with their husbands, all births would be out-of-wedlock births. Actually, the rank correlation between the proportion of infants borne out of wedlock and the proportion of female-headed families between 1949 and 1962 was high.[26]

[26] The rank correlation between the proportion of infants borne out of wedlock and the proportion of families with female head was + 0.91; the proportion of married women with absent husbands, +0.79. There is a considerable amount of evidence that many of the children in the female-headed families and households were out-of-wedlock births. The increasing proportion of out-of-wedlock infants borne by multiparous women is one such line of evidence; the unmarried marital status of so many—43.8 per cent—of the women heads of households with own children under eighteen in 1960 is another. Detailed studies point in the same direction. One, for example, of mothers, mainly Negro, who were receiving assistance in Philadelphia, reported three types of families: in one (34 per cent), all of the children were in-wedlock births; in another (31 per cent) all were out-of-wedlock; and in the third (also 31 per cent), there were both in- and out-of-wedlock births. Among these families, the first and sometimes the second child was an out-of-wedlock birth; the next several were in-wedlock; and the last was once more an out-of-wedlock child (Dolores Griffin Norton and Elizabeth Ann Vernon, "A Study of a Random Sample of Mothers of Legitimate and Illegitimate Children Receiving Aid to Dependent Children from the Philadelphia Board of Assistance." Unpublished Master's Dissertation, Bryn Mawr College, Bryn Mawr, Pa., 1960). Another study of 194 low-income Negro mothers in Philadelphia re-

One could, in effect, say that one has "explained" the downward course of the marriage trajectory, as measured in terms of the proportion of infants born in wedlock, by the increasing proportion of female-headed families. But what is the explanation for the increase in the proportion of such families?

WHY THE INCREASE IN FAMILIES HEADED BY WOMEN?

Although any index of marriage, of course, involves both sexes, the two measures used here are based on data for women; they reveal nothing directly about the men involved. The men who are missing from the female-headed families are not likely to be heads of families themselves. Table 1-11, which presents data on nonwhite men under forty-five living

Table 1-11.

**Comparison of Marital Status
of Negro Men under
Forty-five, 1940 and 1960**

| | *Percentage* | |
Marital Status	1940	1960
Wife Absent	3.5	4.5
Divorced	0.6	13.3
Primary Individuals	7.6	8.6

Source: U.S. Bureau of the Census, *Families* (1960). Data in first two rows are from Table 1, pp. 1, 2; those for third row (for nonwhite men rather than for Negro men) are from Table 2, pp. 11, 12.

as primary individuals, or in separated or divorced status, shows an enormous increase among those in the third category. (It is, however, extremely difficult to "freeze" the marital status of foot-loose men in any census year; their marital careers are likely to be too fluid to be caught in any single "frame.")

---

ported illegitimacy as common to all, whether currently married or not. (Robert Bell, "The One-Parent Mother in the Negro Lower Class." Unpublished paper.) Even the women heads of families who reported their marital status as widowed, separated, or divorced may have had out-of-wedlock children. Their reported status is correct with respect to one man but not with respect to the father of a child. Also, precisely because of the success of the institutionalizing process described by the trajectory, many women have internalized the norms of monogamic marriage and hence give their marital status as separated, divorced, or widowed, rather than single.

One must dismiss, of course, any racial interpretation of the increase in female-headed families. This was neither the *typical* Negro family nor a characteristically *Negro* pattern even in 1960. Furthermore, the racial factor has remained constant and cannot, therefore, be invoked to explain change.

So far as the multiparous woman having an out-of-wedlock birth is concerned, it is argued by some that public-assistance programs "encourage" women to have babies,[27] either because (according to one view) such programs are too easy, encouraging women to go into the business of having babies to increase an income which is more stable than that expected from a man, or because (according to another view) they are too strict, forcing men to leave home so that their families will be eligible for assistance. Actually, such programs have little, if anything, to do with the case, for only "about 16 per cent of the nonwhite [illegitimate] children are receiving aid to dependent children."[28] And in 1958, in thirty-two states, the rank correlation between the proportion of all nonwhite births which were out of wedlock and the proportion of (all) children in Aid-to-Dependent-Children families in which the father was not married to the mother was only +0.25. In any event, it is doubtful that the administration of public-assistance laws can explain the changes under consideration here. The influence of urbanization is often invoked to interpret recent trends, but it is not in and of itself an adequate explanation. Frazier has noted that it was among free Negroes living in cities that the family was first institutionalized.[29] Furthermore, the most rapid rate of urbanization does not always coincide with the marriage trajectory.[30] But urbanization, combined with other circumstances, has undoubtedly had a profound impact on marriage and family relations among Negroes.

Sometimes a cultural explanation is invoked. It is argued that the

---

[27] See, for example, L. Gross, "Are We Paying an Illegitimacy Bonus?" *Saturday Evening Post*, XXX (November 30, 1960), 69-72.

[28] U.S. Bureau of Public Assistance, *Illegitimacy and Its Impact on the Aid to Dependent Children Program* (Washington, D.C.: USGPO, 1960), p. 36. In 1958 there was very little relationship in thirty-two states between the proportion of all nonwhite births which were out of wedlock and the proportion of all children receiving Aid-to-Dependent-Children grants who were borne out of wedlock. If an increase in the proportion of nonwhite births which were out of wedlock tended to increase the proportion of children on assistance rolls who were illegitimate, the rank correlation would have been + 1.00; actually it was + 0.25.

[29] Frazier, *op. cit.*, p. 128.

[30] The increase in the proportion of Negroes who were urban between 1900 and 1910 was 20.3 per cent; between 1910 and 1920, 24.5 per cent; between 1920 and 1930, 28.5 per cent; between 1930 and 1940, 11.2 per cent; between 1940 and 1950, 28.4 per cent; and between 1950 and 1960, 17.3 per cent. The rate of increase, of course, depends on the proportion already urban. See footnote 46 below, for further comment on this point.

female-headed family is a vestige of, or a regression to, the old plantation pattern. The evidence, however, is not at all convincing. If the
female-headed family were a vestige of, or a regression to, the plantation
pattern, then it would resemble the rural farm family of today (found
mainly in the South), which is in direct line of succession from that pattern. Actually, the proportion of female-headed families has been declining markedly in rural farm areas. In the early 1930s, C. S. Johnson
reported that 25 per cent of a sample of 612 rural farm households had
no male head.[31] In 1940, 21.8 per cent of nonwhite households in the
South (rural and urban areas together) had female heads.[32] In 1960,
only 10.8 per cent of nonwhite rural farm families (mostly in the South)
were headed by women.[33] As Table 1-5 shows, there was a drastic decline
in the proportion of such families between 1950 and 1960. The female-
headed family was not a typical pattern among freedmen in rural areas,
or even among their children;[34] it was always more common in cities.

By far the largest proportion of families headed by women (57.5 per
cent) in 1960 occurred in central cities,[35] and these were the family heads
who had young children. Table 1-12 summarizes some of the structural
contrasts between urban families and rural farm families in 1960. The
female-headed family was neither a vestige of nor a regression to an older
pattern; it was a new and different phenomenon.

SOME OTHER CLUES: UNEMPLOYMENT AND POVERTY

Because we are trying to explain, not the existence of female-headed
families, but increases in the number of such families in the third
phase of the marriage trajectory, we must also consider other related
changes. One such series of changes has occurred in unemployment patterns. A team of researchers in the U.S. Bureau of Labor Statistics reported in 1964 that, since 1951, "the percent[age] of nonwhite women
separated from their husbands has a significant correlation of +0.68
with the unemployment rate *for the preceding year*.[36] Thus, the rise in

[31] C. S. Johnson, *Shadow of the Plantation* (Chicago: The University of Chicago
Press, 1934), p. 33.
[32] U.S. Bureau of the Census, *op. cit.*, Table 3, p. 20.
[33] *Ibid.*, Table 4, p. 32.
[34] See Frazier, *op. cit.*, pp. 103, 110-11.
[35] U.S. Bureau of the Census, *op. cit.*, Table 4. About 7 per cent were in the urban
fringe and about 16 per cent each in other urban areas and in rural nonfarm areas.
Only 3.4 per cent of all female-headed families were rural farm families and these
tended to be elderly and not to have young children in them. A smaller proportion
(2.2 per cent) of the unmarried women heads of families with children under eighteen
were rural farm families; 84.1 per cent were in cities. The situation was much the
same for women heads in other marital statuses: 2.9 per cent were on farms; 82.8 per
cent, in cities.
[36] Dorothy K. Newman and Morton S. Raff, in a memorandum dated October 21,
1964, p. 1.

Table 1-12.

Some Structural Contrasts between Nonwhite Urban and Rural Farm Families, 1960

Structural Characteristic	Percentage Distribution	
	Urban	*Rural Farm*
Female Head	23.1	11.8
Median age	42.2 years	54 years
Separated	12.0	5.6
Divorced	5.5	0.9
Married more than once	21.8	18.0
Proportion of female heads with own children under 18	57	46
Median age	34.9 years	43.2 years

Source: U.S. Bureau of the Census, *Families* (1960), Tables 4, 6.

unemployment rates was soon followed by a rise in the proportion of women separated from their husbands (many of whom were doubtless heads of families). But the "explanation" implied by this relationship is limited, "because the number of separated women is many times the number of unemployed men they could be separated from." [37] And even if many nonwhite married men separated from their spouses reported themselves single (as was doubtless the case), the difference would still be a large one.

Nevertheless, unemployment data cannot be wholly dismissed. The proportion of nonwhite males fourteen years of age or older who were in the labor force declined from 80 per cent in 1940 to 72.1 per cent in 1960.[38] Those not in the labor force were not employed, but not all those in the labor force were employed. In 1949, two thirds of the nonwhite men in the labor force had worked forty-eight or more weeks; in 1959, only about two fifths had.[39] The creeping unemployment among the non-

[37] *Ibid.*, p. 2. In 1963, for example, there were 626,000 nonwhite married women separated from their husbands; there were only 48,000 nonwhite married men who gave their marital status as married, spouse absent (*Ibid.*, Table 3).

[38] U.S. Bureau of the Census, *Employment Status and Work Experience* (1960), Table 16. During the same time the proportion of nonwhite women who were in the labor force increased from 37.6 per cent to 41.7 per cent. Nonwhite males constituted 9.4 per cent of the male working force in 1940, 9.3 per cent in 1960. Walter B. Miller, in his Foreword to *Fatherless Families: Their Economic and Social Adjustment* by Sydney E. Bernard (Waltham, Mass.: Brandeis University, 1964) also ties the occurrence of female-headed families to the problematic role of low-skilled labor in an increasingly automated society (p. xii).

[39] U.S. Bureau of the Census, *ibid.*

white population certainly cannot be ignored in any attempt to explain changes in the family pattern. (See Table 1-13.)

Table 1-13.

Marital Status of Nonwhite Men by Employment Status, 1960

Percentage Distribution

Marital Status	Employed	Unemployed	In Labor Force
Married, wife present	82.6	71.1	87.0
Married, wife absent	10.9	18.4	70.1
Widowed	3.5	5.1	44.4
Divorced	2.1	5.2	73.4

Source: U.S. Bureau of the Census, *Employment Status and Work Experience* (1960), Table 4, p. 21.

The so-called culture of poverty is said to find archetypical expression in the female-headed family.[40] And, in fact, these families constitute a very large segment of the poor. In 1960, almost two fifths (36.8 per cent) of all nonwhite families in the under-$2000 income bracket were headed by women, and almost three fifths (59.9 per cent) of all families headed by women fell into this income bracket.[41] Perhaps it is the incomplete structure of the female-headed family that explains its poverty and, perhaps, its poverty also explains its structure.

Still, it can scarcely be argued that poverty has increased since World War II, even among nonwhite families. It is true, however, that the income of Negroes has risen less rapidly than that of other workers.[42] Thus it is possible that a relative, if not absolute, increase in poverty may help to explain the increase in female-headed families.

THE CONCEPT OF THE GENERATION

When we talk about changes over time we are talking about different people. Thus even if the conditions do not change markedly, the people themselves may have changed. The concept *social generation* has been devised to explain or, at least, to describe how people of one period differ from those of another. The term is not identical with *biological genera-*

[40] Walter B. Miller, "Cultural Features of an Urban Lower-Class Community" (mimeographed, n.d.), pp. 13-14.
[41] U.S. Bureau of the Census, *Families, op. cit.,* Table 13.
[42] Herman P. Miller, *Rich Man, Poor Man* (New York: The Crowell-Collier Publishing Co., 1964), pp. 86-87.

tion or *demographic cohort;*[43] it has, rather, a psychological and socio-logical connotation. *Generation,* in this sense, refers to people who have had common experiences and, hence, a common "collective mentality" and morality.

The historical scene during the time people are in their formative years—say, roughly, until their twenties—will determine the decisive experiences of any po-litical or social generation. The concept of decisive, politically relevant experi-ence includes the following elements: the general conditions of social life during the formative period—war, peace, prosperity, depression, stability, or unrest; the important political issues of the time; and the concrete political and social strug-gles, such as revolutions, rebellions, uprisings, strikes, or reform. The concept of social or political generation does not imply that there are no differentiations within each generation, for obviously there are. "To have the same experiences in common integrates a generation into a social collective; but a generation may include several subdivisions, if the crucial experiences are met and mastered in different ways, for example, by different class groups." [44]

It is suggested here that each of the three phases of the marriage trajectory depicts a social generation: the first, an institutionalizing gener-ation; the second, an urbanizing generation; and the third, a self-eman-cipating generation. The first generation included the freedmen and their children, who—still predominantly rural and Southern—slowly assimi-lated the institutional norms of the monogamic family. The second gener-ation was a transitional one, rejecting the mentality of the freedman but not wholly free of it—a generation in headlong flight from a feudal social system. The third generation is almost wholly urban—if not ur-banized—and no longer overwhelmingly Southern.

The succession of the generations is a gradual one, and it takes time for the traumata of any one generation to reveal themselves. It was noted (see p. 14) that the recent increases in the proportion of out-of-wedlock births have been especially notable among nonwhite women in their thirties. These are women born since 1925, who grew up during a period marked by rapid urbanization, a great depression, and a world war; the men in their lives, for the most part, belong to the same generation.[45]

[43] The cohort concept was used by John H. Rohrer and Munro Edmonson in their study of New Orleans Negroes—*The Eighth Generation Grows Up: Cultures and Personalities of New Orleans Negroes* (New York: Harper Torchbook, 1964).

[44] Jessie Bernard, *Social Problems at Midcentury* (New York: The Dryden Press, 1957), pp. 448-49. The concept of generation here is based on Rudolf Heberle, *Social Movements* (New York: Appleton-Century-Crofts, Inc., 1951), pp. 118ff. This, in turn, is based on the work of François Mentre, Willy Hellpach, and Karl Mannheim.

[45] The age of the median nonwhite husband in 1960 was 42.5; of the median non-white wife, 39.4 (U.S. Bureau of the Census, *Families, op. cit.,* Table 38, p. 317). It is probable that the age differences among unofficial matings were not markedly different from those among official matings.

The traumata experienced by this transitional, "urbanizing" generation are reflected in the third phase of the marriage trajectory.

Future trends cannot be projected from those of the past or the present. The traumata of urbanization, if not of those of urbanism, are past,[46] but the self-emancipating generation is still in process of finding itself. A great deal will depend on the success with which it meets the crucial experiences that lie ahead. The degree of this success will determine the future pattern of its marriage and family relations.

[46] The peak is past so far as rural-urban migration among Negroes is concerned. The enormous shock—social, cultural, psychological—resulting from the confrontation of rural Negroes in cities with urban problems is over. There will doubtless be migration still (indeed there must be, to distribute the labor supply), but this will involve primarily the movements of people who live in towns and cities. Thus, future redistributions of population will involve people who were born and educated in urban communities (Irene B. Taeuber, "The American Negro at Midcentury," *Population Bulletin*, XIV (November 1958), 130, 135).

Chapter 2

The Two Cultures

Introduction

The marriage trajectory traced the imposition of institutional norms on the freedmen and their descendants or, at least, of the requirement that children be borne in wedlock and that fathers remain with their families. And, despite our emphasis on recent changes, these norms are still adhered to by most Negro families. What differentiated those who conformed to the norms from those who did not?

The trajectory reveals nothing about the nature of conformity. For a considerable number of those involved, conformity remains a matter of external adaptation, not one of internal conviction—a matter of institutionalization, but not of acculturation.

Acculturation implies that the norms have become an intrinsic part of the personality. Thus, when the acculturated person violates norms, he feels guilty; he experiences conflict and anxiety, and he may even feel impelled to punish himself. Those who internalized the norms related to marriage and the family would be more likely to adhere to the pattern even under stress; those who did not would be more likely to abandon it. A class factor is certainly involved in this differential, but so, too, perhaps is an equally fundamental cultural factor.

However little agreement there may be among students of Negro society in other respects, there is remarkable unanimity about the existence of two distinct strands in that society: one is generally called the "respectable" strand; the other is variously referred to as the "masses," the "low life," the "nonrespectable" strand. This distinction is especially significant for any understanding of family patterns among Negroes, because the important characteristics of each strand concern morals, propriety, and family life.

Two Distinctive Styles of Adaptation

THE TWO IMAGES

Those elements in the Negro population that have had a stable family life . . . have attempted to maintain standards of conduct and to perpetuate traditions of family life that were alien to the majority of the Negro population . . . they have placed an exaggerated valuation upon moral conduct and cultivated a puritanical restraint in opposition to the free and uncontrolled behavior of the larger Negro world.[1]

The most significant status cleavage from the point of view of the people themselves seems to be along the respectable-nonrespectable line . . . [with] behavior or role correlates that amount to two distinctive styles of adaptation. . . . Among the differentiated, or respectable and more stable families, sex behavior lacks the frank, open, and, to some extent, promiscuous character of the relations among their opposites. Public behavior with respect to sex and whisky go far to define respectability. . . . Pride, respectability and the approach to conventional morals tend to be earmarks of the respectable family.[2]

. . . [O]ne of the most fundamental divisions in Bronzeville is that between people who stress conventional . . . public behavior and those who ignore it. Professional men, postal workers, clerical workers and others with "position" rail constantly at the "loud," "boisterous," "uncouth" behavior of other segments of the society. . . . The decisive measure of the man is how he acts in public. . . .[3]

It is difficult to overestimate the importance of this basic cleavage in the Negro population formed by these "two distinctive styles of adaptation." It has wide repercussions, not only for marriage and family, but also for community life (see Chapter 4). The two strands cast different images and evoke different responses in the non-Negro world.

CULTURE VS. CLASS

This cleavage, it must be emphasized, is not one of class. Class differentiation in Negro society is usually based on difference in income levels. Each of the two strands, on the other hand, includes all income levels. Thus, each cuts across income-class lines. The difference between them is not based on income but on ethos, not on money but on acceptance of conventional standards of behavior—especially in relation to sex and work.

The fallacy of equating the two strands with income classes is that such an equation obscures two important segments of the population: the low-income groups with conventional family patterns, and the high-income groups with unconventional family patterns (see Table 2-1).

A strong emphasis on family stability and conventional moral behavior occurs at all income levels, even the lowest. Frazier, for example, speaks of "the great concern of the upper class with respectability," of the efforts of the middle class "to maintain a stable and conventional family life" and to have their children "conform to conventional moral standards." But he also points out that "there are lower-class families that

---

[1] E. Franklin Frazier, *The Negro Family in the United States*, rev. ed. (New York: Holt, Rinehart & Winston, Inc., 1949), p. 190.

[2] Hylan Lewis, *Blackways of Kent* (Chapel Hill, N.C.: University of North Carolina Press, 1955), pp. 86, 233.

[3] St. Clair Drake and Horace R. Cayton, *Black Metropolis* (New York: Harper Torchbook, 1962), p. 519.

Table 2-1.

Class Structure of the Two Strands

	Conventional Strand		*Unconventional Strand*
Higher-income levels	Upper-class families Middle-class families Families in the "genteel tradition"	(Black bourgeoisie)	Shadies Fast set Gentlemen racketeers Sporting set
Lower-income levels	Proletarian families "Peasant" families (Frazier's "black puritans") Families of some service workers Church-centered families	(Black Muslims)	The "masses" The "lower classes" The "unsocialized" Runners, hustlers, etc.

struggle to maintain a stable and conventional family life." Describing the class stratification in Washington, D.C., which he considered typical of border cities, he noted that even a generation ago there were "stable elements" in the lower class whose social lives revolved around the church.[4]

Drake and Cayton, similarly, found "respectable" and "nonrespectable" elements at all income levels. The middle classes manifested "some stability and order," and a strong "desire to be 'respectable' even if it means sacrificing personal happiness." But even in the lower class there was a stable group composed of "church folks" who tried (against great odds, it must be added) to maintain respectability.[5] Hylan Lewis, in his account of Kent, a southern Piedmont community, also noted that the "respectable" and "nonrespectable" categories cut across all income-class levels, groups, and segments of the population.[6] James Weldon Johnson, who discovered elements of both among the higher-income groups in Harlem in the 1920s contrasted the educated, "respectable" well-to-do with the equally wealthy fast set—the "strictly social sets that go in for bridge, . . . cocktail parties, . . . high-powered cars, . . . and exclusive dances. . . ."[7] In the high-income unconventional class, "the people . . . do not ask, 'How did you make your money?' but only, 'Have you got money?'" In the 1930s and 1940s, because legitimate economic opportunities for Negroes were limited, the wealthiest among them were often racketeers and policy kings. With the increase in such opportunities

[4] Frazier, *op. cit.*, pp. 287, 299, 301, 304.

[5] Drake and Cayton, *op. cit.*, pp. 524, 668.

[6] Lewis, *op. cit.*, p. 216.

[7] James Weldon Johnson, *Black Manhattan* (New York: Alfred A. Knopf, Inc., 1930), p. 169.

in the 1960s, the source of money was more likely to be legitimate.[8] The members of their class spend their money generously: saving and thrift are not accounted as virtues; the concept of delayed gratification makes no sense to them.[9]

SOCIAL MOBILITY

Because both strands include all income classes, social mobility—upward and downward—occurs in both. In the conventional strand, mobility takes the traditional American form: attendance at school, hard work, and a "little bit of luck." In this way, the serious, determined individual enters a profession or, at least, the white-collar world and is assured of a stable—and, perhaps, even moderately good—income. In the unconventional strand, the course of upward mobility takes a different and more varied form. It may result from spectacular success in professional sports or in the entertainment world, or even from "advancement" in the underworld.[10] Because there has not been very much research on this subject, it is not possible to make a clear delineation of such career patterns.[11]

Downward social mobility probably also takes different forms in the two strands. Drug addiction and dependence on alcohol may characterize downward mobility in the unconventional strand; extreme apathy, anxiety, withdrawal—even schizophrenia—may characterize it in the conventional strand. Whatever the reasons for it, downward mobility produces atomized individuals belonging to neither strand.

THE CONCEPT OF CULTURE

We have spoken so far of the two "strands" in the Negro world. The term does convey the feeling of a pattern that extends over time, but it is unidimensional. What is needed here is a terminology to describe an ex-

---

[8] Drake and Cayton, *op. cit.*, pp. xviii, 546-50. "The policy kings . . . were . . . able to assume the role of race leaders, patrons of charity, and pioneers in the establishment of legitimate business. They were able to wield some economic control over community institutions through their power to withhold or grant gifts" (p. 486).

[9] A magazine which refers to itself as the "medium that money-spending Negroes rely on" reported that its readers spent 12 percent more than white families for food purchased for home consumption; 19 per cent more for appliances and home furnishings; 38 per cent more for personal-care items, and 50 per cent more for clothing and accessories (*Ebony* advertisement in *Wall Street Journal*, December 10, 1963).

[10] In 1965, Kenneth B. Clark reported that young Negroes took as their models petty criminals, whose colorful, swaggering style of cool bravado fascinated them. They would pretend to be pimps and runners themselves, reflecting respect, contempt, but also despair (*Dark Ghetto* [New York: Harper & Row, Publishers, 1965], p. 66).

[11] If class is delineated in terms of education rather than in terms of income, there is more correspondence between class and strand. Because education is almost an intrinsic value in one strand, it may be taken for granted that more of the "respectables" than of the "nonrespectables" will have schooling beyond minimum legal requirements.

tremely complex set of phenomena. We suggest, with some reservations, the substitution of *culture* for *strand*.

In this discussion of "strands" and "cultures," it should be pointed out that the conceptual lenses through which one views phenomena have a powerful influence on the way one interprets them and, hence, on the ways in which one reacts to them. Peterson and Matza have shown that phenomena may be viewed as cultural traits, as pathologies, or as sins, according to the way in which they are defined.

This triad—custom: tolerance, illness: treatment, and crime: punishment—is a useful framework for structuring a wide variety of analyses. Thus, delinquency, ordinarily defined as illegality, has also been perceived as the prevalent custom of slum youths; and other analysts diagnose the delinquent as "sick" and prescribe one or another nostrum. Homosexuality and other sexual aberrations are seen by those who practice them as the legitimate customs of a minority; by psychologists, as a type of illness . . . ; by law-enforcement agencies, as crime. . . .[12]

An excellent illustration of the different conclusions that arise from differing definitions of a situation is the current controversy among students of family patterns in the Caribbean. Judith Blake, for instance, argues that marriage and family relations among the lower classes in this area should not be viewed as representative of a distinct culture but, rather, as deviations from the conventional institutionalized patterns of Western society. She therefore sees in these relations a great deal of disorganization.[13] Other students challenge this interpretation, arguing that behavior that seems "disorganized" to the researcher may actually be quite conventional and acceptable from the subject's own point of view.[14] Hyman Rodman, the most articulate spokesman for this interpretation, reported that, in one Trinidad village, he found three acceptable types of marital relationships: "friending," "living (with)," and marriage. He found, furthermore, that this range of alternatives was functional, permitting a man to "live with both his conscience and his economic uncertainties."[15]

[12] William Peterson and David Matza, *Social Controversy* (San Francisco: Wadsworth Publishing Co., 1963), p. 5.

[13] Judith Blake, "Family Instability and Reproductive Behavior in Jamaica," *Current Research in Human Fertility* (Milbank Memorial Fund, 1955); "Reply to Mr. Braithwaite," *Social and Economic Studies*, VII (Jamaica: University College of the West Indies). See also William J. Goode, "Illegitimacy in the Caribbean Social Structure," *American Sociological Review*, XXV (February 1960), 21-30.

[14] F. M. Henriquez, *Family and Colour in Jamaica* (London: Eyre and Spottiswoode, 1953); Lloyd Braithwaite, "Sociology and Demographic Research in the British Caribbean," *Social and Economic Studies*, VI (Jamaica: University College of the West Indies).

[15] Hyman Rodman, "Marital Relationships in a Trinidad Village," *Marriage and Family Living*, XXIII (May 1961), 170. Rodman has elaborated the same idea in "The Lower-Class Value Stretch," *Social Forces*, XLII (December 1963), 205-15.

If one accepts Rodman's point of view, many phenomena which, to the external observer, seem to manifest deviancy and/or disorganization take on a less sinister aspect. According to the dogma of cultural relativity, they must be tolerated, if not respected. They are not problems; they are, rather (in Rodman's words), solutions to problems.

Ethically, the concept of cultural relativity forbids the application of the standards and criteria of our culture to people who live according to a different culture. These people, therefore, are not to be viewed as violating the norms of our culture, but as conforming to the norms of a different one. But this prohibition also frees the observer from any sense of responsibility and, in effect, absolves him of feelings of guilt for any suffering he may encounter. This concept, then, puts distance between the observer and his subjects—a distance which, although conducive to objectivity, may also lead to indifference.[16]

Without accepting these ethical implications—that one may ignore the consequences of a particular cultural pattern—we have elected to use the term *culture,* not because it is a perfect solution but because it seems the best choice both for discussing the changes in that pattern and for understanding them.

CHARACTERISTICS OF THE TWO CULTURES

A second semantic problem arises in trying to characterize the two cultures in Negro society. None of the terms so far used is quite correct: *respectable* and *nonrespectable* are pejorative; *the differentiated* and *the masses* are not specific enough; and *lower-, middle-,* and *upper-class* are too closely associated with income level.

Because each culture is, in crucial ways, the antithesis of the other, we could simply define one in positive terms; the other, in negative terms. Hylan Lewis, for example, declares that,

> . . . In general, the respectable persons are defined by what they do not do. They are people who are careful of their public conduct and reputation: they don't drink whisky in public or get drunk in public; they don't frequent the taverns; they don't get in trouble; and they are proud of their lack of contact with the law and the courts . . . ; [their sex life] lacks the frank, open, and . . . promiscuous character of the relations among their opposites.[17]

One culture cultivates "puritanical restraint"; the other, "free and uncontrolled behavior." [18] Conversely, one could begin at the other end:

---

[16] Kenneth Clark (*op. cit.*) makes an impassioned protest against this kind of objectivity, which substitutes "facts" for "the truth." No such protection is sought in the use of the term *culture* here.

[17] Lewis, *op. cit.,* pp. 233, 234.

[18] Frazier, *op. cit.,* p. 190.

the "respectables" strive to maintain stable family life and to conform to high standards of sexual behavior; the others do not.

Neither approach, however, is very successful. It is better to accentuate the positive in both cultures, to define each in terms of what it *is* rather than in terms of what it is not.

There is a strong temptation to resort to such terms as *puritanical* and *hedonistic* as labels for the two cultures. Rather than invoke such "contaminated" adjectives, and recognizing that there are really no completely precise and accurate terms, we propose that *acculturated* and *externally adapted* be used instead. This does not mean that the members of the externally adapted culture are not also acculturated; the members of both strands are acculturated, but to different aspects of the larger culture.[19]

As used here, the term *acculturated* implies that the members of one strand have internalized to a greater degree the moral norms of Western society as these exist in the United States. The members of the externally adapted culture have not taken over these norms, but have adapted themselves to their demands superficially. The ethos of their culture is essentially hedonistic and pleasure-loving. Frazier, for example, contrasted the "Negro's love of leisure and enjoyment of life" with the "old-fashioned virtues" and the "frugal and abstemious . . . habits" of those who "strove to attain middle-class respectability through industry and morality. . . ." The externally adapted culture is consumption-oriented, while the Protestant ethic—which once dominated the white culture in the United States—is production-oriented. In a sense perhaps the externally adapted culture is more "acculturated" than the one we have labelled *acculturated,* for it coincides with what has been called the current "fun-morality" point of view.

The externally adapted view the larger, white culture from the outside, and they have varying degrees of success in getting along in it. Some learn to manipulate and use the white culture. The wealthy Negro interviewed on television who felt no qualms about his position as head of a narcotics syndicate (he viewed his "product" and "market" as no different from those of any other commercial enterprise), and the unmarried woman head of a family in the slum who tries hard to meet the moral standards set as a requirement for public assistance, are both members of the externally adapted culture. Between these extremes are those who

---

[19] C. S. Johnson spoke, in effect, of degrees of acculturation rather than of two categories: ". . . Negroes now represent virtually every stage of the acculturation process in America" (*Shadow of the Plantation* [Chicago: The University of Chicago Press, 1934], p. 6). There is a sense in which the term *acculturated* applies especially well to both cultures for, in a way, each one almost exaggerates versions of some aspect of the outside world. Some acculturateds are more puritanical than the puritanical in the outside world; some externally adapteds are more consumption-oriented than the most consumption-oriented in the outside world; and so on.

learn enough about the law, administrative rulings, social agencies, and other institutions of the white culture to use or outwit them when necessary.[20]

In both cultures, of course, there are the kindly and the cruel, the patient and the headstrong, the compassionate and the bitter, the talented and the dull.[21] The members of each culture have in common only one thing: their position with respect to the ethos of the outside world.

THE "TOKEN" NEGRO

The connotations of the term *Negro* are usually associated with the members of the externally adapted culture. They are viewed as "typically" Negro; their culture, as "typically" Negro. Such connotations of the term *Negro* do not apply to the acculturated, who, in fact, find it difficult to think of themselves as "Negro" in the sense that the term is commonly used. In a cultural sense, they are no more "Negro" than their white counterparts, and their reactions to the externally adapted are—if anything—even less cordial.

The colored man who is invited to sit on public and private boards and committees as a token gesture toward integration is no more representative of the total Negro population than the white man he sits next to. Thus the "tolerance" upon which the members of the board or committee secretly pride themselves is entirely misdirected: they have done no more than accept a "white" man who happens to have a dark skin.

VALUE PRE-EMPTION

The cultural concept of *value* does not refer to something that is considered *absolutely* good or desirable, but to something that is considered *relatively* better or more desirable than something else. Thus, although everyone might hold that warm, affectionate relationships were extremely desirable, some might believe that life-long commitment to a marriage vow is more important. Everyone might agree that a good job is desirable, but some might hold that leisure is better. Fortunate people have relatively few such choices to make. They can enjoy a warm, affectionate relationship within the marital bond; they can have good jobs that provide enough leisure to enjoy the fruits of their labors. Others, less fortunate, are forced to make choices.

Those reared in a culture shaped by the Protestant ethic tend to make one set of choices; those reared in a culture untouched by the Protestant

---

[20] It was noted in some of the early Job Corps camps that among those who first learned how to use their wits and "beat the game" were the Negro boys from urban areas.

[21] It is conceivable that those in the externally adapted culture are more likely to have "the ego strength to rebel by overt acts of defiance rather than succumb to apathy" (Clark, *op. cit.,* p. 101).

ethic, another. (It goes without saying that there rarely is deliberate awareness of the presence or absence of this or any other ethic.) Some people choose future benefits; others, present gratification. Some choose money over personal effort: they do it themselves rather than pay to have it done; they walk rather than take a cab; they shop around rather than buy at the nearest store. To others, personal convenience or gratification is worth more than money: they pay to have it done; they take cabs; they shop at the most convenient store rather than hunt for bargains.

Hylan Lewis has suggested the useful concept of *value-pre-emption*—that is, one value may supersede another. He cites the cases of three mothers, who feel "sacrificed" to their own parents' drive for upward mobility:

> The noteworthy thing about the parents of each of these mothers is that they are all upwardly mobile homeowners, despite large families. . . . In discussions about their parents, all three mothers appear to perceive their parents as strongly motivated to acquire new and better things—a car, a house in a higher-status neighborhood, new furniture. And the mothers seem to perceive themselves as casualties of this parental motivation. One said that she didn't think her family should have "sacrificed" her for a car.
>
> Another, in almost identical words, said she didn't think her parents should have "sacrificed" her for a house. The mothers see themselves as having gone without adequate food and clothing while their parents were making efforts to move upward. . . .[22]

In these cases one value (upward mobility) pre-empted another (warm, affectionate ties with children). Other parents might have chosen to maintain relaxed, warm, easy-going family relations rather than introduce the anxiety and competitiveness of efforts to achieve upward mobility.

Because this concept of two cultures has been ignored in most research, or confused with the concept of class as measured by income, we cannot state the relative prevalence of each culture nor its relationship to other variables. But the concept cannot be ignored in any discussion of marriage and family among Negroes.

The Reshaped Culture

AN OLD BIFURCATION

The cultural bifurcation of the Negro population began even before the first emancipation, not only with the distinction between the free

---

[22] Hylan Lewis, "Culture, Class, and the Behavior of Low-Income Families," (unpublished paper presented at Conference on Lower-Class Culture, New York, June 1963), pp. 36-38. Jack Buerckle found, in a study of forty-six Negro and twenty-two white families in Philadelphia, that "getting ahead" meant an improved or new home for almost twice as many Negro families (40 per cent) as white families (22 per cent), and although both Negro and white families valued security above upward mobility, "getting ahead" was considered "very important" by more than twice as many Negro families (70 per cent) as white families (33 per cent). Jack Buerckle, paper read before American Sociological Association, Montreal, September 1964.

Negroes and the slaves, but with the distinction between the house slaves and the field slaves. The field slaves were cut off from the big house. As children, they were often treated like little animals and fed at troughs like other livestock. As adults, they had only the most limited contacts with the outside world. They saw the big house from afar. The overseer may have been the only person from the outside world with whom they had regular contact, and from him they learned little more than the importance of the whip as a teaching device. They may have watched the comings and goings of their white owners—the carriages, the fine clothes, the elegant balls—perhaps even the duels—but it all probably made little sense to them. The field hands' lives were lived in the cotton or tobacco fields during the day and in the slave cabins at night. What material culture they had was an extremely meager one.

They did, however, have a kind of folk culture which was neither African nor American, but a combination of the two. They had a characteristic form of speech and a unique version of the revivalist religion of the seventeenth and eighteenth centuries.

In its static structure, "extraorganizational" and "extratechnological," slave society was a folk society . . . in all its multiplicity of folkways and folk notions, differentiated by occupation, region, and economy—field hand, house servant, and artisan; Sea Islands, Tidewater, and Deep South; cotton, tobacco, and sugar plantations. As a self-taught, self-contained group, moreover, on the make-it-yourself-or-do-without level of culture, slaves had their folk hand skills and mind skills, their play of popular fantasy in both the real and the unreal world, their songs . . . , stories, sayings, games, pastimes, and superstitious beliefs and practices. Finally, slaves had their own code of behavior.[23]

It was not a "Negro" culture in the sense that all Negroes shared it; but it was Negro in the sense that it was a way of life for many Negroes.[24] Much of this culture was retained after emancipation. Those who were shut off from contact with the outside world retained it for decades, and vestiges of that culture still endure.

THE PLANTATION FAMILY

In the plantation family, love was an important value. In this primary group, interpersonal relations were viewed as more crucial than formal sanctions. It was, for example, more "respectable" to separate from an uncongenial partner than to accept intolerable conditions with even a legal mate; it was more "respectable" to live peacefully and happily with a man to whom one was not officially married than to accept beatings

[23] B. A. Botkin, *Lay My Burden Down* (Chicago: The University of Chicago Press, 1945), p. xiii.

[24] Leonard Broom and Norval Glenn, *Transformation of the Negro American* (New York: Harper & Row, Publishers, 1965), Chap. 2.

from one's husband. The important thing was that the partners be congenial and that they love one another; the nature of the bond between them was irrelevant. Personal pride was also important—in some cases, more important even than love: "The mother of a young girl who had a child by the son of a neighbor refused to let her daughter marry the boy, in spite of mutual desires, because the mother of the boy had made uncomplimentary remarks about the girl." [25]

Men and women were monogamous and faithful so long as their relationship lasted, but it lasted only as long as the partners felt attracted to one another—which might be a few weeks or months or, again, it might last for half a century.

The mother-role was of far greater significance than the wife-role. Women took great pride in producing large families, and fecundity had great weight in the evaluation of women as mates—a relic, Johnson suggests, of slavehood. Johnson also notes that a large number of children was necessary for survival in a society where the infant and child mortality rates were so high. Furthermore, children increased the labor supply, so they were considered economic assets.

But the maternal role, however prized, sat lightly once the child was born. Parents showed only a vague attachment to their children—and then only as long as the children were physically present. Sometimes parents could not even remember the names, let alone the precise ages, of all their offspring. Children were, in fact, often given to relatives; and the practice of "adoption" was widespread.

A clear-cut distinction was made in the assessment of out-of-wedlock births. The strong, independent woman who wanted children, but not a husband, was not censured, nor was the woman living happily and peacefully with a man to whom she was not officially married. The child born to a woman separated from her husband was freely accepted by her family, as was the child resulting from youthful experimentation with sex. Universally condemned, however, were philandering young men who made "foolments" on young girls.

An uncomplicated hedonism characterized the ethos of sex in this culture. Sex was recreational. Johnson reported two unmarried women who said that "they liked to 'pleasure themselves with men' when they were not too tired." And the men referred "to this form of entertainment . . . [as] 'setting around playing with womens.' " [26]

A kind of Dionysianism characterized the "frolic, . . . the great feature of the rural recreation," [27] at which dancing, whiskey, violence, and, of course, sexual activity, offered an escape from the dreariness and drudgery of everyday life.

[25] Johnson, *op. cit.,* p. 81.
[26] *Ibid.,* p. 182.
[27] *Ibid.*

Johnson summarizes "respectability" as the plantation system approached its end. It was "respectable" to assume responsibility for a daughter's children, even though she was not married. It was "respectable" to keep out of contact with the law, to settle personal differences privately. It was "not proper" to ask the father of an unmarried woman's child to support it; but there was approval if he chose to assume the responsibility. Community and family sanctions opposed marriage entered into solely for the purpose of legitimizing a baby.

This, in brief, was the pattern of marriage and family relations among the great mass of Negroes in the rural South for at least several decades after emancipation. These were the patterns—many of which survived well into the twentieth century—that the freedmen had worked out and passed on to their children. The plantation pattern, although far from arcadian, performed some of the minimum functions demanded of marriage and family: it provided for adults a loving—albeit temporary—relationship, and it provided for children a welcome and a place to belong.

When the outside world—especially the urban world—intruded on the plantation world, this family pattern had to be adapted to the exigencies of that new world. But this adaptation did not mean that the new norms were internalized. And when the going got rough, not even external conformity was exacted.

THE IMPERATIVES OF MONOGAMIC MARRIAGE

It was to men and women bred in this culture—men and women who had great "love of leisure and enjoyment of life"—that the proponents of the institutional norms of monogamic marriage said, in effect: "You may not have sex relations until you marry, and you may not marry until you are able to support yourselves and any children you may beget. But we won't do a thing to help you support yourselves and your children and the chances are high that you never will be able to, on a permanent basis. So you may not have sex relations—ever."

These were the norms to which these men and women had to adapt. If they were to conform to these institutional requirements, they would have to live celibate lives. This institutional pattern—even in a puritanical culture, let alone in an essentially hedonistic one—is patently absurd. Celibacy was, in effect, prescribed for people culturally inclined toward pleasure and with very limited resources in education or recreation. (In the 1940s and 1950s, the absurdity was compounded by the new law that, if a man lived with his family but could not support them, they would not be eligible for public assistance.)

The institutional norms of any society imply that conformity is possible for most of its members. When conformity becomes impossible—for whatever reason—institutionalized ways for evading or violating the norms are devised, [28] and a less desirable, but possible, pattern is adopted. In the case of marriage and family, the pattern is one in which love supersedes duty or responsibility. Sexual unions are based on mutual attraction; the partners supply emotional warmth and support and companionship to one another. The man may even make a financial contribution to the household when he can. But the union lasts only as long as the attraction does, and new unions are formed when new attractions develop. While they last, the unions may be monogamous, perhaps even more monogamous than many legal unions among white partners.[29]

THE URBAN ADAPTATION

The female-headed family (see Chapter 1) is a modern adaptation to the white world's demands and the life conditions it imposes. In some ways, it resembles the plantation family. The great emphasis on love as the basis for relationships between men and women is still present, although in some cases this emphasis may be declining.[30] An old tradition of dependency also remains, although its form has been changed.[31]

Nevertheless, the female-headed family differs from the plantation family in many respects. On the plantation, for example, fertility was an ideal; modern Negro women, on the other hand, do not value large families. A 1963 study of 202 low-income Negro mothers in Philadelphia, for example, revealed that, despite their own fate, they did not covet large broods for their own children. At least half of them wanted their daughters to have fewer than three children, and, interestingly, more of the lower-status women (60 per cent) than of the higher status-women (50 per cent) expressed this wish. Relatively few in either category wanted their

[28] Jessie Bernard, *American Community Behavior* (New York: Holt, Rinehart & Winston, Inc., 1962), Chap. 27.

[29] That these extralegal unions may be more monogamous than legal unions among white families is suggested by the fact that in a study of 552 Negro and 387 white out-of-wedlock mothers, the fathers of 13 per cent of the white children (but only those of 2 per cent of the Negro children) were married to other women and living with their wives (Hallowell Pope and Donald P. Irish, "White and Negro Unwed Mothers: Postnatal Marital History and the Disposition of the Child," Paper read before the Society for Study of Social Problems, August 1964).

[30] One psychoanalytically oriented observer notes that in the slum the sex partner may become primarily a means for experience and his specific identity becomes fairly irrelevant (Herta Riese, *Heal the Hurt Child* [Chicago: The University of Chicago Press, 1962], Chap. 6). But this attitude does not seem to be typical, as the work of Ira Reiss (presented in Chapter 4) shows.

[31] The freedmen believed in many cases that the government would support them the rest of their lives (Henderson H. Donald, *The Negro Freedman* [New York: Abelard-Schuman, Limited, 1952], p. 4). C. S. Johnson in the 1930s also referred to the "more sophisticated" who "discover in these agencies a mysterious means of getting something for nothing, which holds dangers both to working habits and to self-respect" (*op. cit.*, p. 86).

daughters to have four or more children (19 per cent and 33 per cent, respectively).[32]

On the plantation, if a woman wanted children but not a husband, she could have them; in the city, she may want male companionship even if —not necessarily because—it involves children. On the plantation, out-of-wedlock children were readily "adopted"; "adoption" is rare in the city slum.

The plantation family, protected from the outside world, was essentially innocent. The urban family, however, has been exposed to the outside world and its members learn to feel shame (or, among the acculturated who have internalized its norms, guilt). Slaves had a great deal to be miserable about, but shame about their sex lives was not salient. It was not among the griefs expressed in spirituals. In the urban slum, behavior is public and may therefore encounter open disapproval (that of the social worker, if no one else's).

Another difference is the extinction of the important stabilizing role performed by the "granny." On the plantation, the oldest living woman was a powerful and steadying force, a repository of wisdom, and—as the permanent member of a household with constantly changing membership —a strong family anchor.[33] Few of her counterparts are found in city slums.

THE "CULTURE OF POVERTY"

It has become fashionable recently to speak of a "culture of poverty" or a "lower-class culture." To the extent that the externally adapted live in poverty, whatever is valid in the concept of a culture of poverty would be valid for them also. But the culture of the externally adapted is not identical with the culture of poverty, for it is found among the wealthy as well and there are many acculturated families who live in poverty. The characteristic of the culture of the externally adapted is its hedonism— its emphasis on consumption, the here-and-now, pleasure and fun-morality. Poverty blunts the thrust of hedonism, but does not destroy it.[34]

The culture of poverty and the culture of the externally adapted do merge, however, in the female-headed family. This type of family (as was noted in Chapter 1) is characteristic of the culture of poverty; it is also characteristic of the externally adapted culture.

[32] Robert Bell, "The One-Parent Mother in the Negro Lower Class" (unpublished paper), p. 9.
[33] Frazier, *op. cit.*, Chap. 8.
[34] It is difficult to imagine people attached to the "culture of poverty" or wishing to cling to it. It is, however, not at all difficult to imagine them clinging to a hedonistic, consumption-oriented, present-emphasizing culture. When poor people resist change it is not the "culture of poverty" they cling to but many of the hedonistic, consumption-oriented practices which, under the circumstances, deepen the poverty.

For many years researchers had spoken of "broken homes" or "broken families" as though intact homes were the norm. Only recently has it become clear that for a considerable proportion of the population, Negro or white, the female-headed family is a standard phenomenon—culturally acceptable, if not prescribed or preferred. Thus, at any given time—say, during the taking of the 1960 census—over half (50.9 per cent) of all the nonwhite families with incomes under $2000 in central cities were headed by women.[35] Over a given period, a considerably larger proportion of women would find themselves, at some time or other, the heads of families. These families are poor because they have women as heads; and, conversely, they probably have women as heads because they are poor.

But not all the members of the externally adapted culture are poor. The pattern of marriage and family characteristic of this culture occurs among higher-income groups as well. Even without the restraints imposed by poverty, marriage and family relations would take this pattern among hedonistic, consumption- and present-oriented people.

The family patterns of these unconventional upper classes are a far cry from those found among acculturated Negroes. These men and women do not mind divorce, scandal, or notoriety; indeed, according to Frazier, such publicity only adds to their prestige.[36]

Although this income level is characterized by the same ethos as that of the low-income level, behavior that seems sophisticated in a luxurious setting may seem sordid in a slum, and its consequences may be different also: the playboy drinking champagne at a club looks different from the street-corner man drinking whiskey at a corner tavern; the playboy who "loves 'em and leaves 'em" is not viewed in the same light as the slum-dweller who does the same thing. And the upper-income women who are loved and left have greater sophistication with respect to contraception, so they are not likely to be left with a brood of children.

The Culturally White

THE PROCESS OF ACCULTURATION

The fallacious identification of class and culture noted above is understandable, for as long as there was little other difference among classes, family stability and conventional behavior became the major criteria by which to differentiate them. In fact, the value placed on family stability

[35] U.S. Bureau of the Census, *Families* (1960), Table 13, p. 113. Almost half (47.9 per cent) of female-headed families in central cities were in the under-$2000 income bracket. About a fifth (21.9 per cent) of nonwhite children under fourteen in urbanized areas (not identical with central cities) were living with mother only (U.S. Bureau of the Census, *Persons by Family Characteristics* [1960], Table 1, p. 2).

[36] E. Franklin Frazier, *Black Bourgeoisie* (New York: The Crowell-Collier Publishing Co., 1962), pp. 108-109.

and conventional behavior may be roughly assessed in terms of their importance as criteria of social class; for many decades, they were the hallmarks of the acculturated Negro and among his most cherished values. Until well into the twentieth century, in fact, they far outweighed other criteria (including occupation, education, or income) of social status.

Among free Negroes in the nineteenth century, according to Frazier, "conventional family life established on a traditional basis provided a solid basis for social stratification." In Charleston and New Orleans, "differences in social status among the free Negroes . . . were based upon family background. . . ." After emancipation, former slaves who achieved family stability could aspire to acceptance by the free Negroes. In rural areas, "as the freedmen acquired land and maintained a conventional family life, the distinctions based upon free ancestry and color . . . [became] less important. Landownership, stability of family life, and education . . . increasingly . . . [became] the bases of upper-class status." But "landownership and education . . . were not as significant as stable family relations and other aspects of behavior." [37] The same emphasis on respectability and morality was found in urban areas. Thus one of the earliest studies of Negroes in a Northern city [38] used moral considerations rather than income as criteria of social class, for "they were the criteria which were generally accepted as the basis of social status among Negroes." [39]

These families had not only "institutionalized" the norms of the outside world, they had internalized them as well. The difficulties involved in institutionalizing behavior—i.e., changing external behavior—have already been discussed (see Chapter 1). It may be even more difficult to change basic motivations, to internalize norms—i.e., to acculturate. How, then, did such acculturation come about?

A considerable literature has accumulated on the "Americanization" of European immigrants; friends and relatives, schoolteachers (through the children), and the foreign-language press all contributed to the process. The case of Negroes was at once similar and different: personal influences were a major factor, and the mass media were important also, but the precise impact of these acculturating forces was somewhat different.

Personal Influence in Acculturation.   Under slavery, the master exerted a powerful acculturating force. House slaves, for example, lived close to their master's family in the big house, observed its members at close range, and often developed strong attachments to them. In many

[37] E. Franklin Frazier, *The Negro in the United States* (New York: The Macmillan Company, 1949), pp. 276, 278-79.

[38] W. E. B. DuBois, *The Philadelphia Negro* (Philadelphia: University of Pennsylvania, 1899).

[39] Frazier, *The Negro in the United States, op. cit.,* p. 281.

cases, they even came to identify with the white family. Some were indeed, related to the master's family, as mothers of his children or as children themselves of the master. They were characterized by cleanliness and order, good manners and decorum and—in many instances—flair and style. Even more important, they took over the values of this world:

> The superior status and prestige of the house servants were not due merely to artificial distinctions. Because of their close association with the master['s] race, the house servants were able to assimilate their ideals and sentiments as well as their external forms of behavior.[40]

This was the culture they brought with them to the world of freedom.

Even after emancipation, many former slaves remained in domestic service, where they continued to have close contacts with the culture of the outside world:

> Both during slavery and after emancipation it was through domestic and personal service that the Negro was brought into intimate contacts with the white race and was thereby able to take over elements of white civilization. . . . Where Negroes were employed over long periods, sometimes several generations, in the white families of culture, they unconsciously assimilated white ideals and standards of behavior. Moreover, when within their own families and within their more or less exclusive community life these ideals and patterns of behavior became a part of their traditions, they were supported by sentiment and acquired significance in their lives.[41]

Even when these families ceased to have intimate contact with white families as domestic servants, the cultural roots survived: "the heritage of conventional behavior which they had acquired . . . [had] become a part of their family tradition." [42]

A second personal force in acculturation was supplied by teachers, especially the band of zealous New England missionaries who established or staffed schools throughout the South after the Civil War.

> At these schools the students . . . received more than a formal education. They lived in close personal contacts with the white New England teachers who molded their characters and made possible their cultural identity with whites. . . . The heroic efforts of the northern missionaries, who attempted to place marriage on a legal and institutional basis, bore fruits wherever they labored. . . . The schools in which the missionaries labored became centers in which sexual mores were taught and enforced and institutionalized family relations were cultivated.[43]

[40] Frazier, *The Negro in the United States, op. cit.*, p. 55. But see Stanley Elkins' more sinister interpretation of the Negro's assimilation of those "ideals and sentiments" in Chapter 3.

[41] Frazier, *The Negro Family in the United States, op. cit.*, p. 336.

[42] Frazier, *The Negro in the United States, op. cit.*, p. 285.

[43] *Ibid.*, p. 314; see also Frazier, *The Negro Family in the United States*, p. 285.

Booker T. Washington stands as a symbol of this acculturating force. He has become much denigrated, even violently rejected, by Negroes in recent years. But although he has come to symbolize acceptance of segregation, he also stood for the so-called Protestant ethic in its nineteenth-century form. He exalted thrift; he emphasized the moral value of work, as well as its economic value; he stood for the solid, stable values of property, and for disciplined sex. The Talented Tenth who, DuBois hoped, were to carry these values to their less privileged fellows also contributed to the acculturation process before they, like Washington himself, were rejected.

C. S. Johnson has illustrated the operation of these acculturating processes on isolated plantations:

> The sense of shame and lowered status follows illegitimacy when . . . there has been exposure to recognized standards of a higher level, as a result of children returning from boarding-school, or when the family has acquired some education. . . .
>
> Work on the railroad had carried . . . [Jacob Wagner] frequently out of the city. He knew the significance of separation and divorce and had taught it to his daughters. . . .
>
> The mother showed no sensitiveness about her daughter's illegitimate children, but the daughter, on the other hand, withdrew in embarrassment when the subject came up. The younger generation is slowly picking up new notions although they cannot always escape the current of the old life to make the shift to the new. . . .
>
> The mother . . . said none of her girls was married, and added emphatically, "Neither of them has had any children either." The remark, as well as the emphasis, was offered without prompting and reflected a new consciousness to the changing mores. . . .
>
> Conflict in Sherman Riggs' mind arose over the question of marrying the woman by whom he had had several children, to satisfy new notions about legitimacy and respectability. . . .
>
> . . . [In brief,] there has been definite cultural penetration through the medium of the school, the church, the influence of persons educated outside the community, the exposure to demonstrations in health and agriculture, and through returned migrants.[44]

PERSONAL INFLUENCE: THE ACCULTURATED

As the core of stable families with conventional moral behavior grew, and especially as some of them acquired education, good incomes, and occupations of higher prestige, they could themselves perform the acculturating role for others by controlling acceptance into their class through a strongly enforced set of exclusive—even snobbish—sanctions.

But their acculturating function was blunted by their relatively small

[44] Johnson, *op. cit.*, pp. 68, 79, 87, 88, 89, 209.

numbers. The nature of this structural impediment to acculturation has been revealed by a recent study of 224 mothers, interviewed during confinement in the hospital, with respect to their exposure to articles on child-rearing. Class for class, fewer Negro mothers than white mothers had been exposed to such articles, and the difference remained even when differences in education were taken into account. Blau explains the discrepancy in terms of the role of the middle class in acculturating upwardly mobile mothers. Among the white women, there was a relatively large, stable middle class to exert influence on a relatively smaller upwardly mobile contingent just entering that class; but among the Negro women this was not true.

> The constitution of the Negro middle class differs sharply from that of the white middle class, and therein may lie the explanation, at least to some degree, of the differences in the extent to which their members expose themselves to child-rearing literature. . . . The size of the established Negro middle class has traditionally been much smaller than its white counterpart, both in absolute and in relative terms. Since World War II, however, employment opportunities for Negroes in nonmanual occupations have increased, with corresponding increases in the numbers who have recently moved from the working class into the middle class. Indeed, in our sample, fully 90 per cent of the middle-class Negro women came from working-class backgrounds, in contrast to 35 per cent in the white middle class. Owing to their insignificant number, the stationary members of the middle class are not in a position to exert any appreciable effect on the behavior of the upwardly mobile members of their class. . . . Thus the new member has fewer opportunities than her white counterpart for exposure to, and assimilation of, middle-class modes of behavior within her own color group. . . .
>
> As a result, the acculturation of Negro upwardly mobile women to the modes of behavior that prevail in the middle class is likely to proceed at a slower pace than in the case of upwardly mobile whites. . . .[45]

The importance of the acculturated in acculturating others has been recognized in urban renewal projects. In the Washington Park Urban Renewal Project in Boston, for example, efforts to improve the area depended in part on the "respectable" families' remaining as "role models"; they were important because "they are families whose way of life—whose 'respectability' is seen as so unchallengeable that they are indeed models to their deprived and less fortunate neighbors." Such families not only provide models of family life but also "bring cultural values and a degree of stability to the community." [46] Efforts were made, therefore, to render the area attractive to these acculturated families, but it is not always easy.

---

[45] Zena Smith Blau, "Exposure to Child-rearing Experts: A Structural Interpretation of Class-Color Differences," *American Journal of Sociology*, LXIX (May 1964), 605-607.

[46] Lewis G. Watts, et. al., *The Middle-Income Negro Family Faces Urban Renewal* (Waltham, Mass.: Brandeis University, 1964), pp. 7, 21.

An Anomalous Case.   An interesting, if not numerically impressive, case of acculturation in recent years is that illustrated by the Black Muslims. Like the nineteenth-century New England Protestant missionaries, they have imposed upon their followers a strict code of behavior with respect to both family and work roles. They transform hedonistic, consumption-oriented, "pleasure-loving" individuals into sober, sexually disciplined, industrious men and women. (It is reported that they have even cured drug addictions and alcoholism among their followers.) Under their influence, men cease to be dependent; they assume leadership in their families. Women become decorous.[47] A Muslim ethic, similar to the Protestant ethic, controls their lives. (The one great difference is that the Muslim ethic is animated by hatred and racism.) But so far as marriage and the family are concerned, the personal influence of the Black Muslims has the same effect, apparently, as that of the Protestant missionaries.

MASS MEDIA AND ACCULTURATION

Personal influence is, then, enormously important in the process of acculturation. But it is not the only channel by which the process takes place. With the increase in literacy and in exposure to the mass media, more acculturating influences come into play. Ralph Ellison has emphasized the importance of this common literary culture among Negroes. To the child absorbed in a fascinating book, the author speaks without prejudice, regardless of race. Neither Shakespeare nor Henry Miller shows the least bit of discrimination against him; they belong to him as much as they do to any white reader. The culture of books belongs to anyone who cares to appropriate it.

The television-viewing and radio-listening habits of young Negroes have been reported to be about the same as those of their white counterparts.[48] They also learn, albeit vicariously, the standards of the larger culture, and they may also adopt them. If the mass media have influenced the manners and morals of white youngsters, they have also influenced those of Negro youngsters.

CONVERGENCE AT THE TOP: THE BLACK BOURGEOISIE

If the phenomenon of the Black Muslims may be viewed as, in effect, the triumph of the Protestant ethic at the lower-income levels, the phe-

[47] One sociologist is of the opinion that the expectation among the Black Muslims that men carry temple leadership and family responsibility roles may prove their most significant achievement (Rita M. James, in review of C. Eric Lincoln's *Black Muslims in America* [Boston: Beacon Press, 1961], in *American Journal of Sociology*, 67 [September 1961], 214). The number of members is not published; it is estimated at about a hundred thousand.

[48] Albert J. Lott and Bernice E. Lott, *Negro and White Youth: A Psychological Study in a Border State Community* (New York: Holt, Rinehart & Winston, Inc., 1963).

nomenon of the black bourgeoisie may be viewed as the triumph of the hedonistic ethic at the upper-income levels.

It was not until World War I that family stability and conventional moral behavior lost their primacy as criteria of social status among Negroes. More and more, income, education, and occupation began to differentiate Negro families. One of the first casualties of the upward mobility of many Negro families was what Frazier has called the "genteel tradition," for the families in this tradition—with their emphasis on propriety, manners, morals, and refinement—could not hold their own against the new classes.

As the Negro masses acquired education, they began gradually to flaunt the standards of behavior and values represented by the genteel tradition. The ascendancy of the "gentleman" was not completely undermined until the mass migrations of Negroes to cities and the resulting accelerated occupational differentiation of the Negro population. . . . The members of . . . [the] class which regarded the genteel tradition as its most precious heritage had to come to terms with the representatives of the Negro masses who had acquired an education, especially a professional education, or had become successful in business. The attitude of those who came to terms with the successful members of the rising black masses was expressed by a young mulatto college student, who was a descendant of a prominent free mulatto family. When asked how she felt when a big, ill-mannered Negro male student addressed her rudely and tossed her about, she replied, "Well, since I have got to live with these niggers, I might as well act like one.". . . The tradition of the gentleman has ceased to have influence on either the manners or morals of the Negro community. . . .[49]

Money alone was not yet the major criterion of class, but the lack of money was a serious barrier to entry into the higher levels. Thus "the old families were undermined because they lacked an economic base."[50] Without good incomes, even family stability and conventional moral behavior were no longer enough to maintain high social status.

. . . In the North, these old families had had several generations of more or less close contacts with the whites, not only as servants but in schools and other institutions. In the South, [although] these old families had ceased to have close contacts with the aristocratic whites . . . the heritage of conventional behavior which they had acquired had become a part of their family traditions. . . . There was [therefore] often cause for genuine contempt for the crudeness and exhibitionism of those who had acquired prominence because of education and a relatively good income. They appreciated the difference between a man or woman without real culture and family traditions who had acquired a formal college education—and that often in an inferior Negro

[49] Frazier, *Black Bourgeoisie, op. cit.*, pp. 99-100.
[50] Frazier, *The Negro in the United States, op. cit.*, p. 289.

college—and a man or woman with a background of several generations of stable family life and conventional conduct.[51]

This is, of course, the classic lament of a displaced élite: "In the large urban communities of the North, the Negro, like other people, wins a place not because of family but through competition." [52]

For a time, the changes in the criteria of class were concentrated within the acculturated strand: upward mobility was achieved through education and occupation, rather than through lineage or family stability. But when the wealthy members of the hedonistic culture also knocked at the doors of the old upper class, a new hybrid culture—the so-called black bourgeoisie—was born.

Whereas in the 1930s it was reported that the Negroes who had become wealthy in illegal enterprises were "by no means scornful of the opinions of the 'upper respectables' " (but, in fact, sought "to secure prestige in the eyes of this group by assuming many aspects of its behavior pattern"),[53] in the 1950s it was reported that some of the members of the older middle and upper classes were now imitating *them* instead. A reversal of the personal-influence process of acculturation had occurred, and the older élite and the newer high-income classes merged.

The black bourgeoisie is . . . recruited from the successful underworld—Negroes who have gained their money from gambling, prostitution, bootlegging, and the "numbers." The old upper class in the Negro community erected an impenetrable barrier between themselves and Negroes who represented the "sporting" and criminal world. Since such Negroes were generally able to handle more money than the majority of Negroes, they always constituted a threat to the respectable way of life cherished by the old middle classes. As a result of urbanization, which upset the old class structure of the Negro community, the "sporting" and criminal elements began to acquire a dominant position among Negroes. . . . [Their] standards of consumption . . . [became] the measure of success among the black middle class.

The standards which they [i.e., the black bourgeoisie] set are emulated by Negroes in the professional classes—doctors, dentists and lawyers, and even teachers as far as they are able to do so. But more important still, in order to secure the money necessary to maintain these standards, Negro professional men engage in the same "rackets" as the successful Negroes in the underworld. Consequently, among the black bourgeoisie an expensive automobile, a "palatial" residence, and a yacht bring more recognition to a doctor than some achievement in medicine.[54]

But the old "respectable" upper classes remained outside the charmed circle, even though "at the summer resorts where the black bourgeoisie

[51] *Ibid.*, p. 285.
[52] *Ibid.*, p. 290.
[53] Drake and Cayton, *op. cit.*, pp. 524-25.
[54] Frazier, *Black Bourgeoisie*, pp. 109-10.

gather to display their wealth, the descendants of the old respectable families must defer to the underworld elements, who, through their money, have risen to the top of Negro society!" [55] The repercussions of this acculturation-in-reverse at the high-income level on marriage and family were great. Frazier has summarized some of them as follows:

> The break with traditional values is seen in the changes in the canons of respectability. Among the older upper-class families in the Negro community, who really stood for a middle-class way of life, the canons of respectability required stable family life and conventional sex behavior. On the other hand, among the new black bourgeoisie these values are regarded as "old-fashioned" virtues and there is much confusion in thinking and behavior with reference to these values. Divorces and scandals in family and sex behavior do not affect one's social status; rather the notoriety which one acquires in such cases adds to one's prestige. The change in attitudes towards the "old-fashioned" bourgeois values is due largely to the fact that the new bourgeoisie is recruited from those elements in the Negro population among whom these virtues never existed and that money has become the chief requirement for social acceptance.[56]

Frazier seems to have overstated his case. It is probably true that neither color nor family stability any longer plays a uniquely pre-eminent part in social status,[57] but both are undoubtedly still important. The acculturated strand, with its emphasis on conventional behavior is still a major segment of the élite.[58]

Acculturated (as the term has been used here) is, of course, by no means identical with conformity to the Protestant ethic of the nineteenth and early twentieth centuries. As the manners and morals of the outside world have changed, so, too, have those of acculturated Negroes. The so-called "genteel tradition" so dear to the old élites appears anachronistic to young acculturated Negroes, just as it does to their counterparts in the white world. And if "the tradition of the gentleman has become the source of amusement" in the Negro world, the same could probably be said about the white world also.[59]

---

[55] *Ibid.*

[56] *Ibid.*, p. 109.

[57] In practically all studies of social distance, willingness to accept marriage is considered an important index. When social distance is absent, marriage is accepted. Among Negroes in the rural South, Frazier tells us, "social relations tend to be informal, social status and social distinctions are less marked, except in such matters as marriage, than in urban areas" (*The Negro in the United States, op. cit.*, p. 278). The "better" families did not hold aloof except when it came to marriage with the "lower" families.

[58] A study of Negro high school students found them, especially the girls, more concerned than white students with doing the "right" thing and with being considered "proper" and "good" (Lott and Lott, *op. cit.*, p. 142). Respectability, financial security, and service were the dominant goals for the Negro girls (p. 143).

[59] Frazier, *Black Bourgeoisie, op. cit.*, p. 100.

Cases in Point

Two basic touchstones of the Protestant ethic are sex and work. We can, therefore, highlight the differences between the acculturated and the hedonistic strands by showing their differences in these two areas. Customs and mores dealing with out-of-wedlock births are the indexes used here to represent the ethic with respect to sex.

CUSTOMS AND MORES DEALING WITH OUT-OF-WEDLOCK BIRTHS

As a result of the early sexual development and experience of many Negro boys and girls,[60] premarital pregnancies have, as already noted, a relatively high probability among young, unmarried Negro girls. It is not now true (nor was it true of the plantation family) that irresponsible out-of-wedlock births to young unmarried girls constitute a positive value to Negro families of either culture. In both Negro cultures it is considered very desirable that girls be married before they have babies, but the cultures differ in their reactions to such births. (We are not speaking here of the births to multiparous women, discussed in Chapter 1, but rather of the first baby born to a young, unmarried woman or girl.)

What are the mores among Negroes with respect to young, unmarried mothers? Is her child welcomed? Is it accepted casually? Is the event condoned? bemoaned? condemned? These were among the questions asked by Elizabeth Herzog of the Children's Bureau several years ago in a review of all the available research on the subject. And, strange as it may seem, no unequivocal answer was forthcoming: for every study that reported a matter-of-fact acceptance, there was one that reported condemnation or another that reported both; for every study that reported shame or guilt on the part of the young mother, there was another that reported none. At a round-table discussion by Urban League community leaders in 1964, there was the same lack of agreement on what the facts were, let alone "the truth." (When one participant said that Negro society accepted out-of-wedlock births, there was loud denial from some of the others.) It would be possible to explain this lack of agreement by attributing bias or defensiveness to the observers. But it is also possible that both sets of observers might be right. It may be the presence of women from both cultures in populations of unmarried mothers that confounds research.

A Cincinnati study in 1936, for example, reported:

[60] Kinsey and his associates reported that "by age fifteen, 62 per cent of the grade-school educated had had premarital coitus, and by age twenty, 82 per cent. Among the high-school educated, the percentage by age fifteen is 48 per cent and by age twenty, 82 per cent." For college women, only 8 per cent had had premarital relations by age fifteen, 49 per cent, by age twenty; and 71 per cent by age twenty-five. (P. H. Gebhard, *et al., Pregnancy and Abortion* (New York: Harper, Hoeber, 1958), p. 155.

As far as we have been able to learn, illegitimate pregnancy is viewed with much less concern [among Negroes] than . . . [among] white people. We have known one or two "shot-gun" marriages among the lower class of Negroes. Mostly, beyond more or less pressure by relatives, the matter of marriage under such circumstances is left to the couple involved. Often enough, the girl will not declare the father of the child unless she is rather certain he will marry her without undue pressure. Frequently enough, she cannot be certain which man is responsible. We know of several instances in which girls frankly welcomed pregnancy as an excuse for getting out of school attendance.[61]

The study revealed, furthermore, that there was no discrimination against the out-of-wedlock child itself.

Yet a 1941 study of forty-four unmarried Negro mothers in St. Louis reported that "in twenty-nine cases the girl's family rejected her and the child after the birth of the child." The drive toward respectability seemed to be part of the drive toward upward social mobility: "In some homes where the family rejected the girl and her child, the rejection was prompted by the feeling that the unwed mother had broken the family's stride forward toward the cultural level they hoped to attain." [62] The author concluded:

It is important to note that in the majority of these cases the girl's family, contrary to popular belief, was not accepting of her situation of unwed motherhood. This is doubly important when we consider that this group in most cases is representative of the low and middle classes in the social structure of the Negro urban community, rather than of the upper class.[63]

In 1944 a study of eleven unmarried mothers in a Southern city, all from the same economic background, found widely different reactions, reflecting the two cultures. The young women in one set were class-conscious and looked down on "common" people; in this set, illegitimacy caused severe loss in social status. The girls in the other set were not class-conscious; they accepted illegitimacy, which was common among their friends. The first set of girls said that the lower classes accepted illegitimacy but that "nice people" considered it a sin and a disgrace.[64]

Somewhat more sophisticated was a 1945 study of forty-nine unmarried mothers in Washington, D.C. This study assumed that guilt feelings, expressed directly or indirectly, served as an index of the degree to which the girl had incorporated the taboo against illegitimacy and, hence, of

[61] A. T. Childers, "Some Notes on Sex Mores among Negro Children," *American Journal of Orthopsychiatry* (July 1936), 444.

[62] Josephine Reynolds, "Problems of Forty-Four Negro Unmarried Mothers in St. Louis, Missouri, March 1940–March 1941." Digest of Master's dissertation presented at St. Louis University Graduate School, St. Louis, Mo.

[63] *Ibid.*

[64] Hilda Hertz and Sue Warren Little, "Unmarried Negro Mothers in a Southern Urban Community," *Social Forces*, XXIII (October 1944), 73-79.

her degree of acculturation. The authors distinguished three groups among the subjects.

In the first there was great concern and anxiety: the girls had delayed seeing a doctor for fear that their suspicions would be confirmed; they were ashamed to ask their families for help, and they could not remain at home, for secrecy was important. These girls spoke of themselves as being bad, as having committed a sin. Self-condemning, they were also anxious about condemnation by employers, coworkers, and associates. They wanted to marry the father of the child to "get rid" of the sin.

At the other extreme were those who showed no apparent discomfort, neither guilt nor anxiety. These girls had applied to social agencies for help with finances, hospitalization, and the behavior problems of the child.

In between were those who gave lip service to anxiety. They assured the social workers that they accepted the norms against illegitimacy; but they had been able to violate them without severe trauma. They often wanted their babies; they did not consider having them to be "bad"; they felt no need for self-punishment or self-abasement. They recognized that unmarried motherhood was considered a disgrace, but they had not violated an internalized norm. They could conceive of going through the experience a second time. They felt they had made a mistake and ought to be punished; but this was not an intense feeling.[65]

Hylan Lewis' study of a Southern mill town in the 1940s revealed that illegitimate motherhood did not militate against marriage:

> There are many girls and many parents whose views are . . . conventional; once pregnancy ensues—barring abortion or miscarriage—individual, family, and community pressures begin to operate. It is considered the right thing for the man to marry the girl, and if he does, he is commended. The chances of the man marrying her are high if she has not been promiscuous.
> . . . The community attitudes toward the illegitimate child are not harsh. It is better, of course, to have been born in wedlock, but the stigma for child and mother, unless they belong to the more stable families, is not great. The sanctions are few, other than mild gossip, which is certain, and possible "churching," i.e., being called before the church and having to express contriteness and to ask forgiveness.[66]

An Indiana study in 1957 reported that the unmarried mother's own parents were rejecting and punitive toward her. Most of the girls pretended to be married: they bought themselves wedding rings, and asked friends to send them flowers at the hospital so people would think their

---

[65] Patricia Knapp and Sophie T. Cambria, "The Attitudes of Negro Unmarried Mothers toward Illegitimacy," *Smith College Studies in Social Work*, XVII (1946-47), 185-203.

[66] Lewis, *op. cit.*, p. 89.

"husbands" had sent them. These facts do not fit into a picture of the Negro as indifferent to illegitimacy.[67]

The two cultures can also be distinguished in another interesting, albeit modest, study of twenty-five unmarried mothers (referred to as "the Clinic Group") and twenty-five girls of comparable economic background (referred to as "the Center Group" because they were studied in a neighborhood house). One-parent homes were characteristic of both groups, and the parents' occupational statuses were similar. The groups differed, however, with respect to their acceptance of premarital sex relations. Although about the same proportion of girls in both groups said such relations were never right, at least twice as many in the Center Group as in the Clinic Group said these relations were not right just because the boy wanted them or because their friends were engaging in them or even if both partners wanted them. Seven of the twenty-five Center Group girls condemned sexual intercourse even when the boy and girl planned to get married, but only four of the Clinic Group girls did. The author concluded that the Center Group girls were more conventional sexually; those in the Clinic Group were more acquiescent. Asked how they would feel if they heard that an unmarried girl friend of theirs was going to have a baby, more than half the girls in both groups replied they would feel sorry, but far more of the Center Group girls (twenty) than of the Clinic Group girls (fourteen) made this reply; a similar discrepancy was found in the proportion of those who felt the girl should or would feel ashamed (Center Group, nineteen; Clinic Group, thirteen). But a much larger discrepancy than either of these was shown in the proportion of those who said it would be the girl's own business (Center Group, ten; Clinic Group, eighteen). Similar, but more pronounced, differences were reported when the girls were asked how they would feel if they themselves were the girls involved.[68]

And, finally, there is the somewhat tangential evidence from a study of one-parent mothers in Philadelphia in the 1960s. Among these subjects there was no stigma associated with unmarried motherhood.

[67] A'Lelia Josephine Osili and Frieda Alice Parker, "A Follow-up Study of Fifty Unmarried Negro Mothers in Active Aid-to-Dependent-Children Cases in the Marion County Department of Public Welfare, Indianapolis, Indiana" (Marion County, Ind.: Department of Public Welfare, January 24, 1957).

[68] Stanley Bigman, in an unpublished study of unmarried mothers in Washington, D.C. The source of information about sex appeared to be significant: "none of the girls who named her boy friend as one of her sources of sex information said that sexual intercourse should wait until marriage; or conversely, none of the girls who opposed premarital relations said she got information from a boy friend." The boy friends appeared to be very persuasive teachers, using the learning-by-doing technique. Cutting off such instruction appeared to be a strategic safeguard for the Center Group girls. But this safeguard itself differentiated the Center Group and the Clinic Group girls.

The study cited in the following paragraph is found in Robert Bell, "The One-Parent Mother in the Negro Lower Class," p. 6.

It is an indication of the lack of stigma associated with being an unwed mother in the Negro lower class that one third of the one-parent mothers defined themselves as "never married" when they could have given another marital status.

Conversely, of course, two thirds gave their marital status as separated, widowed, or divorced; among these one-parent mothers an indeterminate number were, presumably, in the "never-married" category, or at least in the "never-married-to-the-father-of-one-or-more-of-the-children" category.

We have made a distinction between institutionalization and acculturation in our comparison of the two cultures. But even among the acculturated, primary-group attitudes may be at war with institutional prescriptions. Joseph S. Himes reported some interesting reactions among Negro college women when he asked a hundred of them how they would respond, and what response they would in turn expect from others, if they found themselves pregnant. Their replies reflected the conflict between primary-group values and institutionalized values.

> The girls anticipate rejection or lack of sympathy from the formal institutions but expect primary groups and intimate associates to be accepting and supportive. The school is regarded as the most intolerant institution, while parents, siblings, and best friends are viewed as most accepting. The fact that sixty-nine subjects believed that their churches would not reject them in this situation is consonant with the social philosophy of Christianity and the primary-group character of many congregations.[69]

Most, but not all these college women were in the acculturated strand:

> Ninety-four girls . . . assert that . . . they would feel challenged to straighten out their lives and succeed. . . . Seventy girls . . . reject the notion of pregnancy as evidence of "real womanhood." This question was aimed at the idea, said to be common among lower-class [externally adapted] individuals, that sexual accomplishment constitutes evidence of "real" manhood or womanhood.
>
> Between the sense of challenge and the rejection of pregnancy as a sex-prowess symbol, the girls indicated a variety of self-disparaging attitudes. Over three fifths said that they would feel ashamed and embarrassed, and half, fifty-one, defined guilt feelings in religious or moral terms. . . . They strongly rejected violence—suicide, abortion, and infanticide—as an acceptable solution.[70]

Even those who were, presumably, acculturated rejected the notion of marriage as a "solution" for out-of-wedlock births. Thus:

----

[69] Joseph S. Himes, "Some Reactions to a Hypothetical Premarital Pregnancy by One Hundred Negro College Women," *Journal Marriage and Family*, XXVI (August 1964), 364. Among a second sample of high school girls, almost all anticipated stronger social disapproval; they were also consistent in their replies. Their expectation of strong social disapproval was probably realistic because they were younger than the college students.

[70] *Ibid.*, pp. 346-47.

. . . only thirteen of the subjects said that they would feel exploited by the putative father. This finding seems to contradict the middle-class [or acculturated] orientation and to become sharpened when related to the fact that . . . fewer than half would agree to marry any man to legitimize the child, the putative father included, and most seemed to prefer facing life with an illegitimate child. Finally, three fifths would prefer to keep the baby, and a fourth or fewer would relinquish it either to relatives and friends or for adoption.[71]

In any event, whatever else these studies may or may not reveal, they do show that illegitimacy is not accepted—let alone welcomed—even in all low-income families. For many it is as traumatic as it is for middle- or upper-class families. The externally adapted families may resign themselves to such an event; but the acculturated, even the lower-class acculturated, do not.

THE ETHOS OF WORK

Nothing distinguishes the two cultures more dramatically than their work ethos. In the Protestant ethic, work is almost the supreme value. It is considered intrinsically good. However much Booker T. Washington and W. E. B. DuBois might have differed with respect to many other issues, they agreed on the importance of work, which, for both men, involved a religious sanction. ". . . Work is Heaven; Idleness, Hell; and Wage is the 'Well done!' of the Master, who summoned all them that labor and are heavy laden," said DuBois, himself a New Englander.[72] And Washington's name has become almost synonymous with industriousness.

But the slave ethos of work was precisely the opposite. To the slave, work was an evil that was forced upon one by the whip. Laziness, poor work, evasion, and stupidity were the Negro slave's great weapons against the overseer. Many freedmen retained this attitude toward work. Many refused to work at all; they waited to be taken care of one way or another. Without the whip or the threat of punishment, they had no inbred compulsion to work. In the white world, the Protestant ethic of work had succeeded because, in brutal truth, it paid off: hard work had resulted in capital formation which was financially profitable. Work did not always produce the same effect in the Negro world.

But the distinction between the work ethos of the two Negro cultures does not lie in the relative industriousness of their members. It lies, rather, in the nature of the work they are attracted to. The members of both may be equally industrious, but in different ways: the acculturated aspire to kinds of work characterized by stability, steadiness, and security; the externally adapted like adventure and risk—"hustling" or "cash-

---

[71] *Ibid.*

[72] W. E. B. DuBois, "Credo," in *Darkwater* (New York: Harcourt, Brace & World, Inc., 1921), p. 3.

ing in" or "boosting." It is strangely anomalous that the externally adapted sometimes show the enterprise, the initiative, the entrepreneurial skills, and the innovative talents traditionally associated with the original bourgeoisie. All too often their activities are illegal, but in them they may exhibit the same kind of talents as those involved in legitimate enterprises.[73]

These attitudes were revealed in a teen-agers' discussion of money on a 1965 television program.[74] Two of the group were Negroes; one was a Puerto Rican; the other three were white and archetypically middle-class —as was one of the Negro boys. The middle-class youngsters—the three white participants and one of the Negro boys—were products of the Protestant ethic, so we need not elaborate their point of view. Of special interest was the discussion of the second Negro boy (N.B.) and the Puerto Rican (P.R.). Both were school dropouts, and the Puerto Rican boy was married and a father.

Question: How do you get money?

N.B.: Oh, you can always find some way.

Question: How?

N.B.: Well, I go out on the street and hustle. . . .

Question: What's that?

N.B. (somewhat taken aback): Hustle. . . .

Question: Yes, but what is it?

N.B.: Well, you have to make it seem as though she's doing something for you. . . .

Question: What else do you do?

N.B.: Well, you walk down the street and ask people if they want you to do something. And here's a man wants a package delivered. That's $50. . . .

Question: What kind of package would pay that much to be delivered?

N.B. (smiling knowingly): I never ask. It's none of my business. I never know what's in the package. . . .

Question: Wouldn't you rather have a steady job?

N.B.: If it paid and you didn't have to work so hard.

Question: Did you ever have a job?

N.B.: I used to work for the Neighborhood House. But it was too hard.

---

[73] A case study of a small-scale hustler is presented by Henry Williamson in his autobiography, *Hustler: The Autobiography of a Thief* (Garden City, N.Y.: Doubleday & Company, Inc., 1965). See also Kenneth B. Clark, *Dark Ghetto* (New York: Harper & Row, Publishers, 1965), pp. 49-50. Clark notes that getting rid of "bopping" gangs resulted in more drug addiction and stimulation of a hustling subculture (p. 107).

[74] This was a National Educational Television program broadcast January 29, 1965. The name of the program was "The Comers." The version presented here is not verbatim; it is based on notes taken during the broadcast.

Question: What kind of work was it?

N.B.: Taking care of those kids. They kept asking questions. . . .

Question: How old were they?

N.B.: Seven to thirteen.

Question: How much pay would you want?

P.R.: I used to work and got only $45 a week so I quit.

N.B.: You can't go far on $45.

P.R.: Not with a family.

N.B.: You can do better than that by mugging. You could get that in one night.

P.R.: It depends on who you mug. . . .

The Puerto Rican and the Negro boy then carried on a brief, matter-of-fact discussion of mugging. It was viewed as simply one of several ways of getting money, better than some, not as good as others. Neither it nor any other form of hustling was viewed with horror or revulsion. The young men made a distinction between *good* and *legit*. Some kinds of work might be both "good"—in the sense of *profitable*—and "legit." But the likelihood was greater that if it was "good," it would not be "legit." These young men did not conform to the picture of juvenile delinquents who rebel against the world and become nonrationally destructive as a form of revenge against it. They did not seem to conceive of themselves as criminals; they just took it for granted that there were certain ways of getting money with a minimum of effort and that one would be a fool to eschew them.

The middle-class youngsters—including the other Negro boy—kept bringing in the values of honesty, work, and delayed gratification (i.e., the Protestant ethic). Thus, two totally different approaches to life and its problems were reflected, and the two groups talked past—rather than to—one another.

The point here is that the division in this group was not along lines of race but along those of cultural values: one Negro boy clearly belonged with the white participants; the other, to a totally different cultural world.

RELATIVE PREVALENCE OF ACCULTURATED AND EXTERNALLY ADAPTED

It would be useful if we could somehow or other determine the relative prevalence of the two cultures and isolate them for scientific study. Unfortunately, most current research uses such criteria as income, education, occupation, and/or residence as indexes of class. These criteria are even more inadequate for studies of Negroes than they are for studies of white families, for both acculturated and externally adapted elements may occur at all income levels, and studies based on income do not differentiate between the two.

Because the acculturated are likely to achieve more than the externally adapted—both as cause and as effect of their acculturation—there may be some slight justification for assuming that the "masses" are externally adapted and the "middle classes" and the "upper classes" acculturated. This assumption, at any rate, has underlain much of the research on marriage and family among Negroes, so that most of our knowledge on this subject reflects this bias. The "masses" or the "lower classes" are contrasted with the "lower-middle classes," the "middle classes," and the "upper classes." This viewpoint, however, confounds the conventional, acculturated low-income family with the "masses," and does not adequately distinguish between the rich "nonrespectables" and the conventional high-income family.

Whatever might be the relative prevalence of the two cultures, and whatever may be their class composition as measured by income, one fact seems to be clear-cut and unequivocal: they are separated by a great social and psychological chasm.

The Great Divide

WITHIN- AND BETWEEN-CLASS CLEAVAGES

The great chasm between the two Negro worlds is so great as to be, for all intents and purposes, all but unbridgeable, at least until now. Fear and hostility—even hatred and resentment—characterize the relations, or lack of relations, between them. The cleavage reaches both ends of the income scale and crosses income-class lines in both cultures; nor is it mitigated by the ambivalence which often characterizes it.[75]

Within-class Cleavage. "Even the strictest family discipline," Frazier noted, "may prove ineffectual when it is not supported by the opinion of the community and is opposed to what is regarded as normal behavior." [76] The low-income acculturated families wage an incessant battle against what they consider to be the moral "contamination" of their children by the less disciplined children of the externally adapted. "Where they have been few in numbers, they have often shut themselves up within the narrow circle of their own families in order not to be overwhelmed by the flood of immorality and vice surrounding them." [77] These families are characterized by "pride, respectability and . . . conventional morals" and hence frown upon the (to them) immorality around them; they are

[75] Kenneth Clark, *Dark Ghetto* (New York: Harper & Row, Publishers, 1965) p. 196.

[76] E. Franklin Frazier, "The Negro Middle Class and Desegregation," *Social Problems* (April 1957), 291-308.

[77] E. Franklin Frazier, *The Negro Family in the United States*, rev. ed. (New York: Holt, Rinehart & Winston, Inc., 1949), p. 190.

ashamed of it.[78] Davis and Dollard refer to the "virtual chasm" which separates the "social expectations and available goal responses" of the two cultures at the lowest levels: "The chasm is a behavioral one. It lies between the stimuli and goals of the 'respectable,' status-bound lower-middle class and those of the recalcitrant, impulsive, and physically aggressive lower class." [79]

Nor have the issues always necessarily been moral ones. Kardiner and Ovesey quote one of their subjects, a porter studying radio technology in night school, as follows:

> One thing I feel bad about—one thing I have a lot of resentment about—they don't try to help one another, the Negroes. Instead, they go against one another. Take Harlem. There's a lot of people there who don't want to work. They just want to wait 'til the other person gets some money. Then they'll knock him on the head, and get it away. I don't like that. That's what's holding all of us back. One guy is trying to advance and the majority pulls him back.[80]

The battle also has been waged at the high-income levels. We have already noted the largely fruitless effort of the old middle classes to protect themselves against "threat to the respectable way of life" posed by the rising, more monied classes.[81] In fact, the acculturation process was actually reversed, with the acculturated taking over the patterns of the "upper-class nonrespectables." Whatever the outcome of the struggle, however, the point is that the chasm between the two cultures is found at all income levels.

Between-Class Cleavage. The schism also has had a strong class character: the upper-level acculturated and the low-level externally adapted—the "masses"—have been locked in combat. Under slavery, the acculturated looked down on the field slaves, and this attitude persisted after emancipation. When and where the upper-level acculturated have constituted a very small proportion of the population, they have protected themselves by withdrawing and isolating themselves from those they despised. Thus, for example:

> The descendants of the free mulattos became, after the Civil War, the core of a small upper class which undertook to maintain the American pattern of family life and conventional sex mores. In some small communities in the South, a single family with this social and cultural background would live in complete

[78] Hylan Lewis, *Blackways of Kent* (Chapel Hill, N.C.: University of North Carolina Press, 1955), p. 86.

[79] Allison Davis and John Dollard, *Children of Bondage* (American Council on Education, 1940), pp. 264-65.

[80] Abram Kardiner and Lionel Ovesey, *The Mark of Oppression* (New York: Meridian, The World Publishing Co., 1962), p. 89.

[81] E. Franklin Frazier, *Black Bourgeoisie* (New York: The Crowell-Collier Publishing Co., 1962), pp. 109-110.

isolation rather than associate with the masses of Negroes. . . . Sometimes these old "genteel" families sought to preserve their traditions by withdrawing from the competition with the new professional classes in the Negro community. In their quiet, obscure lives, they expressed often their contempt for the black upstarts who, in their view, and often in fact, possessed neither morals nor manners.[82]

Again, in the 1940s in a Southern mill town:

. . . These top families . . . tend to be proud isolates, each with a certain amount of disdain for the other. They, in turn, are outstanding targets for status-starved groups in the community who both respect and envy them, and who show both deference and depreciation. . . . The various upper[-level] families . . . with a gulf of family pride and respectability between them and much of the community . . . tend to be lonely groups.[83]

Sometimes there was positive rejection of the "masses" by the acculturated, as in Louisiana after the Civil War when "the hostility of some members of this class to the newly emancipated blacks was so great that they opposed giving political rights to the freedmen." [84]

Some psychiatrists place great significance on the self-hatred they attribute to Negroes, but many Negroes deny its existence. Whether or not individual Negroes hate themselves, it may be said with some conviction that acculturated Negroes reject the externally adapted, especially those of the lower class. Because they are in contact with the larger, white culture, they apply its standards to the behavior of the externally adapted —and reject it.[85]

. . . [m]any Negro teachers refuse identification with the Negro masses and look upon teaching primarily as a source of income. In many cases they have nothing but contempt for their Negro pupils.[86]

Many Negro college graduates do not engage actively in Negro organizations;[87] and their relationship to the rest of the Negro world is sometimes one of positive exploitation.

[82] Frazier, *Black Bourgeoisie*, pp. 99-100.

[83] Lewis, *op. cit.*, p. 108.

[84] Frazier, *Black Bourgeoisie*, p. 99.

[85] In one study of schoolchildren in a Southern mill town, it was reported that their *"explicit* objects of aggression tend to be . . . in-group rather than out-group. They tend to be the individual who does one harm or segments of one's own group who behave in unapproved ways. Fifty per cent of the children wrote that they felt resentment against no one, and about one in four did not comment at all. Of the one fourth who mentioned specific objects, more than twice as many mentioned the Negro than mentioned the white group: 18 per cent to 8 per cent. Those who expressed in-group aggression mentioned "bad types, embarrassing types, and those who try to appear better than they are" (Lewis, *op. cit.*, pp. 111-12).

[86] Frazier, *Black Bourgeoisie*, p. 194.

[87] Charles S. Johnson, *The Negro College Graduate* (Chapel Hill, N.C.: University of North Carolina Press, 1938), p. 349. Two thirds of his subjects stated that they had no

When the opportunity has been present, the black bourgeoisie has exploited the Negro masses as ruthlessly as have whites.[88]

The attitude of the externally adapted has been no more cordial:

The masses regard the black bourgeoisie as simply those who have been "lucky in getting money," which enables them to engage in conspicuous consumption. When this class pretends to represent the best manners or morals of the Negro, the masses regard such claims as hypocrisy.[89]

Many of the externally adapted hate not only the white world but the upper-class acculturated Negro world as well. Its members live, dress, talk, and (as far as the externally adapted can tell) think like the members of the white world. The very thing that makes it possible for acculturated Negroes to interact successfully with the white world—common values—makes it difficult for them to be accepted by the externally adapted. To the lower-class Negro, if he is at all aware of the situation, the higher-class acculturated Negroes seem as remote as whites. They regard Negro spokesmen, at ease in the white world and able to enter into negotiations with it, as Uncle Toms who have identified with that world, seceded from the Negro world, sold them out.

The Negro[es] as a group or race . . . [have] had many spokesmen, but none to represent how they have felt or feel. The Negro leadership . . . has been and still is bent on integration without true concern for Negro problems or headaches. . . . The Negro establishment has been encountering difficulty in leading the "black masses" because they are detached and distant.[90]

As one Kardiner and Ovesey's subject put it:

---

connection with the social organizations of the Negro community or gave no reply to the question. Jeanne Noble has reported the same for college women in *The Negro Woman College Graduate* (New York: Columbia University Teachers College, 1956).

[88] Frazier, *Black Bourgeoisie*, p. 194. "The lip service which . . . [the Negro middle class] give to solidarity with the masses very often disguises their exploitation of the masses" (Frazier, "The Negro Middle Class and Desegregation," *op. cit.*, p. 299). This cultural alienation among Negroes has intensified the so-called dilemma of leadership. The acculturated, themselves culturally white, have tended to find many of the newer leadership approaches uncongenial. They have winced at the rowdiness and violence that often accompany them. They see all too clearly the reasons for the white community's resistance to integration; they themselves have resisted "the masses" for generations. No more than the old-line Southerner would they want their daughter to marry a "nigger," that is, an uncouth "nonrespectable." Theirs is, in a way, the most difficult position of all: they see the cruelty and injustice of punishing people for deprivations forced upon them by an inimical world, but they do not want to jeopardize their own hard-won cultural tradition by admitting the "nonrespectables" to their circle.

[89] Frazier, *Black Bourgeoisie*, p. 194.

[90] Morgan D. Carney, an American Negro, in a letter to *The New York Times*, August 12, 1964.

"I don't think much of . . . [race leaders]. I think they're just advancing themselves. . . . Regardless of how big a man gets as long as he is social with me and talks to me, then OK, but when he starts thinking he's God, then it's time to pull him down to size. I never really thought about who is the leader. I read a lot about what they is doing and saying, but it's mostly to advance themselves." . . . "These 'race leaders' . . . won't let their daughters marry except for money. They want the men their daughters marry to have fifteen college diplomas and know all the right people. That's why they ain't no leaders. Any time you consider yourself better than others you can't fight for them. All they doing is fighting for their own clique.[91]

THE CULTURAL COMPLICATIONS OF CLASS

If the differences between the two cultures were merely based on class —i.e., a matter of income or even education—the difficulties would be great enough. (To use the term *merely* is, of course, misleading because class is itself a formidable barrier to interaction.) But the differences are more profound because they are based on family values and moral issues —and indirectly, therefore, on sexual values. The acculturated, whatever their class, have placed very high value on family stability. True, they have been more permissive about sex than the members of the larger, white culture—but only when love was present. Their cultural standards, as far as sex was concerned, have been a compassionate and even romantic version of the Protestant ethic. It is not difficult to understand why they have not wanted to accept those Negroes whose manners and morals they completely reject.

Kinsey and his associates found a clear-cut relationship between sexual behavior and class (as measured by education) in his white subjects, a relationship which is not pertinent here. But one of their findings, still puzzling, may be relevant: they reported that upwardly mobile males, even in their adolescence, behaved more like the members of the class they were to reach than like those of the class from which they started. It is easy to explain this phenomenon in terms of "reference-group theory." But even if it is assumed that these males had a higher-class reference group, how did they know what the sexual patterns of this reference group were? It is possible that the relationship between upward social mobility and sexuality is not a one-way relationship: the discipline of sex, as Freudian theory suggests, may be the antecedent as well as the consequence of upward social mobility.[92]

The class-culture problem among Negroes is also complicated by the fact of color. As Frazier has made so clear, the protection of lineage as

---

[91] Kardiner and Ovesey, *op. cit.*, pp. 89-90.

[92] "The middle-class Negro fears he will be identified with the Negro masses from whom he has escaped or tried to escape, and sex is a focal point of anxiety" (Kenneth Clark, *Dark Ghetto, op. cit.*, p. 71).

reflected in light skin color was an important value in acculturated families. Thus the acculturated kept at a distance from the externally adapted in order to protect themselves against intermarriage.

IMPLICATIONS FOR COMMUNITY

The intraclass and interclass cultural cleavages have prevented the development of true community. What have looked like communities to the outside observer have been, in effect, only Potemkin villages.[93] The basic requisites for a true, functional community have been absent or incomplete. The result has been that families of both cultures have been left without the community support which Frazier correctly regards as essential for family discipline.

THE "THIRD-GENERATION EFFECT"

Among ethnic groups of European origin, it has been observed that the first, or immigrating, generation tends to cling to its cultural heritage —the nonessentials as well as the essentials. The second generation, on the other hand, has tended to discard as much as possible of their parents' culture; they feel themselves to be true Americans and dismiss their parents as "greenhorns." But the third generation displays a tendency to reevaluate the cultural heritage of their grandparents. Secure in their Americanism, the members of this generation can embrace much that their own parents had rejected.[94]

[93] It would take us too far afield to explore the complexities of community phenomena among Negroes. Frazier in 1957 presented a strong case for the study of the Negro community in the United States ("The Negro Middle Class and Desegregation," *op. cit.*, pp. 291-308). He denied "the implicit assumption that Negroes are merely atomized individuals" and insisted on the necessity "to emphasize the organized aspects of Negro life" (p. 291). He referred to ecological studies, both plantation and urban, as one approach to the study of Negro communities, but he was more especially interested in the institutions and associations which characterized the Negro community. It cannot be denied that there is a rich and proliferating group life among Negroes—clubs, gangs, cliques, congregations, fraternities, sororities, and the like. But, as Kardiner and Ovesey report, such groups have short lives and are characterized by "continuous discord, jockeying for position and prestige, and insistence that each member must have his own way" (*op. cit.*, p. 308). In recent years the emphasis has been on the lack of community in slums (Elizabeth Herzog, "Some Assumptions about the Poor," *Social Service Review*, Vol. 37 [December 1963], 394); Hylan Lewis has made the same points in his criticisms of the concept of a culture of poverty ("Culture, Class, and the Behavior of Low-Income Families," Paper, New York, June 27, 1963, pp. 41-42). And a study of thirty-four multiproblem families in Harlem corroborates the low level of interaction among them. Scores on a variable, "neighboring," were distributed as follows: 0-24, 18; 25-49, 7; 50-74, 4; 75-99, 1; 100-124, 0; 125-149, 4 (Joan Gordon and Lawrence Podell, "Social Functioning in Multiproblem Families in Harlem," unpublished paper).

[94] With respect to religion, this process has been analyzed by Will Herberg, *Protestant, Catholic, Jew* (Garden City, N.Y.: Doubleday & Company, Inc., 1955).

It is conceivable that analogous—but by no means identical—processes may come into operation among Negroes. Of the three social generations of Negroes, however, none corresponds to the first generation of European immigrants, who clung to an ancestral heritage. The acculturated of both the first and the second generation of Negroes have been eager to put as much distance as possible between themselves and the Negro world; the externally adapted, who have carried on the old culture, have done so unwittingly. But:

Many individuals among the first generation of educated Negroes, who were the products of missionary education, had a sense of responsibility toward the Negro masses and identified themselves with the struggles of the masses to overcome the handicaps of ignorance and poverty. . . . They occupied a dignified position within the Negro community and were respected. As teachers of Negroes, they generally exhibited the same sincere interest in education and genuine culture as their missionary teachers.[95]

Even then, however, there was great ambivalence among the élite:

Although middle-class Negroes have been the leaders in the Negro's struggle for equality, they have always had an ambivalent attitude toward the Negro masses. Even in the days when the Negro "Talented Tenth" went forth from the colleges under missionary control to lead the masses, the middle class could not identify itself completely with the great masses of poor, illiterate black peasants. They were too self-conscious of their achievements and of the burden of proving to whites that they were as intelligent, thrifty, and respectable as whites.[96]

More to the point, however, is the seeming emergence—in the present, self-emancipating generation—of a willingness to bridge the barrier between the two cultures, especially across class lines, which may herald a return to the *noblesse oblige* that once characterized the Negro élite. Thus a beautiful college girl from a Northern city—one of many—spent a week in a Southern jail for taking part in a civil-rights demonstration. For the first time in her sheltered life, she found herself face to face with lower-class—even lowest-class—Negroes. She spent her time in the segregated prison teaching other inmates how to read, touched to tears when they offered her their desserts in appreciation for her willingness to talk to them let alone take the trouble to teach them. When she returned home, her distraught parents were even more alarmed when, in reply to her mother's question as to when she was going to have her hair done before returning to college, she replied she was going to leave it as it was. She was "black and glad." She, and others like her patiently knocking

[95] E. Franklin Frazier, *Black Bourgeoisie* (New York: The Crowell-Collier Publishing Co., 1962), p. 193.

[96] Frazier, "The Negro Middle Class and Desegregation," *op. cit.*, pp. 298-99.

on cabin doors in Mississippi to bring the good news of the second emancipation, were reverting to the "Talented Tenth" tradition of *noblesse oblige*. Their parents, for all their anguish, cannot but admire this new generation—the answer to the hopes of many Negroes.

I genuinely hope, as a Negro and an American, that truly responsible Negro representative leadership . . . will go to the downtrodden black masses and say in the best tradition of Judeo-Christian thought: "Let us really help you and be brothers as the Creator intended us to be." [97]

Already the culturally white National Association for the Advancement of Colored People (NAACP) has begun a program of "citizenship clinics" which "will concern themselves with aid to stabilizing family life, attention to delinquency, vandalism, crime, group moral standards, and other matters demanding frank and helpful evaluation and unapologetic action." [98]

What's kept the NAACP from doing this for years . . . is the feeling that its drive for equality would be smeared and slowed down by whites—and Negroes, too—saying that the Negroes are "admitting they're inferior and they should do something about it." [99]

Assured of their position, the NAACP and similar organizations could now afford to admit that there were some problems that needed solution by Negroes themselves.

The achievement of *rapprochement* between two cultures is no less difficult in the Negro world than in any other. If the goal were the *rapprochement* of classes within the acculturated world only, it might be more quickly attained. The obstacles, as Frazier points out, would be ignorance and poverty, and it might be possible for "truly responsible Negro leadership" to improve the lot of "the downtrodden black masses." A great many so-called do-good programs do, in effect, assume the presence of acculturated families among the "masses," and they are most successful among such families.

But when the upper-class acculturated approaches the lower-class externally adapted, cultural differences intervene. To the young person from a hedonistic culture, the prospect of a modest job and a stable family life has little appeal. And the already acculturated "reformer" may be tempted to reject those who do not respond to his middle-class values.

Actually there is an unfathomed amount of creativity among the externally adapted. How can such creativity be encouraged without foster-

---

[97] Morgan D. Carney, *The New York Times*, August 18, 1964.
[98] Fred Powledge, "Rights Aims Shift to Self-Help Side, Morals and Education to Be Stressed among Negroes," *The New York Times*, January 17, 1965, p. 73.
[99] Roy Wilkins, quoted *ibid.*

ing its destructiveness and eroding the discipline of the acculturated? Is it possible to blend the best of both cultures?

The creativity of the externally adapted is illustrated by their contributions to music and dance, and by the eagerness of the avant garde to imitate their speech, their clothing, and their art forms. Can the entrepreneurial talent of the racketeer be applied to the pursuit of more acceptable citizenship goals? Will the time come when wealthy externally adapted Negroes will endow centers for cultivating the arts—whatever they may prove to be—in which Negroes are particularly creative? Cayton and Drake complain of the efforts to force all Negroes into a conventional middle-class pattern. Perhaps young, externally adapted Negroes might be offered—rather than economic security and middle-class values—the prospect of excitement and adventure in the creative arts, *their* creative arts.

Chapter 3

People

Introduction

Chapter 2 began with the assumption that the presence of two cultures among Negroes might help to explain the marriage trajectory. The nature and operation history of the two cultures seem to warrant the conclusion that the norms of monogamic marriage would be more readily abandoned by those who had made only an external adaptation to them than by those who had internalized them.

Chapters 1 and 2 focused attention on large social forms: classes and cultures. Chapter 3 focuses attention on the individuals who constitute these forms, the forces that shape them, the circumstances that influence their relationships with one another, and the conditions under which they perform their family roles.

Although this book is not about race relations, they cannot be ignored in any discussion of individual men and women, of the same or of different race, for the relations between the races have been profoundly influenced by the relations between the sexes. Fear of "mongrelization" has haunted the white segregationist for decades and stimulated his effort to keep the races apart.

Equally, if not more, profound has been the influence of race relations on the relations between the sexes. The relations between Negro men and women are inextricably influenced by the relations each has with the outside world.

Women and Men

SEX AS A SOCIAL AS WELL AS A BIOLOGICAL FACT

If the human species had only biological differences with which to contend, the relationships between the sexes would be complicated enough. But biological differences are only the grossest and most simple of those involved. In addition, there are all the subtle and complex differences introduced by institutional factors which serve to make relationships between the sexes vastly more intricate than any based on biological differences alone. The institutions of slavery, for example, did not have the same impact on men as they had on women, and the long shadow of those institutions has darkened relationships between the sexes ever since.

WOMEN UNDER SLAVERY

Slave status was less flagrant a violation of the female role than of the male. The enforced subordination and subservience was not so far out of line with the Western world's definition of "woman's place." In any event, perhaps because they were useful in the role of breeders as well as in that of workers, female slaves were strategically better off than male slaves. They could, of course, be whipped—and, indeed, they often were. But they were less willing to take such punishment quietly. They could be saucy—and get away with it. They were powerful, spirited women who could be violent if they had to be.

There was Crecie, for example, who pulled up a stump and whipped an overseer with it when he tried to lash her; or Aunt Susie Ann, who pretended to faint while she was being whipped and then tripped the overseer so that he couldn't stand up; or Lucy, who knocked an overseer over "and tore his face up so that the doctor had to 'tend to him' "; or the mammy who had nursed a child but later, when he tormented her, did not hesitate to beat him until he wasn't able to walk; or Aunt Adeline, who committed suicide rather than submit to another whipping; or Cousin Sally, who hit her master over the head with a poker and put his head in the fireplace.[1]

It was well for these women that they were tough, for after emancipation they were to need the strength and courage of heroes to perform a role almost unique in human history. It was to be a role of stupendous proportions.

THE UNNATURAL SUPERIORITY OF NEGRO WOMEN

The natural superiority of women has been well documented.[2] Among peoples with access to modern obstetrical care, females show greater viability than males, before birth as well as after. They are susceptible to fewer hereditary defects (such as hemophilia, baldness, and color-blindness) and even, perhaps, to mental and emotional breakdown. In the case of Negro women, this natural superiority has been augmented by a social and cultural environment which is less inimical to them than it is to Negro men, becoming what might be called an "unnatural" superiority.

The simplest and most primitive measure of this superiority is the extraordinarily low sex ratio (i.e., the number of males per 100 females) among Negroes. This ratio has fluctuated over time, but it has always been far lower than that of the white population. In rural farm areas,

---

[1] These examples are cited in B. A. Botkin, *Lay My Burden Down* (Chicago: University of Chicago Press, 1945), pp. 174-75, 176, 183-84.

[2] Ashley Montagu, *The Natural Superiority of Women* (New York: The Macmillan Company, 1953).

to be sure, it has always been at least 100 over-all; but in urban areas, at least since 1910, it has hovered around 90. In 1962, it was 95.9. But it was especially low in the critical years of marriageability, twenty-five to forty-four: only 88.4 per cent.

Some of this disparity between the sexes can be explained by under-enumeration of Negro men by the census: they are harder to find. Some of the disparity can be explained by the fact that more Negro men than women annually "pass over" into the white population.[3] Some of the disparity can be explained by the fact that the hazards of life are greater for Negro men than for Negro women. Whatever the reason, the low sex ratio has profound implications for the relations between the sexes and, therefore, for marriage and family.

Another index of female superiority is provided in the field of education.[4] Negro women tend to have more years of schooling than Negro men do. In 1960, for example, Negro women averaged 8.5 years of schooling; Negro men, only 7.9. The average Negro woman is destined to marry a man with considerably less formal education than she has, for the discrepancies in average years of schooling are consistent, marked, and ubiquitous.

Not only formal education but also contacts with the white world have been more available to Negro women than to Negro men. Negro men have been more feared, sexually and occupationally, than Negro women. In fact, Negro women have more often proved attractive to the white world: they have more often been loved—not only as sex partners but also as nurses or "mammies." As a result, Negro women have been less isolated from the white world; they have had more intimate contacts with it; they have lived in the homes of white families; they have had greater opportunity to mingle with white people. More doors—back doors to be sure, but doors—have opened for them. They have, therefore, felt more at ease in the white world. Even in their contacts with social-work agencies and the world of bureaucracy, they have known their way around. Negro men and Negro women have, in brief, tended to live in somewhat different worlds, both under slavery and after emancipation. As a result, Negro women tend, in general, to fall into a higher class (as measured by education, acculturation, income, and familiarity with the amenities of the white world) than Negro men. The most suc-

[3] Maurice R. Davie, *Negroes in American Society* (New York: McGraw-Hill Book Company, 1949), p. 405.

[4] ". . . [G]reater premium has been placed on the higher education of girls than boys. In the past, this was probably due to the fact that the most significant tradition of success locally involved the ability to do something with one's hands and property-getting for the male and school teaching for the female. These are the ways in which independence has been defined in practical terms" (Hylan Lewis, *Blackways of Kent* [Chapel Hill, N.C.: University of North Carolina Press, 1955], pp. 105-106).

cessful, in fact, are marginal women, almost as much outside the Negro world as they are inside it.

Most important of all, perhaps, of the differences between the sexes has been the fact that, if a Negro woman wanted to work, there was always employment for her—even during depressions. Usually it was even a higher kind of work than that available to Negro men; if not, her services were always wanted in the home. Menial though the work might be, the Negro woman had the inestimable knowledge that she was useful, needed.

All these factors increased the unnatural superiority of Negro women, strongly affecting the relations between the sexes. The implications of a low sex ratio are serious. A low sex ratio, especially in the twenty-five-to-forty-four age bracket, means that Negro women are competing for a relatively scarce "good" when they look forward to marriage. They are, so to speak, buyers in a seller's market. A low sex ratio also implies a relatively large number of orphaned children and widowed mothers—families without fathers.

Nevertheless, a low sex ratio is not the "cause" of the patterns of relationships between men and women. It was once fashionable to explain the prevalence of the monogamic form of marriage by referring to the roughly equal number of men and of women. Unfortunately, however, human institutions do not always conform so neatly to logic: it is quite possible for one male to have a harem while other males have no mates at all.[5] Demography does not impose a choice, but it does limit alternatives.

The implications of greater schooling and acculturation among Negro women than among Negro men are also profound for the relations between the sexes. They impose responsibilities on women not always congenial to the feminine role vis-à-vis the masculine role. And, finally, the economic superiority of the Negro woman over the Negro man may be destructive to both.

MEN UNDER SLAVERY

Slavery was more destructive to men than to women. Both male and female slaves, under severe provocation, might kill. But—this is more impression than factually buttressed conclusion—male slaves were more likely simply to run away. Both resorted to ruse or guile—but, again perhaps men more than women.[6]

Slavery had two terrible effects on men: it prevented their coming to emotional maturity by inflicting on them a perpetual childhood, and by imposing their master's ideology on them, resulted in their identifying themselves with their masters.

---

[5] S. Zuckerman, *The Social Life of Monkeys and Apes* (1932).

[6] These conclusions are based on the material presented by Botkin.

An analogy may be drawn between the effects of the Nazi concentration and extermination camps and those of slavery. The inmates of these camps—some sooner, some later—became childishly silly, giggling at the most trivial events; like adolescents, they became unstable in their relationships with one another; they became pathological liars, unable to restrain themselves or to make objective evaluations; they resorted to dishonesty to get more food or to extricate themselves from scrapes, using sly dodges and clever pretexts to avoid being caught; they boasted extravagantly about their earlier lives or about their success in outwitting guards or in sabotaging the work of the camp; and they were not at all ashamed, or even embarrassed, when their lies were discovered.[7] They regressed, in brief, to childhood: the classic stereotype of the slave mentality.

But the most improbable outcome of concentration camp life was that inmates came finally to identify with their captors. They came to imitate the Gestapo in dress, in mannerisms, and often outdid them in their cruelty toward fellow prisoners. The acceptance of the Gestapo's values—as well as their dress and mannerisms—constituted the final stage of "adjustment" for the prisoners.[8] They came to view one another through the Gestapo's eyes, to judge one another by the Gestapo's standards.

How was it possible to bring even strong and talented men to this level? The answer, in part, lies in the combination of punishment and reward used. Terror was used to intimidate; torture, to degrade the inmates as individuals. But there were also rewards for compliance—especially for compliance beyond bare necessity, appeasing and ingratiating.

But perhaps even more important was the "complete break with the outside world." [9] Isolation and secrecy enhanced the unreality of the situation, eliminated alternatives, and enhanced the impact of the guards.

In a similar fashion, according to Elkins, the role of child was forced upon the slave; the master was the father. Nonconformity to the role requirements might bring about severe punishment; survival itself may have depended on completely accurate responses to cues. Another factor, as in the case of the concentration camp, "was the simple 'closedness' of the system, in which all lines of authority descended from the master and in which alternative social bases that might have supported alternative standards were systematically suppressed." [10] No wonder teaching

---

[7] Stanley M. Elkins, *Slavery: A Problem in American Institutional and Intellectual Life* (New York: Grosset & Dunlap, Inc., 1963), pp. 111-12.

[8] *Ibid.*, p. 112.

[9] *Ibid.*, pp. 104-108.

[10] *Ibid.*, p. 128.

slaves to read was viewed as a subversive activity: widespread exposure to the existence of alternatives to slavery would have destroyed the system.

In such a system, the rewards for compliance as much as—if not more than—punishment for noncompliance became the real basis on which the Negro was enslaved. From the point of view of the master, the slave was a masterpiece of his creation—loyal, docile, humble, cheerful, even diligent (under supervision), but also irresponsible, playful, silly, lazy, and with a tendency to lie and steal. The master's love was the slave's major reward for performing his role well. He became a polished performer who learned how to play the assigned role with variations, cheerfulness, even wit. But he was not a man.[11] Hostile or loving, the environment was inimical to his development as a man. Frazier emphasizes the acculturating influence exerted on house slaves by the master's family. But this influence also had a negative aspect: the slaves' acceptance of the master's conception of themselves as inferior.

Nevertheless, the slave was valuable as a worker. It was not to his master's interest to starve or incapacitate him. He was, therefore, in a mixed-motive game against his master. Back at the cabin, before or after emancipation, the Negro could tear off his mask and take his revenge:

> . . . [I]n his folk stories and anecdotes he took a subtle revenge on his master by turning the tables on him. Just as Br'er Rabbit, in a politer form, for the entertainment of the whites, symbolizes the triumph of cunning over superior force, so among themselves the Negroes told more realistic and more caustic tales of Old John, the slave who outwits his master. . . .

His hard-hitting lore reflects the way in which the Negro has adapted himself to a white man's world by "hitting a straight lick with a crooked stick." [12]

Nor was the battle between master and slave completely one-sided; the slave had his own strategies:

> The privations, penalties, and punishments, as well as the occasional favors, privileges, and rewards, were part of an elaborate system of control by which the master made slavery acceptable to the slave. . . . [But] like every tyrant, the master lived in constant fear of revolt and had to make favorites and spies of some slaves and examples of others. In between master and slave were the overseer and the patroller, from whom no mercy was expected, and the "nigger driver," who was apt to be "meaner than the white folks."

But, in spite of all attempts to crush it, the slave had a will of his own, which was actively, as well as passively, opposed to the master's. And it is this stubborn and rebellious will—tragic, heroic, defeated, or triumphant—that, more than all else, . . . haunted the master, "frustrating his designs by a ceaseless though perhaps invisible countermining," as Theodore D. Weld wrote in 1839. As the master saw this opposing will constantly in the "dissatisfied look, and reluctant

[11] *Ibid.,* p. 131.
[12] Botkin, *op. cit.,* p. 2.

air and unwilling movement; the constrained strokes of labor, the drawling tones, the slow hearing, the feigned stupidity, the sham pains and sickness, the short memory," so in the narratives the slave expresses his hatred of enslavement and his contempt for his enslaver in less subtle and more open ways, such as "taking" what belonged to him, escaping or assisting others to escape, secretly learning or teaching others to read and write, secret meetings, suicide, infanticide, homicide, and the like.

Here, too, caught in the same inexorable nexus of human relationships, the master appears as the victim of his own system; for, in a world torn by fear, passion, and violence, all classes were inevitably demoralized and brutalized.[13]

Despite the availability of force to the master, the slave's strategic defense against it in the form of "feigned stupidity" or "sham pains and sickness" often meant a standoff.[14] And if slavery had involved only slave and master, an umpire might easily have called it a draw so far as daily life was concerned. (In a showdown, to be sure, the master always won.)

But the institution of slavery in the United States subverted the relations between the sexes. And in so doing it inflicted grievous wounds on the Negro man. Because the female produced more slave property and because she had to care for the children, she had a higher position than the male; it was to her that the rations were distributed; it was she who was mistress of the cabin. She developed a strong character and did not hesitate to exercise it. The male slave might have been able to hold his own against his white master: it was his black woman who undid him.

The hypothesis suggested here—a hypothesis may be usefully wrong—is that the damage done to the Negro man *vis-à-vis* the white world under slavery was compounded and exponentially increased by the relationship to women which it imposed, and that the same circumstances produced the same effect on the freedmen's generation. The Negro man had to be destroyed as a man, to "protect" the white world. Unwittingly, unintentionally, even against her own will, the Negro woman participated in the process.[15]

AN INIMICAL ENVIRONMENT

The term *inimical environment* is used here to depersonalize the forces operating upon Negroes. It is a broader term than *hostile environ-*

---

[13] *Ibid.*, pp. 137-38.

[14] For an analysis of the theory of this kind of "game situation," see Thomas C. Schelling, *The Strategy of Conflict* (Cambridge, Mass: Harvard University Press, 1960), Chap. 5.

[15] At a meeting of Negro women leaders, it was made abundantly clear that they did not relish the position imposed on them. When one brilliant woman expressed resentment that women had not been permitted to share the platform at the March on Washington in the summer of 1963, the audience did not share her feeling: they were happy to have their men in leadership roles; they were eager to help them cultivate their leadership talents.

ment. Actually, of course, the environment has been hostile, characterized by a prejudice, discrimination, and aggression so well documented that further recital here would be redundant. But there are other ways in which an environment can be inimical. In the case of Negroes, there have been at least three.

The term *inimical environment* does not rule out love on the part of some people in this environment. The custom among well-intentioned Southerners of protecting and taking care of "their" Negroes may have exaggerated the adverse effects of the prevailing environment. They were tolerant; they went out of their way to help "their" Negroes; they assumed responsibility for them. There was a strong strain of *noblesse oblige* among Southerners, and there was often genuine love—demanding, as under slavery, little response other than childlike docility. Southerners of good will who protested that they knew and understood Negroes, loved them, and had better relations with them than did Northerners, were quite sincere. What they said might even be true: "their" Negroes may have been content with their protected and secure lot; they might even have been happy. But this benevolence, although it might mollify or mitigate the adverse effects of the environment, did not overcome or even counteract them. It deprived Negroes of the opportunity for developing responsibility, competency, and autonomy; it made them unfit for maturity and independence; it rendered them incapable of assuming responsibility, of becoming adults. Even a loving environment may be inimical to a child's development. *Inimical* is not, therefore, identical with *hostile;* it does not imply universal and active hatred on the part of the outer world—but even affection can be destructive.

In the North another inimical, though friendly, pattern evolved: the Negro was romanticized. This sentimentality may not have been as destructive as the benevolence of the South, but neither encouraged strength. Negro leaders, recognizing this, often urged Northern employers and teachers and others in positions of superordination to apply the same standards to Negroes as to others. This was difficult for fair-minded people to do: special consideration could be justified on the ground that a Negro who had achieved the same status as a white person was probably "better" because he had had to overcome more handicaps to get there. In any event, however, such concessions—whether sentimental or rational —were not conducive to the development of strength.

A nonhostile third way in which the outside world has been inimical to Negroes is in its complete lack of response to them. Social psychologists have long taught us that we develop our selves, our identities, by interacting with others. We become our selves and know who we are because of the way people deal with us. By not interacting with the Negro, by treating him as a nonbeing, a nonentity, the outside world has, figuratively, obliterated millions of human beings. They feel themselves to be nonexistent: nobody knows their names; they are invisible; they are ciphers.

The Negro man, in brief, was put into a situation in which conformity to masculine norms was all but impossible, and then was, in effect, both rewarded and punished for not conforming to them. The Negro was put in a situation which forbade his becoming a mature human being, and then was both rewarded and punished for not becoming one—and punished if he even attempted to become one. The result was a classic case of the self-fulfilling prophecy: a degraded creature, successful and happy in abject dependence, incapable of rising. For over a generation after emancipation, the Negro obliged his detractors by acting out the prophecy.

SINCE SLAVERY: THE DIFFERENTIAL IMPACT OF THE SOCIAL CONCENTRATION CAMP ON MEN AND WOMEN

Even after emancipation, most Negro men have, in effect, lived in a social and mental concentration camp.[16] Their perspective on life and their view of the world have been analogous to those developed by the inmates of Nazi concentration camps. The walls of this "camp," furthermore, have been more impermeable to them than to their women. They have been feared, hence barred from the outside world and thus cut off from acculturation by personal influence. This isolation has been less severe in the case of their women. The women have been admitted to the outside world, to intimate—even if menial—positions and thus exposed to outside acculturating forces. The wife joins the disciplined army with other Negro women in public conveyances each morning on their way to their posts in the homes of the outside world; the husband joins the shabby group of defeated men huddled on the corner of the "slave market" hoping to be picked up for casual labor. The resulting differential in exposure of men and of women to acculturating influences in the outside world has added to the destructive forces operating on Negro men, increasing the "unnatural" superiority of the women in relation to them.

The white world's insistence on keeping Negro men walled up in the "concentration camp" was motivated in large part by its fear of their sexuality, a fear which has been well documented.[17] One does not have to resort to psychoanalytic figures of speech to see that Negro men were

---

[16] Cf.: "The Negro has been locked in black belts and Harlems just as tightly as he was once confined by his master's leg irons" (Lewis G. Watts, *The Middle-Income Negro Family Faces Urban Renewal* (Waltham, Mass: Brandeis University, 1964), p. 23.

[17] John Dollard, *Caste and Class in a Southern Town* (New York: Harper & Row, Publishers, 1940), pp. 160 ff. "Do you want your daughter to marry a nigger?" appeals to the same fear and has been an almost infallible weapon against any improvement of the position of Negroes.

castrated by the white world—sometimes literally as well as figuratively.[18]

The outside world's fear of the Negro man's sexuality gave rise, again, to a self-fulfilling prophecy. Because the ordinary manifestations of masculine identity were all but impossible for large numbers of Negro men, sex did, indeed, become for some a major instrument of power. This weapon was not directed against the outside world—despite the ever-present fear of such sexual aggression in the South—but against their own.[19] In only a rather devious and roundabout way was it used against the outside world: at least some of the out-of-wedlock births among Negroes, it is alleged, result from conscious or unconscious revenge motives against the outside world. Denied normal male sexuality, they add children to the assistance rolls to be supported.[20] Actually sexuality among Negro men, far from being unrestrained, is plagued with uncertainty and confusion.[21] Whether justified or not, however, it has been fear of Negro sexuality which has largely motivated the greater restraints imposed on Negro men than on Negro women.

SOME EFFECTS OF AN INIMICAL ENVIRONMENT

The biodemographic effects of the inimical environment on Negro men—high mortality, reduced life span, and high illness rates—have had obvious repercussions on marriage and family life, clearly evident in the many homes broken by death, the many widowed women, the many orphaned children. The socioeconomic results—poor education, low occupational level, inadequate income—similarly reverberate through family life.

Even more pervasive and serious was its effect on the personality and character structure of Negro men. Inferiority became an adaptive mech-

[18] The mutilation of Negroes was common in the South, sometimes followed by lynchings.

[19] The statistics on rape, when available, show that they occur mainly against Negro women, not white.

[20] Robert L. Derbyshire, Eugene B. Brody, and Carl Schleifer, "Family Structure of Young Adult Negro Male Mental Patients: Preliminary Observations from Urban Baltimore." Paper presented at the Groves Conference, Baltimore, 1962. "A willingness to express promiscuous sexual behavior and the resultant progeny may also be interpreted as an expression of overt hostility toward the white social world and its moralistic ethos. Since direct expression of hostility against the white society is impossible, this may be functional as a determinant of Negro mental illness, i.e., lower-status Negroes who express overt hostility toward the white social world are more apt to be defined as mentally ill than those who do not respond in this manner" (p. 7).

[21] "As one of the results of not being able to perform the 'masculine role,' middle-class Negro males have tended to cultivate their 'personalities' which enable them to exercise considerable influence among whites and achieve distinction in the Negro world. Among Negroes they have been noted for their glamor. In this respect they resemble women who use their 'personalities' to compensate for their inferior status in relation to men" (Frazier, *Black Bourgeoisie*, p. 182).

anism for them. They learned to underplay their abilities. The relatively more inimical environment in which they moved has, in a sense, perverted role performance and not only given an "unnatural" superiority to the Negro woman (which she neither sought nor wanted) but also damaged their own masculinity.

The wounded masculinity may be on the way to healing; self-emancipation may have helped to reduce its effect. Just as the successful establishment of Israel had a liberating effect on Jews,[22] so may self-emancipation have a similar effect on Negroes. Still, marriage and family life continue to show the effects of an environment inimical to men. Thus the men and women who confront one another in the sexual encounter are still constrained by vestiges of the role created by the slaveowner a century ago. Sambo has long since departed the scene; but his legacy is only now being liquidated.

Mate Selection

COURTSHIP AND MATING UNDER SLAVERY

Mr. Jack Tabb . . . would let us go a-courting on the other plantations near any time we liked, if we were good, and if we found somebody we wanted to marry, and she was on a plantation that belonged to one of his kinfolks or a friend, he would swap a slave so that the husband and wife could be together.

Apparently, then, masters sometimes permitted their slaves to choose their own mates. Sometimes they merely acceded to the inevitable, as when the indomitable Preston Miller and his bride saved their money for a long time to buy her freedom so that she could marry the man she'd "like fine to marry." Perhaps more common was the case of the woman who "didn't care much about" the mate who was just "give to her," so that when he left her after emancipation, that was quite all right with her. Still it was not always easy to force mates upon unwilling women. Rose, for example, only tolerated Rufus as a mate because she felt so grateful to Mr. Hawkins, her master, for not separating her from her parents. But after emancipation she never married again: "After what I does for the massa, I's never wants no truck with any man. The Lord forgive this colored woman, but he have to 'scuse me and look for some others for to 'plenish the earth." [23]

It didn't do, really, to tangle with those spirited women. If they wanted

---

[22] Centuries of humiliation had produced hopelessness and listlessness, despair, and distrust among Jews. Then "the unexpected victories over seven Arab states by a psychologically unhinged people not only established an independent Jewish state but served as . . . catharsis of the spirit" (A. L. Sachar, "Necromancy by a Non-fossil," *Book Week*, Dec. 1, 1963, p. 10).

[23] This account is taken from B. A. Botkin, *Lay My Burden Down* (Chicago: University of Chicago Press, 1945), pp. 161-62, 184, 185, 228.

a man, they seem usually to have got him; if they did not want him, it was, as Mr. Hawkins found, hard to force him on them. Love was an enormously important value to Negro women, even under slavery. Even in the urban slum today, as already noted, the unmarried mother who does not love the father of her child is not pressured to marry him; marriage must be based on love.

COURTING AMONG THE FREEDMAN'S GENERATION

Because children were an economic asset on the plantation, early marriage was frowned upon: the parental family needed their labor. The effect was not, according to C. S. Johnson, to preclude courtship, but to accentuate it. Young people met one another at church meetings, church suppers, festivals and frolics, and on the Saturday visits to town. There was a certain amount of sexual separatism at these events—the men making loud and often ribald jokes to attract the attention of the women, who shyly pretended to be unaware of them. As the evening progressed, a boy would select a girl for more intimate conversation and "less decorous intimacy." [24] Courting was more serious among the older men; they would dress up and escort their partners to parties. Jealousy was a common manifestation during the courtship period.

Young men looked for mates who were good workers; middle-aged men wanted, in addition, some of the feminine graces; older men wanted companionship. Some men wanted wives who would acknowledge them as the head of the household. Young women wanted security; mature women wanted attention and the earning power of a man who was, or was likely to be, the father of their children; the middle-aged woman wanted a good working partner; and the older woman, like her male counterpart, wanted companionship.

Dark color was important: light-skinned men were believed to be poor providers and likely to be "run-roun" men:

Physical strength, dogged industry, and a good disposition . . . took precedence over . . . possession of money, social position, education, physical attractiveness or that kind of ambition which sought to abandon the familiar round of life.[25]

Families in the acculturated tradition sought men who gave assurance of stability as husbands for their daughters; sometimes they asserted their authority by physical means. The daughters escaped family restrictions only by eloping.[26]

[24] C. S. Johnson, *Shadow of the Plantation* (Chicago: University of Chicago Press, 1934), p. 51.
[25] *Ibid.*, p. 57.
[26] *Ibid.*, p. 55.

COURTSHIP TODAY

There is, unfortunately, little research on dating and courtship among the present generation of Negroes in the United States. Hazel Stanton's careful account of courtship practices in four subcultures in Puerto Rico may have at least tangential relevance. She reports that courtship in the so-called peasant subculture may last up to seven years; in the plantation subculture, considerably less. In the urban slum, courtship may be very brief. But in the suburban or middle-class subculture— corresponding roughly to middle- or upper-class acculturated Negroes in the United States—it lasts at least a year and may go on for eight to ten years, although this would be viewed as excessive.[27]

Similar studies are not available for families in the United States. Our knowledge is fragmentary at best, and much of it based on fictional accounts. It may be taken for granted that there are differences between the two cultures, and that there are class differences within each. The precise nature of these differences is blurred by the unnatural superiority of Negro women and by the low sex ratio. In the slum family, it appears that girls may take the initiative without censure; this practice would be in line with the practice antedating emancipation. Among the acculturated, girls apparently do not take the initiative.

A study of a Southern mill town in the 1940s indicated that dating was a casual, catch-as-catch-can matter, a sex game, with clandestine or illicit features associated with it. "Going together," which involved intimacy, was a stable relationship and likely to lead to marriage. "Courting" or "courting strong" was not as fixed or stable a pattern of wooing as "going together." The length of time involved in each varied.[28]

Dating patterns among higher-level acculturated families have been reported for students on a college campus.[29] A sample of some 200 students replied to a questionnaire dealing with values (28 items) and norms (22 items). The subjects were asked to state whether any particular value was *very important, moderately important,* or *slightly important* to them; on the dating norms, they were asked to indicate frequency (for example, *often, sometimes,* or *seldom*). The most prevalent dating pattern was going steady; the least prevalent, double-dating. Random dating fell between these extremes, but was nearer the low- than the high-ranking pattern. Dating within a clique only was almost as infrequent as double-dating. "Double-dating and the restrictions of social-class dating are

[27] Hazel Stanton, paper presented at meetings of National Council Family Relations, Miami, 1964.

[28] Hylan Lewis, *Blackways of Kent* (Chapel Hill, N.C.: University of North Carolina Press, 1955), p. 89.

[29] Charles S. Anderson and Joseph S. Himes, "Dating Values and Norms on a Negro College Campus," *Marriage and Family Living*, Vol. 21 (August, 1959), 228ff.

relatively unpopular with the students," conclude the authors. Petting (extreme forms of sexual stimulation), drinking, and "partying" (private intimate relations between dating partners consisting of one or a few couples, usually not more than two) were the least common dating activities on this campus, considerably less popular than dancing, necking (hand-holding, unstimulating kissing, and embracing), and telephone conversations. The most popular place for dating was the dormitory recreation room; the least popular, night clubs. The women "gave slightly more emphasis to the reception rooms as popular dating locations, while the men . . . were more interested in athletic events." [30] Of some interest was the fact that the women students tended to be more conventional in their ratings than the men, for "they assessed the institutionally sanctioned dating activities (dancing and telephoning) higher, and the unapproved activities, such as petting and 'partying,' lower than the men." [31] With respect to the values, two distinct categories emerged: one (internal personality traits and social skills) dealing primarily with interpersonal relations; the other (external personality traits and accomplishments), with the material and competitive qualities of the individual. "The students gave measurably higher evaluations to internal personality characteristics and skills of social relations than to the overt personal characteristics and evidences of individual achievement." [32] Good taste in dress, "mixing" ability, and intelligence were valued more highly by the young women than by the young men, who assigned more weight to good manners than did the young women. The general pattern that emerges is one of conservative, even inhibited, well-mannered young people engaging in conventional dating activities under supervised conditions.

The dating patterns of 172 urban boys and 169 girls in a middle-sized industrial city of Pennsylvania were reported in the mid-1960s. The subjects consisted of all fifth- through twelfth-grade students in attendance the day the study was made.[33]

---

[30] *Ibid.*, p. 229.

[31] *Ibid.*, p. 229.

[32] *Ibid.*, p. 229.

[33] Several classes were represented but the analysis did not take these differences into account. Of the fathers of the subjects, 16 per cent were unemployed; 6 per cent were in professional or managerial occupations; most were blue-collar workers. Among the mothers, 53 per cent had jobs outside the home; two thirds were unskilled factory operatives, waitresses, nurses' aides or semi-skilled operatives, clerks, and saleswomen. The remaining third were houseworkers, cooks, and cleaning women. A few were teachers or nurses. More than a third (35 per cent) of the families had been broken by death, divorce, or separation (Carlfred Broderick, "Sociosexual Development among Urban Negroes and Whites." Paper presented at meetings of National Council, Family Relations, Miami, 1964).

Table 3-1.

Proportion of Negro Boys and Girls Who Reported Specified Sociosexual Activities, By Age*

Activity	Boys				Girls			
	10–11	12–13	14–15	16–17	10–11	12–13	14–15	16–17
Would like to get married some day	71	60	67	58	76	74	85	84**
Enjoys love scenes in movies	68	75	83	62	70	73	78	79
Has a girlfriend (boyfriend)	65	71**	58	62	64	51	72	71
Has been in love	46	60	57	67	57	48	67	67
Chooses one or more cross-sex friends	52	48	49	81	54	45	58	75
Played kissing games this year	28	49	40	22	33	35	58	23
Kissed, when it meant "something special"	38	51	62	79**	39	48	65	59
Has begun to date	16	49**	69**	93	20	21	48	88
Is now going steady	20	10	17	28	16	15	24	26

* *Source:* Carlfred Broderick, "Sociosexual Development among Urban Negroes and Whites." Paper presented at meetings of National Council Family Relations, Miami, 1964.
** Sex differences significant beyond the 0.05 level using chi square with one degree of freedom.

In general, although dating began somewhat earlier among the girls, the boys soon surpassed them (see Table 3-1). At the age of twelve or thirteen, almost half (49 per cent) of the boys said they were dating; only a fifth (21 per cent) of the girls said they were. The differences began to decline thereafter and by the age of sixteen or seventeen, the sex differences were no longer significant. In the going-steady pattern, however, there were no statistically significant differences between the boys and the girls at any age level. But for these specific boys and girls, there was a greater tendency for dating to take the going-steady form in the twelve-to-fifteen age bracket among girls than among boys. By the twelfth grade, or at least by the age of sixteen or seventeen, only two significant differences remained between the sexes: serious kissing was reported by more boys than girls, and far more girls than boys hoped to be married some day. This item revealed interesting trends in this sample. At no age level did as many as three fourths of the boys say they hoped to marry some day; by the age of sixteen or seventeen, less than three fifths said they did. Among the girls, on the other hand, at no age did significantly fewer than three fourths say they hoped to marry some day; by the age of fourteen, between eight tenths and nine tenths said they did.

As for adults, in a large modern city two lonely people probably just find one another—at the laundromat, at church, on the street, at a restaurant or bar. The courtship may include the amenities: the man may send the woman a corsage before every date. It may be on a simple no-nonsense sexual level: they appeal to one another and both know it, so that little in the way of the niceties or verbal love-making may be expected by either.

Among the acculturated, where unions are expected to be lifelong, the procedures are more complex. Because more is at stake in the relationship, more is expected of it. Among those in the high-income brackets, the campus may be the scene of the mate-selection process. The middle and upper classes follow the ritual of the formal début, which presumably serves the same mating function as it does in white society.

AGE AT MARRIAGE

The selection of mates among Negroes has been achieved at a fairly early age, usually earlier among the lower socioeconomic classes than among the higher. In general, however, age at marriage is not a satisfactory measure of trends among Negroes because a very high proportion —about a fifth—of brides and grooms in any given year are entering a second or third marriage. In 1960 the average age of divorced brides was 34.4; that of widowed brides, 47.6.[34] The overall average age at marriage thus appears older than it really is for first marriages.[35]

The proportion of eighteen-year-olds who are married is perhaps a better index of trends in marriage among Negroes. This index shows that the rate of youthful marriage increased between 1910 and 1950 among Negroes, as it did for non-Negroes also, but more rapidly. By 1960, however, there was a convergence of trends, so that 23.6 per cent of all non-white eighteen-year-olds and 24.5 per cent of all white eighteen-year-olds were married.[36]

Youthful marriages, regardless of race, have a relatively poor prognosis:

Behind age at marriage are numerous confounding influences which make marriage a poor risk at age sixteen or seventeen, possibly even at age eighteen. One of these is the lower-status background of a predominant number of youth who marry before the age of eighteen. Competency in marriage and family relationships today requires a set of values, personality characteristics, and interpersonal skills generated by middle-class society and functional in middle-class society, both at the office, in suburban social life, and at home. . . . [D]ata from numerous studies indicate that child-rearing and family relationship pat-

[34] Public Health Service, *Vital Statistics of the United States 1960: Marriages,* Table 2-6.

[35] *Ibid.*

[36] Lee Burchinal, "Trends and Prospects for Young Marriages in the United States." Paper at meeting of National Council Family Relations (Miami, 1964), p. 26.

terns of lower-status families are in direct contrast to those that research shows are associated with emotional health, school achievement, goal-setting and attainment, social success, and reasonably competent interpersonal relations— all that are valued and required in competent marital relationships. The attitudes, values, and personality characteristics of persons with lower-status backgrounds limit the degree to which they can attain a stable and personally satisfying marriage.[37]

These conclusions suggest that extreme youth is a handicap in marriage, but more so among those of low socioeconomic class background. Even in the twenty–to–twenty-four age group, the unemployment rate for non-white married men was 11.2 per cent in the early 1960s. Youthful marriage plus unemployment equals a very poor prognosis for marital success. In a study of Negro women in Philadelphia, it was found that in one-parent families—that is, families in which the father was not present —the women had married at age 18.0; in paired-parent families, the women had married at age 19.1. In addition, to be sure, the younger mothers also had lower levels of education and church attendance, suggesting that age at marriage is only one element in a large syndrome.[38] In any event, it is doubtful that the postponement of marriage—unless the time were used to increase vocational preparation—would help matters materially: it might only swell the ranks of out-of-wedlock births.

THE LOW SEX RATIO AND THE COMPETITION FOR MATES

The low sex ratio among Negroes, especially in the nubile years, complicates the process of mate selection. There are several ways to deal with a low sex ratio. Bigamy might be openly, if not formally, advocated—as it was during the period of very low sex ratios in Europe after both world wars. Or the surplus women might dedicate themselves to a celibate life of organized social service. Serial polyandry is still another solution, in which several women, one at a time, share the same man.[39]

However it is dealt with, the fact that men are relatively scarce puts women at a disadvantage:

. . . [A]s long as she [i.e. the Negro woman] is confined to an area in which she must compete fiercely for a mate, she remains the object of sexual exploitation and the victim of all of the social evils which such exploitation involves.

In the Negro population, the excess of girls is greatest in the fifteen-to-forty-four [age] group which covers the college years and the age when most marriages occur . . . The explosive social implications of an excess of more than half a million Negro girls and women over fourteen years of age are obvious . . . How

[37] *Ibid.*

[38] Robert Bell, "The One-Parent Mother in the Negro Lower Class," Unpublished, p. 7.

[39] In a sense, serial polyandry is the way slum Negroes have dealt with a low sex ratio. The women, in effect, "share the wealth"—in this case, the relatively scarce men.

much of the tensions and conflicts traditionally associated with the matriarchal framework of Negro society are in reality due to this imbalance and the pressures it generates? [40]

The competition for mates among Negroes is intensified by the unwillingness of some men to marry at all. (The study of the sociosexual development of boys reported only 58 per cent of the sixteen-to-seventeen-year-olds wanted to get married *ever*.[41]) In addition, there has been in recent years an increasing tendency for Negro men to marry white women; and although the total number of such marriages remains small, they tend to occur in precisely those classes in which the supply of potential husbands is smallest. Thus "many of the 645,000 excess Negro women will never marry at all unless they marry outside of the Negro community. And many others will marry men whose educational and cultural standards may not be the same as their own . . . The Negro woman cannot assume with any degree of confidence that she will be able to look to marriage for either economic or emotional support." [42]

COLOR AND MATE SELECTION

Because the environment of Negroes is less hostile to those of light-colored skin, it is expectable that skin color should be a consideration in mate selection. There are so few studies of the processes of mate selection among Negroes that we have few firm data on the effect of propinquity, class, religion, education—or color. Nevertheless, we know that for a long time Negroes associated light skin color with the so-called genteel tradition and, hence, with high status. Because the color of one's mate will influence the color of the offspring, those who covet a nonhostile environment for their future children will prefer a mate of light skin color.

Among the lower classes, however, light skin color may have a negative value. Frazier, for example, refers to a plantation woman whose only preference in a husband was that he be dark, for "if he is most too light, he looks too much like white folks." [43] And Elliott Liebow, field worker for the Child-Rearing Project in Washington, D.C., quoted one man as saying he avoided light women because they were "spoiled." And even in the sample of college students (see p. 80), "redbone" or a light complexion ranked twenty-second out of twenty-eight values in dating, far below internal personality traits and social skills.[44]

Nevertheless, light skin color, especially in women, has tended to be

[40] Pauli Murray, "The Negro Woman in the Quest for Equality." Paper presented at Leadership Conference, National Council Negro Women (Washington, D.C., November 1963), pp. 11-12, 12-13.

[41] Broderick, *op. cit.*

[42] Pauli Murray, *op. cit.*, p. 14.

[43] E. Franklin Frazier, *The Negro Family in the United States* (New York: Holt, Rinehart & Winston, Inc., 1948), p. 105.

[44] Anderson and Himes, *op. cit.*, p. 229.

favored in mate selection. And because men usually have the power of choice, wives, for the most part, tend to be lighter than their husbands. Yet younger Negroes today may put less emphasis on color than their parents do. In one case, a young man's mother objected to his choice of a wife only because the girl was darker than he. It is possible that the "third-generation effect" may be at work, and that the present generation feels secure enough to de-emphasize skin color.

RELIGIOUS AND LEGAL SANCTIONS AGAINST
INTERRACIAL MARRIAGE

One expectable outcome of the preference for light skin color in mates is racial intermarriage. As distinguished from interracial sexual relations outside marriage, it is still rare—and understandably so when the weight of the sanctions against it are examined. The religious and legal sanctions against racial intermarriage a generation ago have been summarized as follows:

There are no ecclesiastical laws prohibiting racial intermarriage. Nevertheless, clergymen have refused to marry couples because the parties differed racially, even in states where racial intermarriage is legal. A notorious case occurred in Rockville, Connecticut, early in 1928 when a Mayflower descendant, granddaughter of a Confederate general, and a Negro laborer took out a marriage license. All the Christian clergy in the community refused to marry the couple, compelling them to have a civil ceremony. . . .

No literature has been found concerning the prohibition of racial intermarriage by governments other than those of some of the United States. In America the first law to deter racial intermarriage was enacted in the Colonial Period. The General Assembly of the colony of Maryland in 1661, reflecting the attitude of the white population, deplored the fact that there were many cases of intermarriage between white female servants and Negro slaves. It legislated that if any freeborn white woman intermarried with a Negro slave, she would have to serve her husband's master so long as the slave lived. Children of all these intermarriages would also be slaves. Children of racial intermarriages which occurred before the law was passed were to remain with their parents' master until they were thirty years of age. In 1681, a new Maryland law provided that any freeborn white woman who married a Negro slave with the permission of the latter's master could retain her freedom. Her children were also free. However, the master or mistress of the intermarried slave and the clergyman performing the ceremony were to be penalized by a fine. This law was an attempt to deter racial intermarriage by shifting the penalty to those allegedly responsible for the action of slaves.

Some of the other colonies also legislated against Negro-white intermarriage. North Carolina in 1715 set up a heavy fine and a period of servitude for any white who married a Negro. It also provided a fifty-pound fine for the clergyman who officiated at a racial intermarriage. Massachusetts in 1705 and Pennsylvania in 1725 passed similar legislation.[45]

[45] Milton L. Barron, *People Who Intermarry: Intermarriage in a New England Industrial Community* (Syracuse, N.Y.: Syracuse University Press, 1946), pp. 47, 50-51.

Although a sizable number of states still retain laws forbidding racial intermarriage—Orientals are the major target in the West; Negroes, in the South—the constitutional status of such legislation is currently in some doubt. In California in 1948 it was declared to be contrary to the state constitution on grounds that it abridged an individual right; that case did not go to the Supreme Court.

In 1964, a Virginia law prohibiting racial intermarriage was challenged. The test involved a white man who was married to a woman who was part Negro and part Indian. The marriage, the result of long acquaintance and dating, had been accepted by the families of both partners—but they had had to elope to the District of Columbia to solemnize it. When they returned to Virginia, they were sentenced to a year in jail, but this sentence was suspended on condition that they did not cohabit; the marriage was declared null and void in Virginia. They therefore made their home in Washington, D.C. In 1963, because the husband worked in Virginia and both wished to visit friends and relatives in that state, they went to court to ask that the law be stricken down. A federal judge refused their request on the basis that no irreparable injury had been done to them. In time, this case will reach the Supreme Court.[46]

TRENDS

Although racial intermarriage is relatively rare, even when it is not forbidden by statute,[47] it does appear to be increasing. The best analysis of the data available on racial intermarriage is that of David M. Heer, who examined the records for Hawaii, California, and Michigan for recent years.

[46] *Washington Post*, October 28, 29, 1964. The Supreme Court sidestepped the issue of the constitutionality of laws forbidding interracial marriage in a case dealing with a Florida law prohibiting a man and a woman of different race from spending the night together in the same room; they struck down this law (*Washington Post*, December 8, 1964).

[47] In New York in 1929, only 2.7 per cent of the Negro grooms and 0.8 per cent of the Negro brides were marrying white partners, and there had been no increase or decrease for at least thirteen years (Barron, *op. cit.*, p. 58). In Los Angeles in 1924-33, only 1.1 per cent of the 4885 marriages of Negroes were interracial (*ibid.*) In 1939 only eight out of 10,000 marriages in the United States involved members of different races, not all of them Negroes (Paul Jacobson, *American Marriage* [New York: Holt, Rinehart & Winston, Inc., 1959], p. 62). In that year, unlike the situation in New York in 1929 when Negro men intermarried at a higher rate than did Negro women, the over-all chances were about even (51 per cent) that the bride would be the nonwhite partner (*ibid.*). The exact proportion varied from place to place. In that year, 583 out of 1,223,633 brides marrying white men were Negro and 559 out of 180,000 brides marrying Negroes were white (*ibid.*). Of the 25,180 Negro brides in California in 1955-59, 252 (or about 1 per cent) were marrying white men; of the 25,867 Negro grooms in the same time period, 921 (or about 3.6 per cent) were marrying white women (**Larry D. Barnett**, "Interracial Marriage in California," *Marriage and Family Living*, Vol. 25 [November 1963], 425, 426).

In all three states the trend in recent years has been for a rise both in the proportion of whites marrying Negroes and of Negroes marrying whites. In California from 1955 to 1959 the proportion of whites marrying Negroes increased from 0.14 per cent to 0.21 per cent and [that] of Negroes marrying whites [went] from 2.21 per cent to 2.58 per cent; in Hawaii from 1956 to 1962 the proportion of whites marrying Negroes increased from 0.13 per cent to 0.24 per cent and [that] of Negroes marrying whites [went] from 6.45 per cent to 13.04 per cent; and in Michigan from 1953 to 1962 the proportion of whites marrying Negroes increased from 0.07 per cent to 0.12 per cent and [that] of Negroes marrying whites [went] from 0.75 per cent to 1.20 per cent. The recent upward trend in Negro-white marriage is apparently a reversal of a previous downward trend which took place early in the present century.[48]

An analysis of California data by county led Heer to conclude that, for whites, "the sheer availability of possible Negro partners is an important factor influencing their intermarriage rate," but, for Negroes, "differences in proportion of Negroes marrying whites may be best explained by differences in the tolerance of the white community with regard to such marriages." [49]

Although in cases of extramarital miscegenation the white partner is likely to be the man, in racial intermarriage it is more likely to be the woman. A white man's occupational status in the past was likely to suffer if he married a Negro woman; a Negro's was not. When a white man did marry a Negro woman, he was likely to be foreign-born, without native American prejudices. It is extremely difficult to isolate all the factors accounting for the sex difference in intermarriage among Negroes. Perhaps the analogous phenomenon of "passing" is relevant. Negro men more than Negro women are among those who every year pass over into the white world. It has been suggested that the Negro girl light enough to pass has a better position in the Negro world than in the outside world. "If she remains a Negro, a light girl is in a privileged position, but if she crosses into the white group, she becomes just another 'white' woman among thousands, and her complexion and features are no longer a peculiar asset." [50] Whether lesser inducements or lesser opportunities operate to prevent intermarriage by Negro women cannot be determined from any data now available.[51]

---

[48] David M. Heer, "Recent Data on Negro-White Marriage in the United States." Paper presented before the American Sociological Association, Montreal, August 1964, p. 1.

[49] *Ibid.,* p. 2.

[50] Maurice R. Davie, *Negroes in American Society* (New York: McGraw-Hill Book Company, 1949), p. 405.

[51] On the inducement side, Pauli Murray notes that "many of the 645,000 excess Negro women will never marry at all unless they marry outside of the Negro community" (*op. cit.,* p. 14).

NONLEGAL SANCTIONS: ATTITUDES TOWARD
RACIAL INTERMARRIAGE

Nonlegal sanctions against intermarriage remain fairly strong. Rarely is it welcomed, although Negroes tend to be more tolerant of it when or if it does occur. One study by Donald J. Bogue and Jan E. Dizard of 721 Negro families in Chicago reported that:

. . . [C]ontrary to what may be the popular stereotype, almost no Negro respondents reported that they would encourage their child to marry a white person. . . . About one half of the Negroes would tolerate it, saying "it made no difference," and the other half would oppose it. Eighty per cent or more of Negro parents would permit their child to marry a white person if the romance had already developed without their knowledge, but there is no evidence of a desire for miscegenation or even interest in promoting it, except among a very tiny minority.[52]

This over-all finding conceals some differences among Negroes. Because racial intermarriage seems likely to involve a Negro male and a white female, such marriages tend to diminish the already small potential supply of husbands for Negro women. Lower-class Negro women are apparently immune to concern on this score. According to Frazier, however:

Among the women of the black bourgeoisie there is an intense fear of the competition of white women for Negro men. They often attempt to rationalize their fear by saying that the Negro man always occupies an inferior position in relation to the white woman or that he marries much below his "social" status. They come nearer to the source of their fear when they confess that there are not many eligible Negro men and that these few should marry Negro women. That such rationalizations conceal deep-seated feelings of insecurity is revealed by the fact that generally they have no objection to the marriage of white men to Negro women, especially if the white man is reputed to be wealthy. In fact, they take pride in the fact and attribute these marriages to the "peculiar" charms of Negro women.[53]

The very nature of racial intermarriage may be in a process of change. At one time it was hypothesized, as indicated by Frazier, that such marriages involved a prosperous Negro man and a lower-class white woman. A study of ninety-five Negro-white marriages in Indiana in 1958-59, however, did not corroborate this hypothesis: the occupational distribution of the partners was the same as for Indiana marriages as a whole; and

[52] Donald J. Bogue and Jan E. Dizard, reported in *Washington Post*, May 25, 1964. A Gallup poll in 1965 reported that nationwide, 46 per cent of those polled disapproved of laws making Negro-white marriage a crime; 48 per cent approved. Among Southern whites, the figures were 24 per cent and 72 per cent, respectively; among whites outside the South, 52 per cent and 42 per cent, respectively (*ibid.*, March 10, 1965).

[53] E. Franklin Frazier, *Black Bourgeoisie* (New York: The Crowell-Collier Publishing Co., 1962), p. 180.

"there was no indication of a pattern of occupational dominance of one spouse over another, regardless of race." [54] Nor were these impulsive teenage marriages: the median age of Negro brides marrying white grooms was a year older than that of white brides marrying white grooms; and the median age of white brides marrying Negro grooms was also older than of white brides marrying white grooms. Similarly, Negro grooms marrying white brides were older than white grooms marrying white brides; and white grooms marrying Negro brides were among the oldest of those marrying. As in other recent studies, there was a preponderance of Negro-white (Negro groom, white bride) over white-Negro (white groom, Negro bride) marriages, the ratio among these ninety-five marriages being 69 to 26.

Wives and Husbands

In Western society, power in the family was traditionally distributed more or less evenly between husbands and wives: the greater tolerance of women for sexual abstinence gave them an advantage in the bedroom; but the control by husbands of the purse strings gave them an advantage everywhere else.[55] The conditions which made this balance possible do not necessarily prevail today, and they have rarely—if ever—prevailed in the world of the Negro. The Negro man has not been able to control the purse strings, and the shortage of Negro men has cancelled the sexual advantage of the Negro woman. For if she is niggardly there are always others who will be generous. As a result, "Most lower-class [Negro] women have to take love on male terms . . . [and] the men . . . are strongly tempted to take advantage of such a situation and to trade love for a living." [56]

There is little information on the Negro woman's performance as a mate under slavery. When, like Rose, she was arbitrarily assigned to a man, she probably submitted sullenly; when there was genuine affection, she was probably the dominant partner. After emancipation, if her husband had not deserted her, she may have been the one to decide where the family would live. For example, when a former master tried to persuade a freedman's family to return to his plantation, the man replied,

---

[54] Todd H. Pavela, "An Exploratory Study of Negro-White Intermarriage in Indiana," *Marriage and Family Living,* Vol. 26 (May 1964), 209.

[55] David M. Heer, "The Measurement and Bases of Family Power: An Overview," *Marriage and Family Living,* Vol. 25 (May 1963), 133-39; Robert O. Blood, Jr., "The Measurement and Bases of Family Power: A Rejoinder," *ibid.* (November 1963) 475-478.

[56] St. Clair Drake and Horace Cayton, *Black Metropolis* (New York: Harper & Row, Publishers, 1962), p. 584. Social workers in urban slums sometimes report cases of men who make the rounds regularly, sharing whatever source of income several women have. They are not considered prostitutes.

"I can't, Master. It don't suit my wife round here. She won't come back. I can't stay." [57]

THE MANY ROLES OF WIVES

In the outside world, marriages tend to be homogamous—husbands and wives tending to come from similar social, religious, ethnic, and educational background. Within this general similarity, there is some tendency for men to marry a little below their own level, so that they are slightly hypogamous while their wives tend to be slightly hypergamous. In the case of Negroes, the reverse tends to be true. Negro women tend to marry below their own level.

So far as education is concerned, for example, in 1960 even among women thirty-five to forty-four years of age who had four or more years of college education, almost a tenth—8 per cent—were married to men who had less than eight years of schooling. Most women were destined to marry men with less education than they had, although the disparity was not often this great. Because educational superiority in women is correlated with better earning power, the inequalities between husbands and wives in this area can have painful repercussions. In the case of college women, for example, their "higher educational rank and earning power . . . [have] created feelings of guilt in some Negro women and . . . some [have] even failed to go on to higher degrees in order to preserve the marital relationship from the destructive effects of envy and jealousy on the part of their husbands." [58]

Not only in formal schooling, but also in the informal schooling of every-day contacts with the outside world, Negro wives seem to be superior. We have already commented on the greater accessibility to Negro women than to Negro men of acculturating contacts with the outside world. An example is presented in a study of Negro men patients at a mental hospital, which reported that in their families the women "were more familiar with the sources of power and resources in the community—i.e., police and eleemosynary institutions—and were more willing to utilize them than were the males." [59] The status of such a woman depended, in part, on "how adequately she performed her role of . . . interpreter of the general American culture to her husband and

[57] B. A. Botkin, *Lay My Burden Down* (Chicago: University of Chicago Press, 1945), p. 244.

[58] Pauli Murray, "The Negro Woman in the Quest for Equality." Paper presented at Leadership Conference, National Council Negro Women, Washington, D.C., November 1963), p. 12.

[59] Robert L. Derbyshire, Eugene B. Brody, and Carl Schleifer, "Family Structure of Young Adult Negro Mental Patients: Preliminary Observations from Urban Baltimore." Unpublished paper, p. 5.

children." [60] The fact that wives are more likely than husbands to "know the ropes" gives them an additional advantage.

The Negro wife, of course, has also been a major contributor to family support. In 1960, even in families with children under six years of age, almost a third (29 per cent) of Negro wives were employed. Some wives work to assure family survival; others, to maintain a higher level of living or to achieve upward social mobility. For high income among nonwhite families usually requires more than one earner and the extra earner is likely to be the wife. [61] In any event, the Negro wife has been a hard worker and, as such, "she . . . [occupies] a position of authority and is not completely subordinate to masculine authority even in those families where the man is present." [62] Thus, in a recent study of 116 husband-wife families in Detroit, it was reported that the wife was dominant—as measured by the criterion of decision-making—in almost half of the families (44 per cent); the husband, in only 19 per cent; and in 38 per cent of the families, both had equal power. [63]

Like Frazier, Blood and Wolfe report a subordinate position for the husband in the higher-income families: thirty-five high-income Negro husbands (over $4000) had lower mean power (4.09) than their sixty-eight less affluent colleagues (4.56) [64] a situation contrary to that found in the white sample.

The authors do not interpret these findings as corroborative of a matriarchal theory; they found Negro wives assumed the decision-making role only because it was thrust upon them. These women—especially those who were in the low-status occupations such as maids and factory workers (29 per cent)—tended to see their contribution to their husbands' mobility in terms of their earnings [65] and savings. They also saw their contribution in terms of being good housekeepers. [66] Negro husbands, incidentally, offered little help to their wives in their housekeeper roles. In the blue-collar occupations, even though their wives were likely to be

---

[60] *Ibid.*, p. 8.

[61] In 1959, two-thirds of nonwhite families in the $5,000 to $7,000 annual income bracket and 91 per cent of those in the $10,000 to $15,000 bracket had two or more earners (Dorothy Newman, "Motivation, Aspiration, and the Negro," Unpublished paper, p. 11).

[62] E. Franklin Frazier, *The Negro Family in the United States* (New York: Holt, Rinehart & Winston, Inc., 1948), p. 344.

[63] Robert Blood and D. M. Wolfe, *Husbands and Wives* (New York: The Free Press of Glencoe, Inc., 1960), p. 35.

[64] About a third (31 per cent) of the wives were employed; one fourth of them put in more than forty hours a week. Only 19 per cent had white-collar jobs, mainly sales and clerical (*ibid.*, p. 99).

[65] *Ibid.*, p. 34.

[66] *Ibid.*, p. 91.

working outside the home as well, husbands did not help around the house. Blood and Wolfe wonder if such work was viewed as a threat to their masculinity.[67]

There was a time when the privilege of not entering the labor force was a status symbol, so-called. In the family which Frazier called "proletarian," the earnings of some husbands freed their wives from the necessity of contributing to family income. In such families the wife lost some of her authority and the husband's was often harsh, even brutal; both wives and children were completely subjected to the man's will.[68] But the employment of married women, white as well as Negro, has shown an extraordinary increase in the last decade or two.[69] In 1960, 40.6 per cent of nonwhite women living with their husbands were in the labor force; in the 35-44 age bracket, almost half (48.9 per cent) were.[70] It is doubtful if the men remaining in the families can exercise "harsh" or "brutal" authority over their wives today.

In contrast to the situation of the proletarian or even the middle-class family, in the culturally hybrid black bourgeoisie, social life—"Society" —is reported to play an inordinately important part in the life of the wife. And Society tends to be in the hands of women. Unlike the strong and powerful "grannies" or "matriarchs" of the past and the hard-working wives of the present, the wives of the black bourgeoisie (according to Frazier) are frivolous, though lovely, butterflies who spend a great deal of time going to card parties, entertaining, and in social life in general, and who dominate their husbands not by their contribution to the family's welfare but by their greater social know-how.

Those who do not work devote their time to the frivolities of Negro "society." When they devote their time to "charity" or worthwhile causes, it is generally a form of play or striving for "social" recognition. They are constantly forming clubs which ostensibly have a serious purpose, but in reality are formed in order to consolidate their position in "society" or to provide additional occasions for playing poker. The idle, overfed women among the black bourgeoisie are generally, to use their language, "dripping with diamonds." They are forever dieting and reducing only to put on more weight (which is usually the result of the food that they consume at their club meetings). Even the women among the black bourgeoisie who work . . . generally . . . have no real interest in

---

[67] *Ibid.*, p. 66.

[68] Frazier, *op. cit.*, p. 344. Frazier added that "especially in Southern cities, one may find that the black worker's authority in his family may be challenged by his mother-in-law," suggesting that even then the presence of at least a long shadow of the matri-focal family could be felt.

[69] Ivan Nye and Lois Hoffman, *The Employed Mother in America* (Chicago: Rand McNally & Co., 1963).

[70] U.S. Bureau of the Census, *Employment Status and Work Experience* (1960), Table 4, p. 24.

their work and only engage in it in order to be able to provide the conspicuous consumption demanded by "society." [71]

A similar picture was painted by Drake and Cayton of the women in the world of the successful "nonrespectables":

The wives of the gentlemen racketeers and their associates are women of leisure; unlike many wives of the "respectable" uppers, none of them have to work for their living. They can spend their time at the dressmaker's and in the swank downtown shops, or in supervising the details of entertaining in their sumptuous town houses or country homes. The women's lives, like the men's, are centered on conspicuous consumption—display of the most lavish kind.[72]

WIVES' EVALUATION OF MARRIAGE

What do Negro women get out of marriage? Some studies dealing with marital satisfaction reveal a tendency toward bimodality, suggesting the presence of at least two patterns of marital satisfaction among them. Robert Bell, for example (in response to the question: "In general, how would you rate your marriage?"), obtained the following results for two sets of low-income women:

Table 3-2.

Marital Ratings of Two Sets of Women, Philadelphia*

| | Years of Schooling | | | | | |
| | 0–9 | | 10–12 | | Total | |
Ratings	No.	Per cent	No.	Per cent	No.	Per cent
Very good	18	26	31	28	49	27
Good	11	16	26	24	37	21
Average	21	30	35	32	56	31
Poor	7	10	13	12	20	11
Very poor	13	20	4	4	17	10
Total	70		109		179	

* *Source:* Robert R. Bell. Tables based on interviews with 194 Negro women, August 1, 1963–October 15, 1963.

In both sets of women, more than one mode appears to be present; in the women with least schooling, perhaps three. At any rate, there seems to be more than a single type.

[71] E. Franklin Frazier, *Black Bourgeoisie* (New York: The Crowell-Collier Publishing Co., 1962), p. 183.

[72] St. Clair Drake and Horace R. Cayton, *Black Metropolis* (New York: Harper Torchbooks, 1962), pp. 546-47.

A similar tendency was noted in the Washington Child-Rearing Project in the early 1960s. Data on twenty-two parental figures revealed a bimodal distribution of ratings of marital relations; one mode was somewhat above, and one somewhat below, average.[73] The bimodality itself was interesting, tending as it did to corroborate the Bell findings in Philadelphia, but so also was the fact that both distributions were approximately the same size. Among these low-income marriages there appeared also to be two types with respect to the reported quality of the relationship: one above, and one below, average.

The same bimodality appeared when a different measure of marital success was used. Bell asked his subjects: "If you had it to do all over again, would you ever get married?" His two sets of women, differentiated on the basis of schooling, showed diametrically opposite reactions:

Table 3-3.

Marital Evaluation of Two Sets of Women, Philadelphia*

| Marital Evaluation | Years of Schooling | | | | | |
| | 0–9 | | 10–12 | | Total | |
	No.	Per cent	No.	Per cent	No.	Per cent
Would get married	24	34	65	59	89	49
Would not get married	44	63	34	31	78	43
Don't know	2	3	11	10	13	8
Total	70		110		180	100

* *Source:* Robert Bell. Tables based on interviews with 194 Negro women, August 1, 1963–October 15, 1963.

A similar contrast of pattern showed up for the question: "Would you marry the same person you are married to now?" On this index of marriage, the bimodality appeared to be related to years of schooling.[74]

One other clue was furnished by the Bell data. He compared the replies of the mothers in one-parent families with those of mothers in paired-parent families. Three fourths of the one-parent mothers (74 per cent)—but fewer than half (44 per cent) of the paired-parent mothers—

[73] The ratings were as follows: A(highest), 3; B, 7; C, 3; D, 7; and E(lowest), 2. Hylan Lewis, "Culture, Class and the Behavior of Low Income Families." Unpublished paper, presented at Conference on Lower Class Culture, New York City, June 1963, p. 18a.

[74] Such bimodality may reflect the two cultures: women who are thus disaffected with their husbands but who nevertheless remain with them are perhaps among the acculturated; those who do not, among the externally adapted.

Table 3-4.

Marital Evaluation of Two Sets of Women, Philadelphia*

	Years of Schooling					
Marital Evaluation	*0–9*		*10–12*		*Total*	
	No.	*Per cent*	*No.*	*Per cent*	*No.*	*Per cent*
Would marry same man	23	32	58	53	81	45
Would not marry same man	45	63	38	34	83	46
Don't know	3	5	14	13	17	9
Total	71		110		181	100

* *Source:* Robert Bell. Tables based on interviews with Negro women, August 1, 1963–October 15, 1963.

said they would not marry if they had it to do over. But even the paired-parent mothers, though they appreciated marriage, were not always satisfied with their current spouses: almost half (47 per cent) said they would not marry the same man again.

THE "MATRIARCH" FALLACY

It was noted (see p. 89) that, in conventional marital relationships, control of the purse strings gave the husband an advantage over his wife in certain areas. The fact that women contribute to the support of the family need not, in and of itself, lower the strategic position of their husbands. In the little ghetto communities of Eastern Europe, the woman who married a scholar and supported him in his studies was honored: it was a genuine privilege to support a learned man—nor was his masculinity diminished because he was supported by his wife. And many immigrant wives in the United States found it necessary to step in to earn money during their husbands' periods of unemployment. Although there was no special honor in the "matriarchal" position, neither was there any disgrace. A husband may have felt chagrin or humiliation, but his wife knew he was a man, the world knew he was a man, so he knew it too.

It is not, therefore, the mere fact that a wife contributes to family support that denigrates a husband, but the context in which this occurs. The Negro husband is not in the scholar's position, nor has the outside world allowed him to cultivate his masculine honor.

THE SLAVE AND THE FREEDMAN AS HUSBAND

Given the primary-group nature of marriage and family relations under slavery, one could expect them to differ widely according to the people involved, and so they did. One could, for example, search the literature of many peoples before finding a story to match in tenderness that of the Negro slave who, when his mate complained of the beating she had suffered, took her to a cave, away from harm. He fixed it up for her to live in; he brought her food; he protected her. Three children were born in the cave and only with emancipation did the family come out to join him.[75] On the other hand, there was Bob Boylan, who fell in love with another woman, "so he burns his wife and four young-uns in their house." [76] There was no standard pattern.

Nor is there any way of determining the relative incidence or prevalence of the different patterns. Sometimes the master helped to maintain a good relationship; but sometimes he did not, so that the care a husband could bestow on his wife was limited: "sometimes a man would help his wife, but most times he was beat afterwards." [77]

There was little in the system of slavery to encourage conjugal responsibility. Even when slave marriages were permitted to be solemnized, there was little emphasis on lifelong commitment. Thus, the behavior of men after emancipation varied as much as it had under slavery: some remained loyal to their families; others did not.[78]

TYPES OF PATRIFOCAL FAMILIES

As the social dust settled after the first emancipation, several different kinds of marriage and family systems emerged. Frazier has described five that were patrifocal in nature.[79] One involved those who had been free even before the Civil War. The free Negroes tended to live in cities and "it was among them that the Negro family first acquired an institutional character." A second kind of male-centered, even patriarchal, family was found in the so-called racial islands or communities, North and South, of complex mixtures of racial types—Negro, white, and Indian. A third type might be called the "straw-boss family," for in some cases the relationship of the husband to his wife and children did, indeed, resemble that of a straw boss or gang leader. The freedmen who, under slavery, had gone to school to Simon Legree, put their lessons to work on their own wives and children as labor-contractors. In the fourth type, the husband had purchased his wife: "in purchasing his wife and children the man not only secured authority over them, but he also acquired a fundamental interest in them since they represented the fruit of his industry and sacrifice." The fifth pattern was that of the landowning peasant, many of whom were (in Frazier's words) black puritans, among whom the Protestant ethic was already highly institutionalized.

[75] Botkin, *op. cit.*, pp. 179-80.
[76] *Ibid.*, p. 256.
[77] *Ibid.*, p. 179.
[78] *Ibid.*, pp. 241, 242, 262.
[79] E. Franklin Frazier, *The Negro Family in the United States*, pp. 128-29, 139-40, 188-89, 193.

THE NEGRO AS HUSBAND TODAY

A disproportionate amount of research on white or Negro marriage and family is based on information gleaned from wives. The Negro husband, in particular, remains a shadowy figure.

One study of 43 consecutive first Negro male admissions (ages 18 to 35 and averaging 26), to a state mental hospital in Maryland reported differences between the sexes in marital and family role conceptions and behavior. Almost half (48 per cent) of these men viewed themselves as unmarried, although 24 per cent were fathers. About a fourth were divorced or separated from legal or common-law wives. The rest were married, almost a tenth to common-law wives. In the families of these men, more concern was shown for their welfare by wives, sisters, and aunts than by fathers, brothers, or uncles. In all the families the women worked to contribute to the family's support and, in some cases, were its sole support. The status of the husband rested largely on his success as a provider; if he performed well in this role, his behavior in other respects did not lower his status. As provider and as family stabilizer, women received appreciation from the husbands. The quality of the relationships of the men and of women seemed to the researchers to differ:

Even though the structure of these families took the form of a primary group, females seemed to function on the level of an emotionally reciprocal primary-group relationship with most members of the family, while the males appeared to function more on the level of a secondary relationship. Male social interaction within the family seemed to be based upon concrete social, economic, and sexual functions, which tended to give an impression of depersonalization rather than an emotionally reciprocal relationship.[80]

The families in this study were not in any sense randomly selected, but they represent, however inadequately, one segment of families.

More adequate was the sample of husbands and wives studied by Blood and Wolfe in Detroit. Although we still see the husband through the eyes of the wives, the view is focused by rigorous research techniques. The wives were, in effect, asked to evaluate their husbands in four areas: level of living, understanding, companionship, and love. The average satisfaction scores for these areas were, respectively: 2.79, 3.19, 3.51, and 3.59.[81] These husbands, in brief, were evaluated highest on love and lowest on the level of living they provided.

It certainly cannot be surprising to learn that these husbands were rated least satisfactory in the role of provider. What is unexpected, in fact, is that relatively so few were. Only 10 per cent of the wives felt that they were really missing out so far as level of living was concerned: about

[80] Derbyshire, Brody, and Schleifer, *op. cit.*

[81] Blood and Wolfe, *op. cit.*, pp. 108, 172, 214, 223.

a third (30 per cent) felt that it would be nice to have more than they had, but a surprising proportion—32 per cent—felt that the level of living provided by their husbands was all right, and a whopping 27 per cent felt quite satisfied and even lucky about the way things were. The higher the husband's income, of course, the higher the satisfaction score his wife assigned him. Husbands with incomes under $3000 had wives whose satisfaction scores were 2.68; those with incomes of $5000 or more, 3.00.[82]

Somewhat, but not a great deal, better was the husbands' ability to satisfy their wives' need for understanding. It was not, however, so much a failing on the husbands' part as it was the enormity of the wives' burdens, according to Blood and Wolfe, which accounted for the low degree of satisfaction reported by the women. Almost three fourths of the wives (72 per cent) were either quite satisfied with their husband's understanding of their problems and feelings or felt that they could not complain; 16 per cent felt it would be nice to have more understanding, and about the same proportion were rather disappointed (5 per cent) as were enthusiastic (7 per cent). For all 731 women in the sample, both white and Negro, help from the husband in withdrawing from the problem situation was the response that had the most therapeutic effect and help from him in solving the problem was most highly related to their satisfaction with the understanding they received.

The Negro wife suffers deprivation in all areas, but it is relatively less marked in the areas of companionship and love than in those of income or understanding: "At least a good many Negro wives say they are quite satisfied" with the companionship their husbands offer.[83] Esther Middlebush, of the Michigan Department of Health, commenting on interviews with low-income Negro women in urban Michigan, has stated that the women feel more secure, more cheerful, with a man around.[84] Although communication tended to be at low ebb among the families in the Blood-Wolfe sample,[85] it is possible that just having a husband in the home was a source of satisfaction in itself.

It was in the area of love that the Negro husband scored best, again emphasizing the importance attached to love among Negroes. Only 2 per cent of the husbands disappointed their wives; more than 2 per cent rendered them enthusiastic; somewhat more than 10 per cent of the wives

[82] *Ibid.*, p. 109. This finding, by itself, is certainly banal. Even compared to white wives, Blood and Wolfe report, Negro wives were less satisfied with the same level of living (but not as dissatisfied as Jewish wives). It could be that size of family was larger among Negroes so that the same income had to cover the requirements of more family members. This interpretation is suggested by the fact that about two-fifths of the Negro wives referred to the hardships involved in rearing children (p. 144).

[83] *Ibid.*, p. 172.

[84] Personal discussion, National Council Family Relations Conference, October 1964.

[85] Blood and Wolfe, *op. cit.*, p. 195.

would have liked more; but another two thirds either felt quite satisfied and lucky or felt they could not complain.[86]

Although the average satisfaction score of Negro wives (3.59) in the area of love was lower than that for white wives (4.03), in general it tended to resemble the average satisfaction score of white wives in similar situations. Thus, for example, the average satisfaction score for white women whose husbands never or almost never talked about events at work (3.70 and 3.48, respectively) were close to those of Negro wives; so also were the scores of those who had slight or no "friendship companionship" with their husbands (3.83 and 2.43, respectively). The satisfaction score of women with three or more years of education more than their husbands was 3.88. In general, the wife's satisfaction scores were low when either she or her husband had low educational levels. Finally, the satisfaction score for white women in the lowest social status levels was 3.54, practically identical with that of Negro wives. In brief, it seemed that the relatively lower satisfaction score for love among the Negro wives could be interpreted in terms of the circumstances of the marriage: whether the husbands were Negro or white, if they never or almost never talked about events at work, or shared with wives companionship with friends, or if they had low educational levels, or low social status, they were less likely to score high in the area of love. Negro marriages, more than white, tended to show these defects.

THE SEXUALITY OF NEGROES

The sexuality of Negroes has been a topic of fascination for many in the outside world for a long time. Thomas Jefferson in his *Notes on Virginia* commented that "Negroes are more ardent after their female; but love seems with them to be more an eager desire, than a delicate mixture of sentiment and sensation." Enough evidence has already been presented to show that even romantic love could develop under slavery. But to this day, Negroes are attributed a higher degree of raw sexuality than white people.

John Dollard has summarized the white image of Negro sexual potency:

The idea seems to be that they [i.e., Negro men] are more like savages, nearer to animals, and that the sexual appetites are more vigorous and ungoverned. There is a widespread belief that the genitalia of Negro males are larger than those of whites; this was repeatedly stated by white informants. . . . One thing seems certain—that the actual differences between Negro and white genitalia cannot be as great as they seem to the whites; it is a question of the psychological size being greater than any actual differences could be.[87]

[86] *Ibid.*, p. 223.
[87] John Dollard, *Caste and Class in a Southern Town,* 2nd ed. (New York: Harper & Row, Publishers, 1949), pp. 160-61.

Among the many bases for the hostility of the outside world against Negro men may well have been envy of an assumed greater sexual potency; castration was a major form of torture in the past. In point of fact, however, fear of male sexuality among modern Negroes is misplaced. Sexuality, like every other aspect of the personality of Negroes, is distorted by the conditions under which they must live. Far from being unbridled, there is evidence to show that it is subject to grave and inhibiting aberrations. Because the hostile environment has imposed submissive, dependent roles upon Negro men, and because so many Negroes are socialized in homes without fathers, normal sexuality (according to Kardiner and Ovesey) is difficult to achieve.

On the basis of clinical experience in a Northern city, Kardiner and Ovesey make the following statement about Negro sexuality:

. . . the sex life of the Negro—of all classes—[shows] marked deviation from the white stereotypes. The Negro is hardly the abandoned sexual hedonist he is supposed to be. Quite the contrary, sex often seems relatively unimportant to him. The factors that weigh heavily to make this the case are the uniformly bad relations with females on an emotional level. If the male comes from a female-dominated household, the relation to the mother is generally one of frustrated dependency and hostility. . . . The sexual function is tied to many other aspects of adaptation. It is, therefore, consistent with the general hardships of the adaptation of the male that his sex life suffers as a consequence . . . because his economic opportunities are worse than the female's he is not infrequently at the mercy of the woman. Masculinity is closely tied to power in every form in our society. The male is much the more vulnerable to socioeconomic failure. He unconsciously interprets it as a loss in masculinity. The inability to function successfully in the male sexual role can be one of the . . . outcomes of this interpretation.[88]

Stereotypes have also prevailed with respect to female sexuality among Negroes. In the nineteenth century, when frigidity was prized among white women, any degree of responsiveness in a woman would seem like ecstatic abandon. Actually there is no reason at all to believe that Negro women are any more "highly sexed" than other women.

The frequent disregard of the [Negro] female for sex is equally remarkable. She is just as handicapped as her white contemporaries. This reluctance exists notwithstanding earlier opportunities for induction into sex, and less real oppression by the sense of shame for breach of conformity—as is the case, for example, with illegitimate offspring. . . . [S]exual disturbance, that is, frigidity, is quite frequent.[89]

[88] Abram Kardiner and Lionel Ovesey, *The Mark of Oppression*, "Explorations in the Personality of the American Negro," (Cleveland: Meridian [subsidiary of World Publishing Co.], 1962), pp. 69- 0. See also Kenneth Clark, *Dark Ghetto* (New York: Harper & Row, Publishers, 1965), pp. 68ff. and *Journal of Social Issues*, Vol. 20 (April 1964), pp. 46-53.

[89] *Ibid.*, p. 69.

Frazier has reported supporting evidence from the upper income classes:

> . . . if the husband has risen in social status through his own efforts and married a member of an "old" family or a "society" woman, the husband is likely to play a pitiful role. The greatest compliment that can be paid such a husband is that he "worships his wife," which means that he is her slave and supports all her extravagances and vanities. But, of course, many husbands in such positions escape from their frustrations by having extra-marital sex relations. Yet the conservative and conventional middle-class husband presents a pathetic picture. He often sits at home alone, impotent physically and socially, and complains that his wife has gone crazy about poker and "society" and constantly demands money for gambling and expenditures which he can not afford. Sometimes he enjoys the sympathy of a son or daughter who has not become a "socialite." Such children often say that they had a happy family life until "mamma took to poker." [90]

The grievances were not, however, all on one side. Men, being at a premium, were not always faithful.

> Preoccupation with poker on the part of the . . . woman is often an attempt to escape from a frustrated life. Her frustration may be bound up with her unsatisfactory sexual life. She may be married to a "glamorous" male who neglects her for other women. For among the black bourgeoisie, the glamor of the male is often associated with his sexual activities. The frustration of many Negro women has a sexual origin. Even those who have sought an escape from frustration in sexual promiscuity may, because of satiety or deep psychological reasons, become obsessed with poker in order to escape from their frustrations. One "society" woman, in justification of her obsession with poker remarked that it had taken the place of her former preoccupation with sex. Another said that to win at poker was similar to sexual orgasm.[91]

SEPARATION AND DIVORCE

In view of these sexual, as well as economic difficulties involved in marriage among Negroes, it is not unexpected that separation and divorce are common. Because love has greater significance than the concept of duty and because, at least among the externally adapted, it is not a virtue to remain with a man or a woman if love is not present, either spouse may take the initiative in breaking the relationship.

Both the separation and divorce rates among Negroes are high, the first being considerably higher than the second. Paul C. Glick constructed three indexes of marriage instability: a separation ratio, a divorce ratio, and the percentage of young children not living with both parents. The separation ratio (the proportion of all married women who were separated) and the divorce ratio (the proportion of all married women who

[90] Frazier, *Black Bourgeoisie, op. cit.,* p. 182.
[91] *Ibid.,* pp. 182-83.

were divorced) constituted the "disrupted-marriage" ratio. Among non-white women, two thirds of the marriage disruptions were caused by separation,[92] but all kinds of marriage disruptions were much higher in central cities than in other areas and lowest by far in rural areas[93] (see Table 3-5).

Table 3-5.

Marriage Instability among Nonwhite Women, 1960*

Measure	Total	Urbanized Areas		Other Urban Areas		Rural	
		Central Cities	Urban Fringe	Places 10,000+	2,500– 10,000	1,000– 2,500	Other Rural
Separation Ratio							
United States	138	163	121	147	137	120	82
Northeast	192	207	157	150	125	100	103
North central	146	157	115	101	105	89	79
South	131	161	123	164	148	134	86
Divorce Ratio							
United States	60	77	58	63	51	41	23
Northeast	49	50	51	47	36	35	31
North central	91	96	78	89	73	67	48
South	49	71	45	62	51	41	20

Per Cen Children not Living with Both Parents

Northeast	35.5
North central	33.5
South	35.1
Urban	35.1
Rural nonfarm	32.7
Rural farm	26.5

* *Source:* Paul C. Glick, "Marriage Instability: Variations by Size of Place and Region," *The Milbank Memorial Fund Quarterly*, Vol. 41 (January 1963), 48-49. Data for the West are not here included because they include many nonwhites who are not Negro and thus blur the picture.

The significance of such terms as *separation* and *divorce* is somewhat blurred by the fluid nature of many conjugal relationships among Negroes. Some of the anomalies associated with legal marriage, as contrasted with nonlegal or extralegal alliances, among Negro men were highlighted in a Milwaukee study of persons who applied for marriage licenses but did not

[92] Paul C. Glick, "Marriage Instability: Variations by Size of Place and Region," *The Milbank Memorial Fund Quarterly*, Vol. 41 (January, 1963), 46.
[93] *Ibid.*, p. 47.

return to pick them up after the waiting period.[94] A disproportionate number of such nonreturnees were Negroes.[95] Among them, the archetype was an inmigrant to the city, with low status (four out of seventy-two were unemployed, forty-seven were unskilled or semiskilled) and uncertain plans, and paired with a woman much older or much younger than he— a set of characteristics associated with unsuccessful marriage. By not returning to pick up the marriage license, a marriage with all the earmarks of failure may have been prevented. But this does not mean that the union did not take place. In any event, the likelihood of a breakdown in the relationship was great. In other words, putting a legal seal on a union would not necessarily have improved its quality. It might have given the stamp of legitimacy to the offspring, but no greater chance of support and stability.

Among the men who actually did return for the license and did get married, more than a quarter (26 per cent) had been married before; only 17 per cent of the nonreturnees had. Some of the men, apparently, engaged in serial polygamy with legal sanction; others, without it.

Mothers and Fathers

THE SLAVE MOTHER

No moonlight-and-magnolia myth is more appealing than that of the old Negro mammy who nursed her white charges with infinite tenderness and devotion. Often, however, she did so at the expense of her own children. Among the field Negroes, there was little time for the children. Furthermore, it was made very clear that the children were the master's property and did not belong to the parents.[96] On some plantations, the women were simply breeding instruments.

That women could love children conceived under such circumstances is, in a way, quite remarkable, yet many of them were fiercely maternal. "The old overseer he hate my mammy, 'cause she fight him for beating her children. Why, she git more whuppings for that than anything else." Even the children of hated white fathers were cherished. "She was so glad freedom come on before her children come on old enough to sell. Part-white children sold for more than black children." One woman was so broken-hearted to have her children sold that when the fourth was born she said, "I just decided I'm not going to let Old Master sell

[94] Gordon Shipman, "Nonmarriage and the Waiting Period." Paper presented at annual meeting of National Council on Family Relations, Miami, October 1964.

[95] About a third (34 per cent) before 1959 were Negroes; after that date, 45 per cent. A law regulating marriage was strengthened in 1960.

[96] Henderson H. Donald, *The Negro Freedman* (New York: Abelard-Schuman, Limited, 1952), p. 68.

this baby; he just ain't going to do it. . . . [So] she got up and give it something out of a bottle, and pretty soon it was dead." [97]

THE MOTHER AMONG FREEDMEN

The early accounts of mothers among the freedmen contrast strikingly with the memories of former slaves. To outside observers, parents showed very "feeble" affection for their children. Floggings were reported, more cruel than any given under slavery. Neglect of hygiene led to extremely high infant mortality rates. Discipline was reported to be nonexistent.[98]

But whatever may have been their behavior in the early years of freedom, in later years many Negro mothers became the very model of maternal responsibility. A classic figure among Negroes of this generation was the hard-working, self-sacrificing mother who served not only as support but also as model for her children. Life was no crystal stair for her, Langston Hughes has her say to her son, but she kept on climbing, reaching landings, turning corners, sometimes in the dark: "So boy, don't you turn back. Don't you set down on the steps 'cause you finds it kinder hard." [99]

MATERNAL ROLE PERFORMANCE

At least one element of the old plantation-family pattern persists even in the urban slum family of today: the relatively greater value attached to motherhood than to wifehood. In studies of lower-income Negro mothers in Philadelphia, Robert Bell asked his subjects: "If you could only be a wife *or* mother (but not both) which would you choose?" Fifteen per cent of the one-parent and 13 per cent of the paired-parent mothers answered "don't know." "Of the one-parent group, 73 per cent said 'mother,' and 12 per cent, 'wife' . . . The . . . responses for the paired-parent mothers were 67 per cent and 20 per cent, [respectively]." [100]

It does appear, then, that motherhood is more highly valued than wifehood, but the value placed on wifehood (as noted earlier) is not great and even motherhood itself is far less valued by modern women than it

---

[97] B. A. Botkin, *Lay My Burden Down* (Chicago: University of Chicago Press, 1945), pp. 55, 154, 189.

[98] Donald, *op. cit.*, pp. 67, 68, 69.

[99] Langston Hughes, "Mother to Son." Pauli Murray comments on the fact that this poem had great meaning for her and "a generation which still recalls the washtub and the steaming wood stove as the source of hard-earned dollars which sent it to school" ("The Negro Woman in the Quest for Equality." Paper presented at the National Council of Negro Women Leadership Conference, Washington, D.C., November 1963). She rightly notes that the poem "reveals the great gift of the Negro woman for mothering, consoling, encouraging."

[100] Robert Bell, "The One-Parent Mother in the Negro Lower Class." Unpublished paper, p. 8.

was on the plantation. Of the one-parent mothers, 26 per cent said that, if they could start over again, they would have no children; even 14 per cent of the paired-parent mothers felt this way.[101] For half the mothers of both sets, the ideal number of children was three or fewer. Bell concludes that, "given their social class level and its related problems, . . . some lower-class Negro women actually reject the adult female roles of both spouse and mother." [102]

In view of the low value attached to the maternal role, poor performance is inevitable. After emancipation, as under slavery, some Negro women became more devoted to their white charges than to their own children. Even among those who were not expending their care on white children, a casual neglect of their own was common[103] and cruelty was occasionally reported.[104] Infanticide and desertion, though not always documented, have also occurred. Even today, hospitals are hosts to hundreds of abandoned Negro infants whose mothers disappear once they have delivered them. And there is no count of the infants suffering from the battered-baby syndrome. Still, considering the difficulties of performing the maternal role under the given circumstances, one should probably be surprised not that neglect and abandonment occur but that they occur in relatively few cases. Indeed, "analysis of aid to dependent children caseloads in one state showed more abuse and neglect of children among whites than among Negroes." [105] Actually, among one-parent families a great hazard is often the mother's temptation to compensate for the lack of a father by overprotectiveness. One speaker at an all-Negro parent-teacher meeting noted that " 'mama tries to compensate' to her son for the lack of the male parent. 'Mama says, This is my boy, right or wrong, thus preventing the boy from developing into a responsible, self-respecting individual. . . . She's going to cut him up so through love that he isn't going to be able to do anything.' This puts the schools in the position of 'trying to fight mama's love.' " [106]

Two stereotypes about the Negro woman as mother have wide currency: the glorified black mammy who lavished love and affection on generations of children in the big house and was loved in turn, and the irresponsible woman who makes a career of bearing children—especially

[101] *Ibid.*

[102] *Ibid.*

[103] Charles S. Johnson, *Shadow of the Plantation* (Chicago: University of Chicago Press, 1934), p. 59.

[104] E. Franklin Frazier, *The Negro Family in the United States* (New York: Holt, Rinehart & Winston, Inc., 1948), p. 77.

[105] Elizabeth Herzog, "Some Assumptions about the Poor," *Social Service Review*, Vol. 37 (December 1963), 400.

[106] George O. Butler, Director of Education and Community Relations for the President's Committee on Equal Employment Opportunities, *Washington Post*, December 8, 1963.

out of wedlock in order to increase her public-assistance allowance.[107] Both stereotypes, of course, are flawed. The "loving" mammy often rejected her own children, while the modern Negro nurse or babysitter shows no more and no less affection for her charges than her white counterpart does. As for the "irresponsible" mother, a considerable body of research shows her to be, not a careerist in maternity but, rather, a good mother. A study of the parity of unmarried mothers on relief and unmarried mothers who were not on relief in New York City in 1955-59 showed that it was not greater for the first set than for the second, as it should have been if unmarried women were having babies to increase their grants.[108] Studies in many other states corroborated this finding.[109]

The unmarried mothers appear to perform their maternal role as well as others of the same class background. One study selected thirty mothers—twenty-eight Negro and two white—who had all conceived out-of-wedlock children while receiving aid. Living on grants was, indeed, a way of life for them: they had more children of more fathers, more older children, and had been grant recipients a longer time than the mothers in a comparable cross-section sample. Yet, the enormous sense of responsibility shown by these women toward their children was impressive. Most of them wanted to marry and some still hoped they would, but the basic value to all was to be good mothers. It is clear that, in each case, a family exists, even though there is no father present. "Most of the women seemed serious and weighted . . . It seemed . . . however, that the burden was that of carrying all the responsibility for the children." [110] Their use of money was socially constructive. Education was extremely important to them, and all had contacts with the school, talking to the teacher or attending PTA meetings. They had high ambitions for their children, wanting them to become doctors, lawyers, technicians. Unrealistic as these aspirations might seem to outsiders, they did disprove the theory that such mothers were content to reproduce generations of dependents. On the contrary, public assistance was a necessary evil for them, but they hoped for better things for their children. If they failed, it was not for lack of desire to succeed.

Not all of these women were, of course, equally competent. The researcher distinguished three groups, which included all but three of the women. Of these twenty-seven mothers, twenty-two were taking good care of their children—half with little psychological conflict about their situa-

[107] John Fischer, "What the Negro Needs Most," *Harper's Magazine* (July 1962), 12-19.

[108] Jean Pakter, *et al.*, "Out-of-Wedlock Births in New York City," *American Journal of Public Health and the Nation's Health*, Vol. 51 (May 1961), 688-89.

[109] From an unpublished study by the Children's Bureau, 1961.

[110] Renée M. Berg, "A Study of a Group of Unwed Mothers Receiving Aid to Dependent Children," doctoral dissertation, University of Pennsylvania, 1962.

tion (the externally adapted perhaps), half with psychological conflict about it (doubtless the acculturated ones). The remaining five were described as "caught." These were women of limited intellectual ability, emotionally unable to deal with their problems (the two white women, incidentally, fell in this category). The over-all picture, however, was one of satisfactory maternal role performance.

Bell's study reported no difference in child-rearing practices between one-parent and paired-parent mothers. About half of each set punished by spanking; more one-parent mothers (eleven) than paired-parent mothers (six) rewarded with affection; more paired-parent mothers (twenty) than one-parent mothers (eleven) used praise. But "there were no differences in playing with their children or taking them places . . . These were areas of child-rearing met by others than the mother in both family groups." And there were "no significant differences in occupational or education aspirations for either sons or daughters." [111] With or without husbands, with or without their children's fathers, these mothers performed about the same.[112]

A reassuring picture was presented in a study of out-of-wedlock children in North Carolina between 1917 and 1957. This study, admittedly conjectural in many respects, concluded that the vast majority of the out-of-wedlock children—most of whom were nonwhite, raised by mother or relatives—had become law-abiding citizens and were living normal lives.[113]

We have already noted (see Chapter 2) that relatively fewer Negro than white mothers, class for class, have been exposed to child-rearing experts. Understandably, therefore, their knowledge about child-rearing is limited. It is not surprising, then, to find that in Harlem slum families, twenty out of thirty-three mothers agreed that "some kids are just born lazy," and twenty-five agreed that "the most important thing a child can learn is to obey." On the other hand, twenty-three disagreed with the statement that "some kids are just born bad and there is nothing anybody can do about it." They apparently felt more fatalistic about laziness than about badness; or, conversely, they felt more responsible about goodness than about industry. Of special interest was the agreement of twenty-

[111] Robert Bell, *op. cit.*, p. 11.

[112] For comparative purposes, the reader might consult the detailed description of eighty white women in Boston caring for at least one child under eighteen without a husband present, half receiving AFDC and half not receiving it, by Sydney E. Bernard in "Fatherless Families: Their Economic and Social Adjustment" (Waltham, Mass.: Brandeis University, 1964). An interesting finding of this study was that the missing men were more alike than the women were, and it was their inferiority, rather than anything about the women themselves, that differentiated the families so far as dependency was concerned.

[113] Technical Subcommittee on Birth Out of Wedlock, *The Problem of Births Out of Wedlock* (April 1959).

five of the subjects with the statement that "all a little child needs from
his mother is to see to it that he eats and sleeps and stays out of trouble." [114]

TRAINING FOR DEFEAT AND FAILURE

Whatever their aims and motives, the child-rearing practices of parents
in the so-called culture of poverty have the effect of training children
for defeat and failure in the outside world. Catherine Chilman, who has
summarized the literature on child-rearing practices among the poor as
well as the literature on the conditions of achievement in our society,
finds in all spheres—emotional, intellectual, and mental health—that the
child-rearing practices among the poor shape personalities ill-suited for
success in the outside world.[115]

"GRANNY"

An important role among Negroes, now all but vanished from the
scene, is that of the "granny," whom Frazier has called "the guardian
of the generations." The position of the oldest woman in a family was,
traditionally, an extremely important one: it was she, not the female head
of the family, who had the role of the matriarch. The grandmother played
an important part even under slavery, "highly esteemed by both the slaves
and the masters."

In the master's house she was very often the "mammy" whom history and
tradition have idealized because of her loyalty and affection. Because of her
intimate relations with the whites, "all family secrets," as Calhoun observes,
"were in her keeping; she was the defender of the family honor. The tie of affection between her and her charges was never outgrown. Often she was the
confidential adviser of the older members of the household. To young mothers
she was an authority on first babies." Age added dignity to her position, and
"her regime," as Thomas Nelson Page says "extended frequently through two
generations, occasionally through three." [116]

The prestige of these women was great among the slaves also. They
outlived the men, and—perhaps because they were too useful to be sold
—represented the one stable factor in family relations. After emancipation, it was they who contributed what stability and integrity there was to
Negro families, who assumed responsibility for children abandoned by
their own parents, who served as repository of family traditions.

---

[114] Joan Gordon and Lawrence Podell, "Social Functioning in Multiproblem Families
in Harlem," unpublished report on a pilot project, 1964.

[115] Catherine Chilman, "Child-Rearing and Family Relationship Patterns of the Very
Poor," *Welfare in Review* (January 1965), 9-19. This material is from a monograph soon
to be published by the Division of Research, Welfare Administration, U.S. Department
of Health, Education, and Welfare.

[116] Frazier, *op. cit.,* pp. 114-15.

These grannies were genuine matriarchs—powerful, stabilizing figures who performed a profoundly important service, but they have all but disappeared from the scene. The term *matriarch,* as used today, refers to the female head of a family, but she is not a true matriarch, any more than the true matriarch was the head of the family (at least, as the term *family head* is defined by the census).

THE SLAVE AS FATHER

Inasmuch as there were white fathers who sold their mulatto children down the river, it should come as no surprise that the free born Negro, George Wright, sold his five sons—Eber, Eli, Ezekiel, Enoch, and Ezra—into slavery to raise money to pay a debt.[117]

The role of father is much more abstract than the role of mother. Biologically, it may be defined as insignificant. It may, in fact, be ignored (and it is by some preliterate peoples). Although parenthood is a culturally defined role, fatherhood far more than motherhood is a creation of social, cultural, and institutional forces. Under slavery, for example, the role of father was, in effect, institutionally obliterated:

> The "real" father was virtually without authority over his child, since discipline, parental responsibility, and control of rewards and punishments all rested in other hands; the slave father could not even protect the mother of his children except by appealing directly to the master. Indeed, the mother's own role loomed far larger for the slave child than did that of the father. She controlled those few activities—household care, preparation of food, and rearing of children—that were left to the slave family. For that matter, the very etiquette of plantation life removed even the honorific attributes of fatherhood from the Negro male, who was addressed as *boy*—until, when the vigorous years of his prime were past, he was allowed to assume the title of *uncle.*[118]

In the primary-group plantation family, the relations between men and their children were not necessarily those between a father and a son or daughter, but those between a more or less casual male adult and a child. Bonds of affection between them, when these existed, were based on personal interaction, on primary-group relations, rather than on recognition of institutional bonds. Fatherhood was not defined in terms of parental responsibilities; these were assumed by the mother and the white master.

THE FREEDMAN AS FATHER

The major test of freedom to many former slaves was the right simply to move from one place to another. The freedmen were not migrants in

[117] Botkin, *op. cit.,* p. 240.
[118] Stanley M. Elkins, *Slavery: A Problem in American Institutional and Intellectual Life* (New York: Grosset & Dunlap, Inc., 1963), p. 130.

the sense of purposively moving toward a planned destination; they simply wanted to *feel* that they were not bound to any particular place.

In 1865, desertions were innumerable. . . . When the Negroes were moving around to test their freedom, many of them seized the opportunity to desert their wives and children. . . . The young and strong deserted the aged, the feeble, the children, leaving these to shift for themselves. . . .[119]

Those who remained with their families often exercised extremely severe discipline. This prerogative, formerly the privilege only of the white man, may, like moving about, have been just another test of freedom. At any rate, flogging was common, though not necessarily any more severe than that administered by white parents or any more an indication of lack of affection.[120]

These first years after the Civil War were the first time the freedmen had ever had responsibility for the care of their own children; it was a novel situation for them and hard to get used to. They were accustomed to thinking of their children as belonging not to them but to their masters. The idea that *they* must now provide for the children did not easily take possession of them. On the part of the father there was often, therefore, no parental supervision; on the part of the child who had learned to read, contempt for his illiterate parent.[121]

The institutionalization of family life in the first decades after emancipation involved the inculcation of norms of paternal responsibility. In a sense, the marriage trajectory (see Chapter 1) also described the fatherhood trajectory, for every birth reported in wedlock implies that there was a man present who acknowledged his relationship to the child. This fact, of course, reveals nothing about how well they were performing as fathers, but it does indicate that the rudiments of the paternal role had been incorporated into the family.

PATERNAL ROLE PERFORMANCE

Nowhere, perhaps, is the difference between the two cultures among Negroes more striking than it is in paternal role performance. Among the acculturated, the father is reported as showing as much concern for his children—as high aspirations—as fathers in the outside world.

A civil servant, father of a three-day old baby, observed:

I'm already thinking about how to give my daughter all the best advantages. She's only three days old, but I'm thinking about how I want her to finish college and about all the things I'd like her to do. She's going to get music and dancing and everything else that'll help her to develop her personality.[122]

[119] Donald, *op. cit.*, pp. 63, 65.

[120] *Ibid.*, p. 69.

[121] *Ibid.*, p. 70.

[122] St. Clair Drake and Horace R. Cayton, *Black Metropolis* (New York: Harper Torchbook, 1962), p. 665.

My youngest boy is seven. All my kids are in school. I try to instill in their minds that the only sound way to succeed is by laying a good foundation of learning and then to get actual experience. I hope to be able to see them all through college. I own the property where I live and have a few dollars in the bank. I own a car, too. My greatest ambition is to see my children come along and keep this cleaning and pressing business of mine going, or else get into something they like better.[123]

Even among the lower-income levels of the acculturated, the same aspirations appear. A stockyard worker says: "I'm trying to educate my children and bring them up so they won't have trouble finding work." [124] If these ambitions and aspirations for children involve self-sacrifice, so be it. And in a Southern mill town in the late 1940s,

A man who has been married nearly fifty years and who has raised a family of ten children—nine of whom are in Northern cities—explained his design for living and rearing children. He said that he and his wife had never had a cross word; that they had never called each other a liar; that he had never allowed his wife or his children to hear him utter a profane word or see him take a drink. He had tried to teach all of his children "good citizenship," i.e., not to bother anybody and to take care of their own business. . . . This epitomizes the creed of the respectables.[125]

Some of these fathers are permissive; some are authoritarian; some are both. In any case they take their paternal responsibilities seriously.

You can't give a kid too much. You can't give a kid too much loving or anything. There's no such thing as too much for a kid. . . . Sometimes it's good to take a switch to a kid until he's ten or eleven years old. I ain't taken a switch to either of mine in a year and a half, but I'll do it if I thinks they needs it. But not after they're ten or eleven. When a boy gets that old, it starts getting hard for him to cry. If you take a switch to him and he don't cry, he starts thinking he's a tough, and taking a switch to him just makes him hard.
. . . [Children] get to know when you're just fooling around and when you mean business. Most of the time my kids know just from my tone of voice or the way I look whether I'm playing around and they know they gotta listen to me when I ain't playing around.[126]

These men have internalized the norms of parenthood implied in monogamic marriage and, according to the characteristic patterns of the class they belong to, conform to them. Upper-, middle-, or lower-class, they are full-time fathers.

Among the Externally Adapted.   Among the externally adapted, however, especially among those in the lowest-income brackets, fatherhood

[123] *Ibid.,* p. 666.
[124] *Ibid.,* p. 667.
[125] Hylan Lewis, *Blackways of Kent* (Chapel Hill, N.C.: University of North Carolina Press, 1955) , p. 113.
[126] Hylan Lewis, "Class, Culture and the Behavior of Low-Income Families." Unpublished paper, pp. 32-3.

takes a somewhat different form.[127] Lip service may be given to the norms regulating parental responsibilities for children, and men who can conform to them—like those quoted above—may be accorded genuine respect; but the actual relationships are more likely to be determined by primary-group attractions and reactions than by formal norms. Thus, despite frequent verbal declarations of affection for children, there may be little sustained and responsible contact.

These men might love babies—sometimes even "borrowing" one to play with or to carry around for a while; they might oppose abortion (even when they are not married to the mother of the child); and some might even assume a modicum of intermittent responsibility for the support of the child. But fatherhood as such is rather low in their hierarchy of values. Unlike the case of women among whom, as noted earlier, the parental role takes precedence over the conjugal, men value the man-woman relationship far more highly. The father's concern may be absent, minimal, or deep, depending on his relationship with the child's mother.

If fatherhood as such is relatively low on their scale of values, why do they have children? Like other men, they may want children for a variety of reasons.[128] And, also as among other men, reasons may change over time.[129] To some parents, children constitute "a reassurance of their biological fitness." [130] This pattern occurs among streetcorner Negro men also: paternity confirms their masculinity.[131] Having a child by a woman may be seen by some men as a way of preventing her from engaging in

[127] Unless some other source is cited, all the material on "streetcorner" Negro men is taken from a preliminary draft chapter, "Fathers Without Children," of a doctoral dissertation by Elliot Liebow for Catholic University, 1966. Dr. Liebow collected the data while he was a field worker for the Child-Rearing Project, Washington, D.C., directed by Hylan Lewis. The project was sponsored by the Health and Welfare Council of Washington, D.C. and funded by the National Institute of Mental Health, Grant #OM-278, National Institutes of Heath, Public Health Service, Health, Education and Welfare. Dr. Liebow deliberately avoided any hard-and-fast definition of "*streetcorner*" *men* which would have distracted from the main object of his study, namely, values. In general, however, "streetcorner" men may be thought of as men whose major interests are no longer in their families but in the amorphous though persisting congregations of men who meet informally at congenial hangouts.

[128] For a summary of such reasons, see Jessie Bernard, *American Family Behavior* (Harper's, 1942), pp. 250-52.

[129] A study of reasons for wanting children among Princeton classes in the first quarter of this century included such items as perpetuation of the family, the companionship of young children, feeling that parenthood constitutes a major life interest, desire to embody the ideal relationship between husband and wife, companionship in old age, a feeling of social obligation (Charles Pugh Dennison, "Parenthood Attitudes of College Men," *Journal of Heredity*, 31 [1940], p. 528). It is doubtful that such reasons hold equal weight today.

[130] Jean Walker Macfarlane, "Inter-personal Relationships within the Family," *Marriage and Family Living*, 3 (Spring 1941) , 30.

[131] Elliot Liebow, *op. cit.*

infidelity; or it may be seen as a guarantee of a continuing relationship with her. In any event, such reasons have little to do with the child itself.

Equally if not more cogent are reasons for not having children.[132] If children were an economic asset on the plantation, they are a liability in the city.[133] They are expensive to rear. In crowded slum housing, they may interfere with privacy in a legitimate household and with secrecy in a clandestine relationship. They become informers.[134] In any event, reasons for not wanting children, as well as reasons for wanting them, have little to do with the welfare of the child.

The usual evidences of warm father-child relationships, such as those implied in the families quoted earlier, do not appear among streetcorner fathers. Little time or attention is devoted to children; they are rarely mentioned in casual conversation. Few of these fathers are observed sitting on the steps with their children or playing with them in the streets. Unlike other fathers in the neighborhood, streetcorner Negro fathers do not promenade with their children on Sundays and holidays.[135]

Nevertheless—perhaps because it is rarer—the child responds far more appreciatively to any affectionate gesture from the father than to a similar gesture from the mother. One man in a generous mood distributes change among his children. Their day becomes luminous; they brag to one another that their daddy has given them a dime. The mother may be far more generous, may give them dimes frequently; her generosity is taken for granted. It is the father's attention that wins them. Even the most casual caress by the father may fill the child with "unutterable delight." [136] An absent-minded tousling of the head leaves the child shining-eyed. Physical contact is, however, relatively rare; when it does occur, it may be a slap rather than a caress.

The children may be convinced by a father's claim that he loves them but the mother is not. If the men loved their children as they sometimes insist, why do they let them go hungry and poorly dressed? Actions would speak to them a great deal louder than words or occasional kind gestures.

Quite aside from the occasional show of affection, the men tend to consider their wives too easy on the children. They complain that there was too much hugging and kissing. Most of these men believe physical punishment to be necessary and proper, provided it was neither excessive nor untimely. Actually, like the fathers described above, some tended to be permissive, some authoritarian, and some both.[137]

[132] W. G. Sumner noted that "if procreation had not been put under the dominion of a great passion, it would have been caused to cease by the burdens it entails" (*Folkways*, Boston: Ginn, 1907, p. 309).

[133] Eliot Liebow, *op. cit.*

[134] *Ibid.*

[135] *Ibid.*

[136] *Ibid.*

[137] *Ibid.*

The Absent Father   Many streetcorner Negro men were reported to
have entered marriage with ideals as high as those of any other young
men: they hoped, even if they did not know for sure, that they were
making a lifetime commitment and they were as eager as any other young
men to make a go of it. They knew what the obligations of marriage and
parenthood were and they honored the men who could carry them out.
Succeeding as a husband and father was a badge of manhood.[138]

It was only when the number of children and responsibilities increased
that some of the men withdrew from their families and entered the form
of male society composed of men aged, roughly, twenty-five to forty-five,
who were in circumstances similar to theirs—"fugitives" from their
families, "fathers without children." [139] Or, perhaps, fathers in varying
degrees. It is not necessarily that they rejected their families; it is more
likely that the role of father, as institutionalized in our society, became
too difficult and expensive for their resources. They might still have high
aspirations for their children, as do the mothers also, but they cannot
implement them. So as the babies multiply and the burden of support becomes heavier and heavier, it finally becomes easier just to leave.

It is interesting, although not necessarily corroborative of this pattern
of fatherhood, that the average age—about 24.5 years—at which women
with one to three years of high school become separated [140] is about the
same as that at which nonwhite women have third and fourth children
(23.9 and 25.7 years respectively).[141] It is not certain, of course, whether
this correspondence is merely coincidental or whether it reflects a causal
relationship. In either case, however, it illuminates the problems of the
father role among Negroes.

Sometimes the father who deserts his family is, in fact, emotionally sick.
Some men, it is alleged, use reproduction—in or out of wedlock—as a
form of reprisal against a hostile world: they burden it with the support
of their children.[142] They are at the opposite extreme from fathers who

---

[138] Elliot Liebow reports a curious inconsistency. Although streetcorner men respect
the man who can carry his family responsibilities, still they themselves explain their
flight from family as being evidence that they were too masculine to be domesticated.
One is "too much of a man" to give up drinking, gambling, and running around with
other women. There are, apparently, two quite different male archetypes involved.

[139] Elliot Liebow, *op. cit.*

[140] Paul C. Glick, *American Families* (New York: John Wiley & Sons, Inc., 1957),
p. 151. The women with one to three years of high school were selected for presentation
here because separation rates for nonwhite women in 1948-50 were highest for this
set of women. The age at separation given by Glick does not break the data down
by color.

[141] U. S. Department of Health, Education, and Welfare, *Natality Statistics Analysis
1962* (Washington, D.C.: USGPO) , p. 41.

[142] Robert Derbyshire, Eugene B. Brody, and Carl Schleifer, "Family Structure of
Young Adult Negro Patients: Preliminary Observations from Urban Baltimore."
Unpublished paper, p. 7.

love their children but cannot afford to live with them. Between these extremes doubtless lie many types of absent fathers; the only thing they have in common is that they are not living with their children.

Where were these absent fathers? Where were they living? In some cases they may become the temporary fathers of another man's brood. We shall have more to say about them presently. In 1960, about half of the nonwhite males who were separated (49.3 percent) or divorced (50.8 per cent)—not all of whom, of course, were fathers—were living as primary individuals or as secondary individuals (lodgers or partner of family heads) in other households. About two fifths (40 per cent) of the separated and 37.7 per cent of the divorced) were in primary families, a considerable proportion having gone home to their own parents (14.7 per cent and 13.1 per cent, respectively), or to brothers, sisters, or other relatives (13.9 per cent and 12.2 per cent, respectively). If we limit our scrutiny to the nonwhite males in the age brackets most likely to have dependent children (twenty-five to forty-four) we find about a fifth (19.7 per cent) of the separated and divorced in parental families; about two fifths (43 per cent) living as primary or secondary individuals; and about an eighth (12.1 per cent) living in group quarters.

On quite abstract grounds, it is possible to think of father-child relationships as arranged along a continuum. At one end, a man might (1) refuse or be unwilling even to acknowledge his paternity; or he might (2) acknowledge paternity but have no further contact with either mother or child; or he might (3) be willing to acknowledge paternity and even show affection for the child but have only occasional or intermittent contacts with it; or might (4) acknowledge paternity, show affection for the child, and even provide some support for it; or he might (5) be married to the child's mother but be separated from her and acknowledge financial responsibility, although not be able always to provide more than emergency or occasional support; or he might (6) turn the child over to his mother to rear and give it his name and at least partial financial support; or, finally, (7) he might live with the child. All of these "degrees of fatherhood" were reported among streetcorner Negro men.[143] The most common situation was one in which the father was separated from his children with only occasional brief contacts, but one in which paternity was acknowledged and responsibility admitted, at least verbally, although actual financial support was likely to be forthcoming only under pressure from the mother.[144]

Expectedly, the emotional ties between father and child also vary along this continuum. At the first two levels, there is no relationship at all between the absent father and his child. In the middle ranges the father may show great affection for the child during the brief and occasional

[143] Elliot Liebow, *op. cit.*
[144] *Ibid.*

contacts he has with it. He may hold his infant in his arms and show great pleasure in its presence. Even if he sees the child only when its mother comes to dun him for support, he may show great affection. And if she has to take him to court to enforce support of the child, he holds no grudge against her; he recognizes his responsibility even if he does not assume it.

If the contact between father and child lasts too long, however, the sweetness of the relationship becomes attenuated. The first few days of a summer visit may see a father parade his child before his fellows, accepting their flattering compliments for the child with great pleasure. The usual comments on the speed with which children grow, on how they change from year to year, are made and agreed with. Shopping trips are arranged. The pleasure the child takes in his father's attention is noted. But when the visit is over, the child returns to his world and the father to his. Until the next visit, they may forget one another entirely.

Liebow found it difficult to evaluate the many variables which determined the nature of father-child relationships. Color of child, legitimacy status, sex of child, and, especially, relationship with the child's mother were all involved. Some of the men were more likely to prefer light-skinned to dark-skinned children. In general, legitimate children were preferred to illegitimate, but legitimacy status was neither a bar to close relationships nor a guarantee of them. Some of the men favored sons; some favored daughters. There was no clear-cut sex preference.

The one clearly determinative factor in the relationship of father and child was the father's relationship with the mother. If that was close, it "rubbed off" on the relationship with the child. In fact, biological paternity was less important than relationship with a child's mother. Liebow reported the anomaly of men who seemed more affectionate with children of women they were living with than with their own children.[145] He interprets this paradox in terms of the voluntary nature of these relationships. With his own children he must, in effect, reject affectionate relationships which highlight his failure to perform his obligations. "I'm not even trying to be your father so now I can't be blamed for failing to accomplish what I'm not trying to do." [146] Once his failure as a father to his own children has been faced, he can dismiss it. With another man's children, however, to whom he has no obligations, whatever he does is a plus; having no responsibilities, he cannot fail. Much of the spontaneous, natural, pleasant kind of father-child relationship which is impossible with his own offspring finds expression in his voluntary relationships with other children, an excellent example of the ways in which institutions may defeat their goals.

---

[145] *Ibid.*

[146] *Ibid.*, p. 68. Dr. Liebow's analyses and examples of this anomaly are especially perspicacious.

Chapter 4

Socialization

Introduction

One of the major tasks of the family is socialization: the process by which "individuals selectively acquire the skills, knowledge, attitudes, values, and motives current in the groups of which they are or will become members." [1] But because socialization is a lifelong process,[2] the family is only one of many groups and agencies that perform socializing functions.

In a homogeneous and simple society, the socialization of infants and children may be entirely inadvertent: the infant or child observes the reactions of those about him and responds accordingly. But when a society becomes heterogeneous and complex, socialization also becomes more complex. In such a society socialization tends to take place on at least two levels. At the inadvertent level, socialization proceeds by circumstances, not by design: it is not deliberate or self-conscious; it is not purposive or verbal. At this level, the behavior of the model or the partner-in-interaction serves as the instrument by which the practicing norms of the group are internalized. At the "advertent" level, however, socialization is deliberate, self-conscious, purposive, and usually verbal. Parents and other adults serve not only as models, but also as preceptors and teachers. This is the level at which the inculcation of ideal norms is sought.

Socialization involves more than the mere imparting of skills and knowledge: experience and interaction with others are involved, in order that the individual may develop a suitable self-conception. It is the socialization process during infancy and childhood that is the characteristic task of the family. In the case of Negroes, an additional burden has been placed on parents: they have had to socialize their children into the role of Negro.

[1] William H. Sewell, "Some Recent Developments in Socialization Theory and Research," *Annals of the American Academy of Political and Social Science*, Vol. 149 (September 1963), 161.

[2] *Ibid.*, pp. 173-79. Earlier research emphasized such factors as "child-rearing practices" associated with weaning and toilet-training. More recently family relationships, including interparental, parent-child, and sibling relationships have engaged researchers more (*ibid.*, p. 171).

.umstantial Socialization: Families and Homes

CIRCUMSTANTIAL SOCIALIZATION

It has long been recognized that socialization by circumstances is more fundamental than socialization by precept. What the child becomes accustomed to in infancy limits what he can ultimately achieve in adulthood.

It is difficult for most people to realize that the outside world is not near, immediate, or at all clear to the Negro slum child; that to him, it is remote and hazy. It impinges on him by way of the welfare agency, perhaps, or the police, or the school; he experiences it only vicariously through movies, television, or the radio. By the time he enters the outside world as a worker, he already regards it as a foreign—indeed, frightening—country:

> . . . [A] black child, looking at the world around him, though he cannot know quite what to make of it, is aware that there is a reason why his mother works so hard, why his father is always on edge. . . . He is aware that there is some terrible weight on his parents' shoulders which menaces him. And it isn't long . . . before he discovers the shape of his oppression. . . .[1a]

THE DEMOGRAPHIC STRUCTURE OF FAMILIES
IN WHICH NEGRO CHILDREN ARE SOCIALIZED

The commonest type of Negro household is one in which there is a male head and his wife; about three fifths (61 per cent) of all Negro households were of this type in 1960. Most Negro children under fourteen live with both of their parents in primary families and are the children of the head of the family (see Table 4-1). Our attention, therefore, will be focused first on the role structure of two-parent families and its effect on socialization.

THE TWO PARENTAL ROLES

A study of fifty-six cultures around the world reported that in most of them (forty-six) at least two kinds of parental roles were differentiated: the so-called instrumental role, having to do with management, discipline, and control of children; and the so-called emotional-expressive role, having to do with mediation, conciliation, and resolution of hostilities. In most cases (fifty), the father performed the instrumental role; the mother, the emotional-expressive role.[2a]

[1a] James Baldwin, "A Talk to Teachers," *Saturday Review* (December 21, 1963), 42-43.

[2a] Morris Zelditch, Jr., "Role Differentiation in the Nuclear Family: A Comparative Study," in Talcott Parsons and Robert W. Bales, *Family: Socialization and Interaction Process* (New York: The Free Press of Glencoe, Inc., 1955), pp. 318, 347-48.

Table 4-1.

Family Status of Nonwhite Children under 14
by Size of Place, 1960*

Family Status	Urbanized Areas	Other Urban Areas	Rural Farm	South
"Normal" **	65.3	60.7	71.3	63.6
Living with mother only	18.5	17.5	5.5	13.9
Living with grand-mother and mother	2.7	4.1	3.2	3.9
Living with neither parent	8.8	12.5	14.8	13.3
Other	4.7	5.2	5.2	5.3

* *Source:* U.S. Bureau of the Census, *Persons by Family Characteristics* (1960), Table 13-1. The situation reported deals only with the day on which the census was taken. The day before or the day after, the children might have been living under different conditions.
** "Normal" defined as living with both parents in primary families and being the child of the family head.

A great deal of current research on socialization is based on the concept of these two roles, defined, let us say, in terms of power (for the instrumental role) and support (for the emotional-expressive). *Power* is generally defined as "actions which control, initiate, change, or modify the behavior of another member of the family;" *support,* as "actions which establish, maintain, or restore, as an end in itself, a positive affective relationship with another family member." [3]

Unfortunately the exact distribution of these two variables is not known. Hylan Lewis, for example, in a study of forty-one parental figures in thirty-nine low-income households in Washington, D.C., reported that most (twenty-four) of these parental figures said they had an average degree of control over their children, seven said they had extreme control, and nine said they had little control. Their self-ratings on the emotional-expressive variable, as measured by judgments of "relations with children," "emotional response," and "regard for children," are shown in Table 4-2.[4] The conclusion is that, in general, these parents considered themselves about average or above-average with respect to both variables. The bimodality of the findings on emotional response suggests the

[3] Murray Straus, "Power and Support Structure of the Family in Relation to Socialization," *Marriage and the Family,* Vol. 26 (August 1964), 318.
[4] Hylan Lewis, "Culture, Class, and the Behavior of Low-Income Families." Unpublished paper, p. 182.

presence of two types: average, and greater-than-average emotional response. Because these data are not classified by sex, we do not know which parent tended to perform which role in the two sets of distributions.

Table 4-2.

Distribution of Reported Ratings in Three Selected Categories
as Indexes of Expressive Role, 41 Parental Figures*

Index	A (High Degree)	B	C	D	E	No data
Relations with children	4	15	15	4	2	1
Emotional response	10	5	13	4	2	7
Regard for children	7	8	18	6	1	1

* Hylan Lewis, June 1963, p. 18a.

In another study, which attempted to determine the relative prevalence of several family types, both white and Negro college students were asked to select three husband-wife families they knew well and to specify, in each case, which parent performed the disciplining role and which the supporting one. Then they were asked to rate (on a scale ranging from 1 to 10) the performance—from "neglect" to "very strict" for the instrumental role, and "neglect" to "very supportive" for the expressive role. Some of the results are summarized in Table 4-3.

Contrary to expectation, the proportion of role-reversed families was higher (21 per cent) among the families reported by white students (assumed to be white) than those (15 per cent) reported by Negro students (assumed to be Negro). Expectedly, mothers were rated higher in the supportive role than fathers in both white and Negro families. White parents were reported to be somewhat higher than Negro parents in the supportive role. White mothers, white fathers, and Negro fathers all scored about the same on strictness in the instrumental role; Negro mothers scored less strict than any of them in this role. Taken as a whole, regardless of whether the family structure was archetypical or reversed, Negro fathers scored higher (6.6) in the instrumental role (stricter as disciplinarian) than in the supportive role (5.3); Negro mothers reversed this pattern, rating higher in the supportive (6.5) than in the disciplinarian role (5.7). The numbers involved here are too small to make much of the findings, but they are suggestive of the structure of acculturated families.

These data reveal nothing about the combination of power and sup-

Table 4-3.

Role Structure and Role Performance In 99 Negro
and 56 White Families

Role Structure	No.	Per cent	Mean Instrumental Role Performance Score **	Mean Expressive Role Performance Score †
Negro Families				
Archetypical *	29	29	7.5 (father)	7.5 (mother)
Reversed	15	15	5.2 (mother)	6.4 (father)
White Families				
Archetypical	11	20	7.2 (father)	8.3 (mother)
Reversed	12	21	7.4 (mother)	7.6 (father)
Negro Parents				
Negro Fathers	68		6.6	5.3
Negro Mothers	74		5.7	6.5
Negro Parents	142		6.1	5.9

* *Archetypical* refers to structure in which father performs instrumental and mother expressive role; reversed, to structure in which mother performs instrumental and father expressive role.
** Score of 1, "neglect"; score of 10, "very strict."
† Score of 1, "neglect"; score of 10, "very supportive."

port within the family, nor do they indicate which parent is associated with which variable. And, apparently, the combination of these variables affects the personality of the child.

The four archetypes for combinations of the two variables may be viewed as follows: power high, support high; power high, support low; power low, support high; power low, support low. One researcher has found it possible to organize a great many studies in terms of this paradigm as shown in Table 4-4.[5]

This author notes that the relative magnitude of the two variables is related to the family's position in the social structure. In our society, the middle class "tends to fall within the high support-low power quadrant, while the working-class pattern of parent-child interaction tends to be in the low support-high power quadrant."[6]

[5] Murray A. Straus, "Power and Support Structure of the Family in Relation to Socialization," *loc. cit.*, pp. 319-24.
[6] *Ibid.*, p. 325.

Table 4-4.

Power-Support Paradigm

Combination	Family Type	Personality
Power high, support low	Dictatorial or demanding; authoritarian or exploitative; traditional	Withdraws; avoids; relinquishes
Power high, support high	Overprotective; indulgent; democratic	Conforms; acquiesces; assists; obliges; has intellectual control; has self-control
Power low, support low	Neglectful; detached; ignoring; self-centered	Is aggressive, impulsive, quarrelsome, irritable; analyzes; disapproves; resists
Power low, support high	Cooperative or democratic; casual; permissive or overindulgent; developmental	Is friendly, affectionate; participates socially; advises; directs; initiates

Of the ninety-nine families judged by the Negro college students, 13 per cent were in the first of the above categories (instrumental score 8 or more, expressive score 1-5); 35 per cent, in the second (instrumental score 8 or more, expressive score 8 or more); 9 per cent in the third (instrumental score 1-5, expressive score 1-5); and 4 per cent, in the last (instrumental score 1-5, expressive score 8 or more).[7] The remaining 39 per cent fell into intermediate categories. The commonest single type among these families (according to the paradigm) was, then, overprotective, indulgent, and democratic, and the type of personality expectable would be one which conformed, acquiesced, assisted, obliged, and had intellectual control and self-control.

In view of the emphasis of researchers on the strong wife-and-mother in the Negro family it is especially interesting to note that, among the families reported on by these college students, almost a third of the Negro families—but only a fifth of the white families—were archetypical in structure (that is, with the father performing the instrumental role; the mother, the expressive role). Almost half again as many of the white families as of the Negro families were reported to show reversed

[7] Compare E. Franklin Frazier's description of middle-class Negro families: "There is often not only a deep devotion to their one or two children, but a subservience to them. It is not uncommon for the only son to be called and treated as the 'boss' in the family. Parents cater to the transient wishes of their children and often rationalize their behavior towards them on the grounds that children should not be 'inhibited.' They spend large sums of money on their children for toys and especially for clothes. They provide their children with automobiles when they go to college. . . . Their fierce devotion to their children . . . generally results in spoiling them. . . ." (*Black Bourgeoisie* [New York: The Crowell-Collier Publishing Co., 1962], p. 184).

role structure,[8] with the mother performing the instrumental role; the father, the supportive role. The Negro mothers tended to be rated higher than the fathers in their performance of the expressive role,[9] lower in their performance of the instrumental role.

Murray Straus, analyzing the effect of husband-wife relationships on certain aspects of adolescent personality, distinguished four types of husband-wife relationships: (1) the husband-dominant type; (2) the wife-dominant type; (3) the autonomic type, in which there is role specialization, but in which neither attempts to dominate; and (4) the conflict type, in which both attempt to dominate. The aspects of adolescent personality affected by these patterns were: grade-point average in school; an active-future rather than a passive-present world view; general anxiety; and acceptance or rejection of parents. The subjects were 287 (white) nonfarm junior and senior high school boys.

. . . [T]he wife-dominant type family, although high in achievement orientation (as predicted) and high anxiety and parent-child conflict (also as predicted) does *not* represent the type of family power structure associated with the highest level of achievement orientation . . . except for the lowest socioeconomic-status group. . . .

The highest performance on the achievement variable is obtained by boys from autonomic-type families. . . . The present study suggests that the undifferentiated type of equalitarianism which results when both husband and wife attempt to play a dominant role is associated with lack of effectiveness in socialization for both internal stability and external achievement roles. On the other hand, the role-differentiated . . . autonomic type . . . seems to be associated with sons who are high in personality variables needed to meet all four functional imperatives of the family system.[10]

In other words, the family in which husbands and wives have differentiated roles but in which neither attempts to dominate the other may be the best suited for socializing boys. This, however, does not seem to be the family structure commonest among Negroes.

It is interesting that at the lowest socioeconomic levels, the wife-domi-

[8] Hylan Lewis found two facts clear in Kent: "first, a large number—probably as many as one half, if autobiographies are a true index—of the children are raised by mothers and/or maternal relatives without significant help from the father for major portions of their lives; and, second, the mother is the more important figure in disciplining and dispensing rewards" (*Blackways of Kent* [Chapel Hill, N.C.: University of North Carolina Press, 1955], p. 100). The college students reflect an acculturated pattern; the Kent children, the externally adapted.

[9] Again, Frazier: ". . . even among some of the poorest families, the mother's whole affectional life may be centered upon a son or daughter. In fact, her attitude often presents a striking contrast to that of the father" (*Negro Family in the United States* [Chicago: University of Chicago Press, 1948], p. 350).

[10] Murray A. Straus, "Conjugal Power Structure and Adolescent Personality," *Marriage and Family*, Vol. 24 (February 1962), 24.

nant family was associated in the Straus study with the highest level of achievement orientation. This type is common among Negroes, as Blood and Wolfe have reported, but because the Negro wife is dominant not by choice but by default, it is doubtful that the same relationships would be obtained in a sample of Negro boys. In any event, Straus concludes that our knowledge of the interrelations between conjugal power structure and the socializing process is very tentative—among Negroes, we might add, especially so.

ONE-PARENT FAMILIES

In the families discussed so far, both parents have been in the home, whatever roles—conjugal or parental—they were performing, and most Negro children are being socialized in these families. But, one in every six Negro children does *not* live with his father, and the absence of the father appears to have important consequences for socialization.

THE FATHERLESS FAMILY

Thomas Pettigrew has summarized the studies dealing with the effects on personality of being socialized in a fatherless family.[11] Children reared in one-parent homes are reported to find it more difficult to delay gratification. They are, reportedly, less socially responsible, less achievement-oriented, more susceptible to delinquency. Furthermore, a study of Negro boys and girls, ages five to fourteen, indicated that those without fathers had greater difficulty than others in differentiating the roles of the sexes. Both boys and girls from the fatherless homes described themselves in similar ways; those from two-parent homes described themselves in terms more conventionally appropriate for their sex.

A study of white boys who were sons of sailors or who had grown up during World War II, while their fathers were serving with the Armed Forces, indicated that these boys were more effeminate than other boys, both in their fantasy life and in actual life; they were also more submissive and more dependent, traits conventionally viewed as feminine rather than masculine; they were also less mature.

The applicability of these findings to Negroes has been shown by two other studies summarized by Pettigrew: one of jailed prisoners in Alabama, and one of working-class veterans in Wisconsin. In both studies Negroes tended to score higher than others on measures of femininity. Negro girls who model themselves on their mothers learn to assume masculine as well as feminine obligations. A follow-up study of individuals twenty years after an original study in the 1930s revealed that the lower-class girls who had been reared in fatherless homes tended to establish the same kind of

---

[11] Thomas F. Pettigrew, *Profile of the Negro American* (Princeton, N.J.: D. Van Nostrand Co., 1964), pp. 17-24.

households when they grew up, living with their mothers or very close to them. The men had experienced conflict over sexual identity: they had become compulsively masculine gang members, rejecting femininity in every form—and because they tended to consider law, morals, and religion effeminate, they rejected these, too.

The difficulty boys experience when, after initially identifying with the mother, they must develop the male self-image demanded by the outside world has been discussed by Burton and Whiting.[12] Passive behavior may continue, but either overcompensation in the form of exaggerated masculinity (harsh language, toughness) or defense mechanisms (need for social power and dominance) may result. Such needs for power have been reported among men, white as well as Negro, reared in one-parent families.[13] And, finally, boys reared without fathers are reported to feel more victimized, as having less control over their environment, and more distrustful of others.[14]

For our purposes, the most relevant effect of fatherless socialization, as reported by Pettigrew, appears to be lack of "marital aptitude." Men socialized without fathers reveal a marked inability to maintain a marital relationship. In a study of twenty-one adult working-class Negroes whose fathers had been absent in their early childhood and twenty-one subjects —matched for age, income, education, and region of birth—whose fathers had been present, Pettigrew found that a third of the fatherless men were either single or divorced, as compared with only four of those whose fathers had been present.[15] In brief, about a third of the boys in fatherless homes are being socialized into a sex pattern which will later be inimical to the socialization of their own children.

Another study, comparing Negro college students who had been arrested for participating in civil-rights demonstrations with young Negroes arrested for more conventional offenses, indicated that the major differentiating factor was the presence of a father in a larger proportion of the first set of subjects than in the second.[16]

The adverse effects reported for children socialized in fatherless families presupposes that the father would have been a suitable model. In some cases, however, the departure of the father results in little loss. A Philadelphia study of low-income families found that the fathers took very

[12] R. V. Burton and J. W. M. Whiting, "The Absent Father and Cross-Sex Identity," *Merrill-Palmer Quarterly*, Vol. 7 (1961), 85-95.

[13] W. B. Miller, "Lower-Class Culture as a Generating Milieu of Gang Delinquency," *Journal of Social Issues*, Vol. 14 (1958), 5-19; D. B. Lynn and W. L. Sawrey, "The Effects of Father-Absence on Norwegian Boys and Girls," *Journal of Abnormal and Social Psychology*, Vol. 59 (1959), 258-62.

[14] Pettigrew, *op. cit.*, p. 20.

[15] *Ibid.*, p. 20.

[16] Franklin Edwards, unpublished report.

little responsibility for child-rearing duties—such as feeding, bathing, and changing the children, or playing with them—and that the mothers expected little help in the process. In fact, the researcher concluded that "it is possible that in the Negro lower class the one-parent family may in reality be the most efficient and functional family type, because the presence of the husband-father may in the long run more negatively than positively affect the mother and child." [17]

Another researcher, asking adult "streetcorner" males about their own fathers, found censored memories too bitter to talk about freely.

When one looks at the . . . men as sons rather than as fathers, the father-child relationship is a . . . [very] distant one. In part, this appears to be due to the fact that the father-child relationship deteriorates over time, and to the different assessment that father and son each make of their relationship. When the child is very young, the father may still be living with the family or, in any event, making an attempt to help out in some way. But after the father has left, as he usually does, the growing distance in time and space between father and family makes it increasingly difficult to sustain even a semblance of family ties between the man, on one hand, and his wife and children on the other. . . . From the child's point of view—and he sees even more from the vantage-point of adulthood—the father is the man who ran out on his mother, his brothers and sisters and himself, who had, perhaps, to be taken to court to force him to pay a few dollars toward the support of his wife and children; who, even when he was home, is perhaps best remembered with a switch or belt in hand.

The men seldom refer to their fathers spontaneously. A group of men can reminisce for hours without the word being mentioned. Some men seem never to have known their fathers but none said so explicitly. Responses to direct questions are commonly of the order of, "I don't remember him," "He left (or died) before I was born." . . .[18]

THE DANGERS OF OVERGENERALIZATION

The evidence that fatherless families are handicapped in the socialization of children, especially of sons, should not, however, be overemphasized. Only a minority of Negro children are socialized in such families, and not all of them suffer irreparable damage. And some of the damage associated with fatherlessness undoubtedly arises from deprivation—both of money and of maternal care as the mother struggles to perform both parental roles. Alvin Schorr reveals the dangers of overgeneralization about the effects of Negro family life on children.

We had achieved an oh-so-thorough understanding of the Negro matriarchal family. The boy, indulged but never treated as fully masculine, grows into a

---

[17] Robert Bell, "The One-Parent Mother in the Negro Lower Class." Unpublished paper, p. 13.

[18] Elliot Liebow, "Fathers without Children," Chapter 3 of a preliminary draft for a doctoral dissertation, Catholic University, Washington, D.C., 1966.

cavalier but withal insecure and undependable man. And he learns, for his survival, to turn aggression on or off. How, indeed, could such youths organize demonstrations with semimilitary care and precision? How, indeed, can they walk picket lines with a discipline that does not yield to the most humiliating provocations? [19]

Apparently, some of the children reared in fatherless homes manage to overcome their handicaps.

THE TEMPORARY FATHER

In some poor Negro families, the father comes and goes. He may come home when he finds a job and can contribute to the family, but leave again when he loses it and cannot. Or he may be officially present when he has a job and the family does not need public assistance, but only clandestinely present when he does not have a job and the family must apply for public help. The effects of his coming and going on the socialization of the children may be as destructive as if he had been entirely absent, and perhaps even more so.

TOO MANY FATHERS

It has already been noted that a pattern of serial polygamy has evolved among lower-class externally adapted Negroes. In some cases, the relationships are of long duration and take on many of the characteristics of a stable marriage. But in other cases the rapid succession of different mates approaches promiscuity. Such a situation is likely to add confusion to the socialization process. Few, if any, of the research studies make a distinction between absent fathers and multiple "fathers." The following analysis, based on years of observation of the "hurt child" in Baltimore illustrates the trauma which may be associated with a multiple "fathers" home.

When a cohesive family group does not exist, . . . the natural father's traces may be lost. Numerous legitimate and illegitimate "daddys" of very different characteristics and attitudes may have moved in or visited. Some may have . . . stayed on with the family when the child hoped they would leave; others may have disappeared when the child had just taken to them. . . .

Not only is the child menaced by the man's role as the mother's sex partner . . . , but also by the changes in the mother's personality affected by each new relationship. Moreover, each separation is preceded by violent dissensions and multiple symptoms of asocial or antisocial adjustment. The child's liberation from a usually unwanted father-substitute is at the price of a deeply resented humiliation of the mother, whatever the causes of the breach. Gratification forever is at the price of wrong and guilt feelings and to be relieved is tantamount to being bad. This promotes a new ambivalence, a new motivation for fearing

[19] Alvin L. Schorr, "The Nonculture of Poverty." Paper presented at American Orthopsychiatric Society meetings, Detroit, March 1963, p. 8.

gratification, and a repression of guilt feelings and a weary indifference to being bad.

Each time the boy is liberated from the father-substitute, . . . he . . . misses the man as a protector and resents that he deserted and exposed him. In his exposed condition, he turns against the mother. . . . The son needs to promote the mother's hostility to justify his own hostility and to assuage his guilt feelings. . . .

The emotional problem is complicated by the economic difficulties. The common-law husband may be costly rather than a relief from financial stress, as hoped. When he leaves, the family economics may have deteriorated to an all-time low . . . and the mother is likely to project her despair on the boy. That the child is there, instead of the man, is sometimes cause enough to resent him. His helpless attempts to offer emotional and economic comfort to the mother contribute to further impairment of the relationship. The offer to substitute for the man who has left is irritating not only as a reminder of the child's inadequacy, but of her own in reference to a grown and, as such, a desirable man. Moreover, the child's eagerness to "jump into the hurdle" is justifiably sensed as his secret delight in her bad fortune. Under the guise of tendering the mother a gift, he actually tends to absorb and consume her. Only by such behavior does the child resemble the man, as known to her from a disconcerting experience of a lifetime, and it is as an image of the male that the child once more has to be rejected. . . . [T]he boy, who also has fought for love and life, . . . once more writhes in mortal pain . . .[20]

The position of the daughter is, doubtless, equally harrowing and cases are not unknown when even quite young daughters become competitors with the mother for the transient man. Thus, a succession of "fathers" can be even more disruptive of the socialization situation than the complete absence of any father.

THE DENIGRATED FATHER

Even the best-intentioned of Negro fathers may find the paternal role excruciatingly difficult because of his denigrated position vis-à-vis the outside world. James Baldwin has pointed out that "the overriding horror of the present system is that it is teaching millions of Negro children to disrespect their parents and despise them." [21] A Negro physician driving his family through city traffic may be stopped by a policeman who will address him contemptuously as *boy* in the presence of his children. No wonder that Miss Dorothy Height, President of the National Council of Negro Women, has stressed that the problems of Negro mothers are vastly complicated by the low esteem in which the father is held by the outside world.

[20] Hertha Riese, *Heal the Hurt Child* (Chicago: University of Chicago Press, 1962), pp. 53-55.

[21] Quoted by Peter Putnam, "If You Had a Choice," *Saturday Review* (October 26, 1963), 53.

A Negro woman has the same kind of problems as other women, but she can't take the same things for granted. For instance, she has to raise children who seldom have the same sense of security that white children have when they see their father accepted as a successful member of the community. A Negro child's father is ignored as though he didn't exist.[22]

One study of Negro male patients in a mental hospital noted that the roots of the illness could be found in the family structure in which they had been reared, "complicated by the growing boy's perception of his father as emasculated by the surrounding white society." [23]

Thus, although the presence of a stable father is important, the denigrated position in which he so frequently finds himself may tend to cancel his contribution to the socialization of his children. In the outside world he must be subservient, if not servile; he is often assigned jobs conventionally associated with women, such as cooking, waiting on tables, dishwashing, and service occupations.[24] Or he may be unemployed and supported by his wife, or otherwise dependent on her. He is not the decision-maker. No matter how much a child loves such a father, he will find it difficult to accept him as preceptor and model.

Students of schizophrenia have reported that this illness is related to socialization in families with strong mothers and weak fathers.[25] Both the illness and the type of family structure with which it is associated are common among Negroes of both cultures, suggesting, as Pettigrew points out, the need for further research to clarify the relationships.[26] (The upgrading of the Negro father, one might add parenthetically, might constitute a major contribution to the welfare of the nation.)

CROWDING

It is not only in family structure, especially in anomalous paternal-role situations, that lower-class children of both cultures encounter handicaps;

[22] Dorothy Height, article in the *Washington Post,* October 25, 1963.

[23] Robert L. Derbyshire, Eugene B. Brody, and Carl Schleifer, "Family Structure of Young Adult Mental Patients: Preliminary Observations from Urban Baltimore," unpublished paper, p. 1.

[24] Pettigrew, *op. cit.,* p. 21.

[25] M. L. Kohn and J. A. Clausen, "Parental Authority Behavior and Schizophrenia," *American Journal of Orthopsychiatry,* Vol. 26 (1956), 297-313. It has been reported that social-psychological similarities between schizophrenic males, both white and Negro, and nonschizophrenic Negro males "appear in [certain] family structures; problems in forming a satisfactory identification with a father figure; the need to resolve anxiety-induced conflicting identifications with figures of opposing symbolic significance; factors promoting the use of defensive techniques which impair the evaluation of and ability to act upon reality; and lack of opportunity to develop an individual identity which is a successful variant of group identity" (Eugene B. Brody, "Social Conflict and Schizophrenic Behavior in Young Adult Negro Males," *Psychiatry,* Vol. 24 [1961], 345).

[26] Pettigrew, *op. cit.,* p. 22.

the setting in which the family has to function is also likely to be unpropitious, especially with respect to the crowding that results either from living in extended families or having to take in lodgers to share household expenses.

Studies by Sussman, Burchinal, and Litvak have shown that kinship assistance is fairly common in modern families. Among the more affluent, such assistance may take the form of money, but among poorer families —and especially among Negroes (for whom housing is a serious problem) —it may take the form of sharing households. A strong feeling of obligation often leads them to make room for relatives, even if such hospitality has disturbing effects on the family. Thus most nonwhite children under eighteen live in large families (Table 4-5), and in 1960 a large proportion of all nonwhite families—14 per cent—were multigenerational.[27]

Table 4-5.

Proportion of Nonwhite Children under 18
in Families with 6 or More Members*

All Nonwhite Families	Urbanized Areas	Other Urban	Rural Nonfarm	Rural Farm	South
63.0	56.3	62.7	72.3	81.9	68.6

* *Source:* U.S. Census, 1960, *Persons by Family Characteristics,* Table 4a, pp. 33-35.

In fact, among nonwhite families with their own children of any age, only about half had no other members.[28] The chances were great that all these multigenerational families were living under crowded conditions: almost a third (30 per cent) of all nonwhite members of households in 1960 lived in dwelling units with 1.51 or more persons per room. Crowding is the lot of slum families of whatever color, but it is more likely to occur—and it is likely to be more severe—among Negroes.[29]

[27] John C. Beresford and Alice M. Rivlin, "The Multigeneration Family." Unpublished paper, presented at University of Michigan Conference on Aging, Ann Arbor, July 1964, p. 11 and Appendix Table 1. Among the families which were not husband-wife families, 23 per cent were multigenerational.

[28] *Ibid.,* Appendix, Table 1. For husband-wife families, the proportions with no other members were: over-all, 52 per cent; urban, 50 per cent; rural nonfarm, 52 per cent; rural-farm, 50 per cent. For other, that is, not husband-wife families, the proportions were: 51 per cent, 53 per cent, 43 per cent and 38 per cent, respectively.

[29] Housing is one of the most resistant indexes in measures of Negro improvement. Segregation appears to be increasing rather than the reverse. See Karl Taeuber, "Negro Residential Segregation: Trends and Measurement," *Social Problems,* Vol. 12 (Summer 1964), 42-50.

A study of thirty-three so-called multiproblem families in Harlem revealed that a considerable number maintained extended-family relationships: twenty-five subjects said that they went to relatives' graduation; twenty-three got together with their relatives on holidays; twenty-one took care of relatives' children if their own parents could not; and seventeen took care of elderly relatives.[30] However admirable such mutual aid within the family may be, however, it also leads to crowding—and adverse effects on the children.

Hylan Lewis has pointed out that "to a great degree the child finds himself either deprived of balanced biparental care in a family situation marked by the total or frequent absence of one or both parents, or he finds himself in a large or extended-family situation—which itself may be lacking one or both parents—competing with a number of siblings and relatives for care and desired responses." [31] Actually, they may be competing not only for care and response but, in the lowest-income levels, for sheer survival.

Sometimes the crowding results not from generosity to relatives but from the necessity of sharing expenses with roomers or lodgers. Almost 8 per cent of nonwhite households in 1960 included nonrelatives.[32] In either case, the situation can be confusing for children.

Even intelligent children become totally confused as to who all these people are, whether they are related or not, and if they are related, to whom they belong. The meaning of the family to the children, and of the children to the family, is constantly changing. The children are so weary of all these harmful moves and emotional swaps within their home that they do not make the effort to know, or even refuse to know, the people who increase the hardship of family living, no matter who they are.[33]

James Plant's analysis of the adverse effects of crowded living conditions on socialization has been summarized as follows.

. . . [C]hildren reared in crowded areas lack self-sufficiency or the ability to be alone. . . . Figuratively speaking, they live socially naked, without privacy. They have no opportunity to withdraw in crises to compose themselves. They become accustomed to seeing human nature "in the raw," so to speak, with its defenses down.

[30] Joan Gordon and Lawrence Podell, "Social Functioning in Multi-problem Families in Harlem," unpublished report on a pilot project, 1964. On a "family integration scale," not two, but three, types seemed to emerge. Thus there were ten cases with scores of 0-5; three, 5-19; one, 10-14; six, 15-19; three, 20-24; two, 25-29; eight, 30 and over. The extremes may reflect the acculturated and the externally adapted; the in-between mode (six cases in the 15-19 bracket) is puzzling and cannot be accounted for within the framework of our analyses.

[31] Lewis, *op. cit.*, p. 103.

[32] U.S. Bureau of the Census, *Families* (1960), Table 24.

[33] Riese, *op. cit.*, p. 69.

As a result of this constant contact, illusions about people are destroyed. . . Ideals about people tend to suffer the same fate. . . . . Much of the dignity of life in roomier quarters derives from the fact that there can be long backstage preparation for human contacts. Statistically speaking, the volume of this preparation that is necessary for dignified human contacts is great. We have to dress our minds and personalities as well as our bodies in order to be presentable. The child in crowded areas sees life backstage.

Along with this destruction of illusions about people goes sexual maladjustment. . . . [S]exual behavior may be idiomatic, a means of communication for emotions far too deep for verbal formulation. But sex on this level requires a substratum of idealism or . . . illusions, in order to develop. The child in a crowded district does not have the opportunity to form such ideals, for he early becomes familiar with the grosser manifestations of sex. It is difficult to graft illusions on this foundation. . . .[34]

This is likely to be the ambience in which many Negro children are socialized, in families with or without fathers.

Among the very poor, constant moving further complicates life for the child.

With this baggage train of dependents these people are constantly on the move. They are resented by the more affluent and less numerous families of the neighborhood. The quality of the quarters they can obtain declines with each change that circumstances impose on them. . . . Moving about incessantly for the purpose of evading their creditors may be just one symptom of their collapse.[35]

Order, if not Heaven's first law, is in any event extremely important in human societies and a vast institutional apparatus is designed to achieve and buttress it. "Law and order" are frequently bracketed in our thinking, reflecting a recognition that order depends on some kind of normative system which makes expectations logical and probable. Order, unless carried to compulsive extremes or imposed in a mechanical and ruthless manner, is a basic value in the socialization process.

A child in a well-managed home finds a daily, weekly, monthly, and yearly order surrounding him: meals, most activities, and bedtime follow a regular schedule. There is a rhythm of five days of school, a day of play, and a day for church. There are birthdays, anniversaries, holidays—all of which mark his life with regular, expectable events.

The child in the slums seldom finds such regularity and order. There is no regular mealtime: people eat when they are hungry and there happens to be something to eat. The child's social world is often as confused as his physical world: members of the household come and go and he

---

[34] Jessie Bernard, *American Family Behavior* (New York: Harper & Row, Publishers, 1942), pp. 522-23.

[35] Riese, *op. cit.*, pp. 46-47.

finds it hard to keep up with all the relationships involved. Order—social as well as physical—is one of the major casualties of crowding.[36]

NEIGHBORHOOD

Because of the limited housing space available to Negro families, acculturated families with high standards for their children often find themselves forced to live in neighborhoods of externally adapted families whose social and moral standards they abhor. Confined to a ghetto, the acculturated family has to work twice as hard to maintain its standards of behavior as it would have to if it had the support of neighbors of similar culture. Parents must enforce taboos against behavior to which the child is constantly exposed. Even when a family is surrounded by cultural reinforcement, it is not easy to require children to study, to repress aggression, and to inhibit sexual impulses; when one is surrounded by people with quite different patterns and standards it often becomes all but impossible.

The concern of acculturated parents was documented in a study in Boston of why families were eager to move out of Negro neighborhoods: "Every mother among the self-integrators declared that dissatisfaction with the local schools—their undisciplined, unambitious pupils; dilapidated plant; and squalid, disorderly surroundings—was a principal reason for their wanting to [move] . . . Almost two fifths (36.4 per cent) of the residents expressed dissatisfaction wih their neighbors. The young educated mothers were "most aware of the effect of local conditions . . . on the socialization and aspirations of their children." In fact, "the problem of bringing up young children in [such areas] is a recurring theme" among young families with school-age children.[37]

The greatest (or most visible) differences between the externally adapted and the acculturated are those between lower-class and lower-middle-class families. The line dividing them is the critical point in the upward or downward social mobility of individuals or families. The grade is steep; and firm footholds are hard to come by. In order to prepare children for middle-class standards, such families may have to run counter to the trends which surround them. The result may be greater harshness in the exercise of power by the father; he may become more authoritarian than he would have to be under less inimical circumstances.

Even so the odds are often against the family. Hylan Lewis has re-

[36] The more obvious effects of poverty on health, sleeping provisions, and recreation have been elaborated in detail by social workers. A very perceptive and intuitive statement of the subtler effects was presented by Alvin L. Schorr, "The Nonculture of Poverty." Paper presented at the American Orthopsychiatric Society meetings, March 1963.

[37] Lewis G. Watts, *et al.*, *The Middle-Income Negro Family Faces Urban Renewal* (Waltham, Mass.: Brandeis University, 1964), pp. 44, 54, 60, 68.

ported that, among low-income families, parents cease to have control over their children as early as the age of six—or as soon as the child can escape the confinement of the home and wander through the streets.

Sometimes, however, it is noted that even in such a neighborhood, there may be little pockets in which acculturated families struggle successfully to maintain their own standards. It is reported, for example, that in Harlem there are certain blocks which surround themselves with a cultural "curtain" to protect their children from undesirable influences. It is hard to imagine any frontier more difficult to defend, or one whose defenders exhibit more quiet heroism.[38]

"Do As I Say"

REACH AND GRASP

Despite the inauspicious circumstances under which many Negro families must conduct the socialization process, they have a very high level of aspiration for their children.[39] Like most other families, they set their sights high—but their reach is far more limited. Thus Hylan Lewis reports that, in thirty-nine low-income Negro families studied intensively over a long period, "the parents tend to show greater conformity to, and convergence with, middle-class standards in their verbalizations of value —in what they say they want (or would like to want)—than in their actual behavior." In this, of course, they do not differ from other families, but because they face so many more obstacles, they are more likely to become discouraged. Again, as Lewis notes, "lack of confidence in some instances is associated with slackening efforts, or diminution of the will, to cope with crucial aspects of child-rearing." It is not their aspirations that decline, but their ability to implement them. These families are well aware of their failures: ". . . with few exceptions, they do not prefer or approve the circumstances in which they now live and in which their children are being brought up." [40]

What do Negro families say they want their children to be like? What kinds of character do they say they want for them? What aspirations do they say they have for them? These are some of the questions we address ourselves to here.

[38] For an insightful discussion of the battle mothers must fight to inculcate their values when surrounded by an unsupportive world, see Riese, *op. cit.*, pp. 157ff. "Her standards, unsubstantiated by the realities of a true home, are similar to a foreign language" (p. 157).

[39] For a discussion of Negro aspirations, see Leonard Broom and Norval Glenn, *Transformation of the Negro American* (New York: Harper & Row, Publishers, 1965), pp. 23, 61, 152-53, 163-65, 172-86. For a comparison of aspirations among Negroes with those of other ethnic groups, see Bernard C. Rosen, "Race, Ethnicity, and the Achievement Syndrome," *American Sociological Review*, Vol. 24 (February 1959), 47-60.

[40] *Ibid.*, p. 25.

VERBAL SOCIALIZATION

There was a time when normative verbal socialization was more self-conscious and deliberate than it is now; there was a more conscientious and purposeful endeavor on the part of parents, teachers, and clergymen. The child was surrounded by mottoes, aphorisms, sayings, proverbs in samplers on the wall, and moral lessons in his schoolbooks: "Honesty is the best policy"; "Do unto others as you would have them do unto you"; "Honor thy father and thy mother"; "Never put off until tomorrow. . . ." In this way the Protestant ethic was drummed into millions of children throughout the nineteenth century. The task of "forming the moral character" of children was taken very seriously by parents, and they went about it with dispatch, usually confident that they had the outside world's support.

There is relatively little of such deliberate, self-conscious, didacticism today, and there is less dependence on verbal socialization. A modern child is not likely even to hear most of the aphorisms of the past. This does not mean, of course, that the process of verbal socialization is no longer omnipresent or that deliberate verbal socialization is no longer important.[41] Little pitchers, so to speak, still have big ears.

EDUCATION

I have been impressed [says a retired teacher] by the enormous prestige that learning has for the unskilled Negro workers I come in contact with [in a Northern city]. The foreman of the gang moving my furniture last week, for example, chided me when I told him I had retired. "Our children need all you teachers," he kept repeating. My windowwasher was awestricken at the books in my home. He had left school in the tenth grade and regretted it. "If only they had been more patient," he said, "I think I could have made it. I'll sure see to it that my children do."

Stereotypes and clichés about the apathy of parents with respect to education may contain a kernel of truth—but not the whole truth; for when Negro parents of all class levels are asked what they want for their children, the answer is "Education." Even in the lowest-income classes, despite the recurring characterization of the Negro family as apathetic, no research result is more consistently reported than the salience of high—some say unrealistically high—educational aspirations for their children. It may be true that the school gets little help from parents in preventing dropouts. And it may be true that out of several hundred schoolboys who say they would like to enter an apprenticeship, only a small fraction will actually show up when it is offered. Still, parents say—and children echo

---

[41] We leave for later discussion the nonverbal families, those in which verbal communication is at a minimum, so that socialization is almost wholly on a gestural, nonverbal level.

—that they want education, and Hylan Lewis reported "evidence of posi- tive concern and [even] a willingness to sacrifice . . . despite deprivation and trouble . . . in a good proportion of the families" he studied.[42]

The amount of education aspired to for children varies, understand- ably, by class. Thus a Philadelphia study of 202 Negro mothers with at least two children found that many women even in the lowest-status level (zero to eight years of schooling and seven or more children)—pre- sumably acculturated—had high educational aspirations (college)—for their children; and among the higher-status women (nine or more years of schooling and six or fewer children), most of them did.

In the low-status mother group, 44 per cent wanted a college education for their sons, as compared to 65 per cent of the high-status mother group . . . Thirty-nine per cent of the low-status mothers and 61 per cent of the high-status mothers wanted a college education for their daughters [as well]. There were no differences by the sex of the child in either of the two mother groups in desired educational achievement for their children.[43]

For many of these mothers there is little recognition of the way one goes about getting an education—that is, of the course one has to follow to arrive at college, and the tremendous discipline involved in completing such a course. For others, though, "there is frequently communicated a combination of realism and pessimism, a kind of wise weariness that may appear to belie the very educational or career goals they express for at least some of their children." [44] Enough do succeed, in any event, so that in 1960 the proportion of men and women twenty-two to twenty-four years old who had at least some college education was 11.8 per cent and 13.1 per cent, respectively.

OCCUPATION

High aspirations characterize Negro parents with respect to occupa- tions as well as education for children. Money is important, of course, but so is prestige and social recognition. Bell found that almost half (47 per cent) of the mothers he interviewed coveted professional careers for their sons. (The proportion was the same in the lower- and higher-status sets of mothers.) A fifth of the lower-status mothers (21 per cent) wanted skilled occupations, but only 12 per cent of the higher-status mothers did. So far as maternal aspirations for daughters were concerned, 38 per cent of the lower-status mothers and 21 per cent of the higher-status mothers selected office work or clerical occupations.[45]

[42] *Ibid.,* p. 26.
[43] Robert Bell, *loc. cit.*
[44] Quoted by Lewis, *op. cit.*
[45] There were no differences in occupational aspirations for sons and daughters in the higher-status set of mothers; almost twice as many lower-status mothers aspired to

One of the most revealing results of this study was the evidence of greater assurance among these mothers with respect to their daughters than to their sons. The lower-status mothers replied that they did not know what they wanted for their sons three times more often than they did for their daughters. The male occupational world is probably a very vague and hazy one to many of these lower-status mothers and probably not much clearer to the fathers.

Of course, even among those who do know what they want for their children, the high occupational aspirations expressed by many reflect a lack of understanding of the outside world. Many of the mothers, seeing only the rewards of the more prestigious and highly paid occupations and professions, do not know the long hard years of preparation required for entering or the discipline involved in pursuing such careers. In any event it is clear that many—perhaps most—Negro parents, whatever their own achievement may be, do harbor high aspirations for their children.

MANNERS AND MORALS

The twentieth century has seen a powerful movement away from the Victorian rejection of sex in Western society. Some reformers, like Albert Ellis, for example, even mount aggressive attacks on sexual abstinence, painting consequences as dire as those formerly associated with free sexual indulgence.[46] Their general view is that "coitus is . . . an inevitable, natural, and desirable activity to be enjoyed both in and out of marriage." This view coincides precisely with the value assigned to sex by externally adapted and (now even) many acculturated Negro families.[47] For other Negro families, however, sexual permissiveness is not a positive value but a negative value, as it was for the Victorians. Mothers in acculturated families try to teach their daughters not to permit sexual advances from boys or men; their standards, if not their socializing techniques, are rigorous. The middle-class girl is often so rigidly protected, in fact, that normal sexuality is impaired.[48]

---

office, clerical, and skilled occupations for their daughters as for their sons (48 per cent and 25 per cent, respectively).

[46] Albert Ellis, *Sex and the Single Man* (New York: Lyle Stuart, 1963), Chapter 1.

[47] P. H. Gebhard et al., *Pregnancy and Abortion* (New York: Harper, Hoeber, 1958). The quotation in the preceding sentence is a statement of Negro values in the area of sex (p. 154).

[48] Hylan Lewis cites the case of Mrs. M., whose "twelve-year-old daughter was molested sexually by an elderly man—a tenant in the same building—whom she had asked to 'look out' for the children while she was away. When she learned about this, one of the things she did was to give the girl 'a good spanking for letting the man do things to her.' When she was asked why she did this, she replied: 'I sure spanked her for not coming to me, and for not knowing no better. She should have knowed better than letting that man bother her!' " (*op. cit.*, p. 23).

Kardiner and Ovesey, on the basis of clinical experience in New York, summarize the teachings of Negro parents with respect to sex:

In the lower class, the overt teachings about sex are Victorian for both males and females. However, although sex taboos are universally taught, explicitly or implicitly, it is rare that they are enforced with beatings. . . .

The sexual education of the lower-class female is a bit more thorough. She is generally taught Victorian morality. . . . Shame is generally invoked as the chief sanction. Later, the emphasis is more that sex should be associated with love. . . .

In the middle class, . . . there is more freedom . . . in discussing sex with parents, and . . . few instances of intimidation. . . .

The middle-class female is much like her white sister. Sex education is rigidly puritanical . . . and sex as an expression of love is highly stressed. The same is true of continence as a virtue. There is, however, little terrorization. . . .[49]

The upper-class sex mores are about the same as in the middle class.[50]

Reflected in this statement is another tenet of sexual reformers in Western society: love must accompany sex. This belief that marriage without love is no better than prostitution,[51] and that sex outside of marriage—but with love—was not wrong, is also represented among Negroes of all classes, and results in a relatively high permissiveness toward sex. Ira L. Reiss believes that romance is more sex-linked—or, as Hazel Stanton prefers to state it, sex is more romantic—among Negroes than among whites. Reiss found, for example, that (verbally at least) Negroes tended more than whites to require affection as a basis for sexual behavior and were less inclined to accept kissing and petting without affection.[52]

Reiss' findings were based on a study of sexual permissiveness (defined as acceptance of premarital coitus under some conditions) in a student sample of 118 women and 115 men and a national sample of 62 men and 81 women. The women were, as expected, less permissive than the men. It was interesting to note that women students (high school and college) were less likely to be either extremely permissive or extremely nonpermissive; they were more likely to be in the middle range. Thus, for example, whereas almost a third (32 per cent) of the national sample of women were at the low extreme of permissiveness, less than half that many (only 14 per cent) of the students were. Conversely, three times as many of the national sample (12 per cent) as of the student sample (4 per cent) were extremely permissive. If the students reflect the wave of the future, it appears that both the extremely nonpermissive and the

---

[49] Kenneth Clark, *Dark Ghetto* (Harper and Row, 1965), p. 71.

[50] Abram Kardiner and Lionel Ovesey, *The Mark of Oppression* (Meridian Books, 1962), pp. 68-69.

[51] The Marxists of the nineteenth century belabored this point at great length in their attacks on the bourgeois family as a perpetuater of inequalities.

[52] Ira L. Reiss, "Premarital Sexual Permissiveness among Negroes and Whites," *American Sociological Review*, Vol. 29 (October 1964), 688-698.

extremely permissive are on the way out and a generation of moderate permissiveness will succeed them. It may be that there is a convergence process at work: the students may be reacting to the forces that are modifying the sexual mores of Western society, while the slum and plantation families may be reacting to the forces that are acculturating them to the larger, white society.

If all degrees of permissiveness are taken into account rather than only the extremes, 45 per cent of the students and 83 per cent of the national sample were more permissive rather than less so. The men did not show the same trend, however. Among them, 37 per cent of the students but only 29 per cent of the national sample were more permissive, and only 4 per cent of them—but 18 per cent of the national sample—were less permissive. The trend, however, is clear-cut; the student generation is more permissive than the national sample.[53]

Associated with these attitudes is a strong negative value placed upon contraception and abortion. Here, again, class differences (as measured by years of schooling) occur. Gebhard and his associates reported that, in their sample, among grade-school women, 8 per cent had had induced abortions; among the high school women, 16 per cent; among the college women, 20 per cent.[54]

Hylan Lewis reports a sex difference in attitudes among the families he studied. For example, when one young man was told by his girlfriend that he was the father of her child, and that she knew how she could get rid of it for fifty dollars, he replied that she should have the baby: he would do what he could.

> Everybody should have a chance. My mother didn't get rid of me like that, so why should I do that to somebody else? That wouldn't be right. . . . When he grows up, maybe he be a doctor or lawyer. He come to me when I'm old. He say, "You 'help' me when I was little, now you old I help you." [55]

Bell found class differences among Negro mothers in preferred age for marriage: half of the lower-status mothers felt twenty-one or younger was the best age for sons and 39 per cent felt that nineteen or younger was the best age for daughters; the figures for the higher-status mothers were 17 per cent and 7 per cent, respectively. Conversely, only 37 per cent of the lower-status mothers felt that the sons should wait until they were at least twenty-four years of age before marrying, and only 10 per cent felt their daughters should; among the high-status mothers, the figures were 63 per cent and 27 per cent, respectively.[56]

[53] *Ibid.*, Table 2.
[54] Gebhard, *et al., op. cit.*, p. 166.
[55] Lewis, *op. cit.*, p. 29.
[56] Robert Bell, *loc. cit.* These status differences reflect differences in the occupational aspirations for the children, higher occupations requiring more education and hence, presumably, delay in marriage.

Because the values Negroes associate with sex range from the Victorian rigor of the middle-class acculturated to the high permissiveness of Reiss' young men students, and because great differences exist not only among classes but also between the sexes, and because all Negroes are responding to the impact of forces operating in the whole Western world, it is difficult to predict exactly which of these values will finally prevail in Negro society—or, for that matter, in society as a whole. It may be that the extremes may ultimately converge at a level less permissive than the reformers advocate but also less restrictive than the Victorians sought.

PROPERTY, THRIFT, CONSUMPTION

A third set of values deals with another aspect of the Protestant ethic: property, thrift, and consumption.

The set of norms which constitute the institutions of private property are very early inculcated into children in Western societies. Among the first orders a child hears are "mustn't touch"; "it's not yours"; "give it back to him, it's his." Little by little, a world of objects becomes organized around the basic criterion of ownership as reflected in control. Even when Jimmy is nowhere in sight, his shovel and pail still belong to him. The child learns that there are severe sanctions invoked against violation of these norms. The cynical aphorism, "Honesty is the best policy," takes on sad cogency when his knuckles are rapped or his behavior sorrowfully frowned upon by his mother when he comes home with another child's toys and he is told that he must not take things that belong to other children.

The concept of property had little meaning for the slave[57] or the freedman. Because both the slave and the chicken were the property of the master, the slave reasoned that he could take the chicken. The military appropriation of goods and real property during the Civil War was not calculated to clarify the nature of property for the freedmen, and stories of stealing and general thievery were common.

In the slum, where goods are scarce, the Hobbesian model of human society finds ready credence. One boy was quoted by a Negro social worker as saying: "As long as you can hang on to something that I want, I'll let you have it; but if you can't hang on to it, I'll take it and it's mine."

But the mothers who daily sally forth to work in the homes of white families know that honesty is a fundamental qualification for any job. They know that if anything is missing in those homes they will be the first to be suspected. For them, honesty is truly the best policy.

Some psychoanalytic interpreters of juvenile delinquency suggest

---

[57] Without any inbred feeling for property, the care of what little they had was careless, a fact also commonly reported among freedmen. It was not too much later, however, that Booker T. Washington, with his emphasis on ownership, began to develop the institution of property among Negroes.

that children often act out their parents' wishes and that parents, however much they may protest, derive vicarious satisfaction from their children's actions. It is thus possible that, however much a mother might wish for honesty in her child, she might be willing to look the other way if he secured dishonestly what she could not supply him honestly. But she is unlikely deliberately to teach him dishonesty.

Thrift was a basic tenet of the Protestant ethic, the virtue that made possible delayed gratification. The stereotype of the Negro has been notoriously nonthrifty. The externally adapted Negro spends what he has as soon as he gets it and if there is a surplus, he may stop work until it is used up. But cultural and class differences are salient here, as they are in the area of sex. In acculturated families, ideals of thrift flourish. Despite the stereotype of the profligate, thriftless Negro, the following comments by a twenty-eight-year-old father of two children illustrate its importance in such families:

> I believe in religion. I live by The Book. . . . I don't drink. . . . I don't gamble and I don't stay out late or run around. I work hard. . . . I always save some pennies from every dollar. . . . My wife's check goes straight to the bank. We don't even look twice at it. And we save something from my check too if we can. . . . When I get paid, we sit down together with pencil and paper and we write down how we're going to spend the money. . . . I work hard and that's relaxation for me. . . . Next year, or the year after that, we're going to buy a house with a piece of ground. . . .[58]

Frederic LePlay, a great French student of the family, was of the opinion that a family's budget of expenditures was an accurate reflection of its values. The convertible at the slum doorstep of the Negro is always being cited by impatient critics; they never see the check that "goes straight to the bank."

CLEANLINESS

Millions of housewives for several generations depended on Negro women to keep their homes clean. To work in these homes, the Negro women had to learn to keep their own persons clean. Millions of Negroes of an older generation, as Pauli Murray has noted, remember their mothers washing clothes at a scrubbing board. Still, many people associate Negroes with lack of cleanliness.[59]

Cleanliness is an almost compulsive value in the United States. A vast industry is engaged in inventing ways to implement it for both homes and persons. There is a specialized brush to get at almost every conceivable speck of dust and the goal is a cleaning system which will inhale

---

[58] Lewis, *op. cit.*, p. 31.
[59] Robert Coles, "Racial Identity in School Children," *Saturday Review* (October 19, 1963), 56.

dust by an air-cleaning system. Commercials for soaps and detergents monopolize daytime television programs. The bathroom is the master-piece of the house designer.

This almost fetishistic emphasis on cleanliness is possible because the technology—in the form of plumbing and power facilities—is widely available. In homes and areas where it is not, cleanliness is somewhat farther away from godliness. Like so many other values, this one is shared by Negro families but is less possible for them to achieve.

A generation or two ago, it was believed that immigrants used their bathtubs for storing coal. The immigrants' children now bathe with oils and salts or shower with soaps that "protect them from body odors" for indeterminate periods. The road to godliness by way of cleanliness is one of the easiest: all it takes to get started is modern plumbing and plenty of cheap hot water.

VIOLENCE

The Western world maintains an ambivalent attitude toward violence. Usually, aggression is verbally condemned, but defensive violence is not. There are important cultural and class differences in the norms regulating violence and the forms it takes.[60] Violence has been reported as characteristic of lower-class life in general, and it has always been endemic in the environment of all Negroes, especially in the South.[61] One of the tests of emancipation among some of the freedmen, it is alleged, was the right to use violence themselves, as it had been used on them under slavery.

Violence against the white man was all but impossible; but its deflection toward Negroes was not. As an outlet for aggression aroused against the white world, violence among Negroes has been common[62] but it is not a positive value; it is simply a fact of life.

When I fight, I fight to hurt and kill. That's why I don't like to fight. I hate fighting. A man come up to me to talk trash, I turn around and walk away. But if he keep on . . . , I'll fight him and try to kill him. Suppose you and me fight and you beat me decent. I'll shake hands with you, say you whipped me and go home. But I'll come back tomorrow and fight you again and if you beat me decent again I'll go home and come back the next day and the next day until I beat you.[63]

---

[60] Jessie Bernard, *American Community Behavior* (New York: The Dryden Press, 1962), Chap. 26.

[61] The question has been raised whether the Negro's violence may not be simply a Southern characteristic. See Thomas Pettigrew, *Profile of the Negro American* (Princeton, N.J.: D. Van Nostrand Co., Inc., 1964), pp. 147-49.

[62] Hortense Powdermaker, *After Freedom: A Cultural Study in the Deep South* (New York: The Viking Press, Inc., 1939).

[63] Lewis, *op. cit.*, p. 32.

To the extent that violence is a value among Negroes, it is not an aggressive violence but, rather, defensive. There are, for example, few if any Negroes who glorify violence as the white vigilantes or the night-riders have done. What the parents teach their children is not aggression but defense:

When Dick's eight-year-old son came home from school crying, and explained that he had been beaten up by some bigger boys, Dick told him he didn't want him to come home crying from school. He was to return to school the next day and if the boys bothered him again, he was to stay and fight hard as he could and do as much damage to them as he could. And if he was beaten, he was to do the same thing the next day and the next.[64]

Vis-à-vis the white world, however, nonviolence, nonretaliation, and infinite patience in the face of provocation were more likely to be the values which Negro parents attempted to inculcate in their children. It is only recently that violence has become a positive value among Negroes —and then only among the so-called Black Muslims.

Negroes have been torn by conflict in their attitude toward violence. They have writhed at the derision heaped upon them for their passivity in the face of oppression. Negro historians have been at great pains to show that slaves had not supinely accepted their fate. It was not lack of resistance on their part, but the overpowering force of their masters that kept them in bondage.

It was Martin Luther King who offered a new solution—a way of combining heroism with resistance in an aggressively nonviolent way. Not their own parents, but an American tradition straight from Thoreau, solved for at least some of the new generation of Negroes the old, old problem: What is the value of violence?

NONVERBAL FAMILIES

Not until Negroes from the backwoods areas of the South came to the cities did they become visible. Hidden in isolated rural areas, they were —as far as the outside world was concerned—almost nonexistent. It is, therefore, only recently that we have become acutely aware of the absence, or low level, of verbal communication among them. Children are found who have almost never been talked to by adults. Because the child learns who and what he is by interacting with those around him, such children have little self-identity. Many are unable even to state their names.

Much of this inarticulateness can be attributed to fear, but not all; many have a genuine inability to respond verbally. In their world, physical gestures, grunts, facial expressions, and tones of voice constitute

[64] *Ibid.*, pp. 33-34.

the major means of communication. These, of course, are inadequate and greatly restrict the child's ability to learn.

Socialization, under such circumstances, is enormously handicapped. *Don't do that!* can be communicated easily enough, but *That's not right* cannot. *Go to school* can be communicated, but *Education is important* cannot. Whatever socialization takes place in such circumstances is almost wholly inadvertent, even accidental. People react, when they do, on an emotional level; few abstractions enter the relationship. And even if the mother has strong feelings about what she wants for her children, she herself has no way of communicating them except on a nonverbal level. Children reared in homes of this kind have been labeled "culturally deprived;" it would be more accurate to say "humanly destroyed," for if the deprivation lasts even two or three years its effects may, some students believe, become irreversible, the mental and emotional capacity irredeemably lost.

Masks, Roles, and the Hawthorne Effect

THE MASK

A function of both Negro and white families is the inculcation in children of the customary role patterns for the two races. Thomas Pettigrew has underscored the role nature of Negro-ness. "The Negro must . . . act out the role of the 'inferior'; he must play the social role of 'Negro.' " [65] It is a role—a mask—imposed by the outside world. Socialization into this role is, of course, a function of agencies other than the family as well; literally every institution and group with which the Negro has contacts participate in the process. But it begins in the family.

Hylan Lewis, reporting on a Southern mill town in the 1940s, pointed out that "one of the important functions of the Negro family in a bi-racial community is to define the role of the child in relation to whites and to provide techniques for 'getting along' and for lessening tension and frustration." [66] Two basic patterns emerged. The first was one of reserve: because no white person could be completely trusted or incorporated into Negro society, no genuine intimacy was possible. The second pattern set the limits of approved, or even of permitted, behavior toward whites. The result was a life view which, temporarily at least, reduced racial tensions and trauma.[67]

But the performance of this role drew heavily on the Negro's emotional reserves. An insight into the protective façade Negroes develop may be gleaned from studies comparing replies given by Negro subjects

[65] Thomas Pettigrew, *op. cit.*, p. 4.

[66] Hylan Lewis, *Blackways of Kent* (Chapel Hill, N.C.: University of North Carolina Press, 1955), p. 109.

[67] *Ibid.*, p. 110.

to questions when put by white and by Negro interviewers. In 1942, for example, almost twice as many respondents (45 per cent) replied that Negroes would be treated worse if the Japanese conquered the United States when replying to a white interviewer than when replying to a Negro questioner (25 per cent).[68] And in North Carolina in 1961, subjects were more likely to mention higher educational goals for their children, to state that changes must be made in the way the country is run, and to approve of sit-in demonstrations and school desegregation when talking to Negro interviewers than when talking to whites.[69] This tendency to dissemble in the presence of whites has been reported by Pettigrew. He found, for example, that only 66 per cent of the subjects interviewed by whites agreed that "the trouble with most white people is that they think they are better than other people;" 87 per cent of those interviewed by Negroes agreed. Three fifths of those responding to white interviewers said they felt they had been victims of group discrimination; more than three quarters of those responding to Negro interviewers did. When responding to a white interviewer, 56 per cent said they agreed that they sometimes felt prejudice had hurt them personally; when replying to a Negro interviewer, 70 per cent agreed. About a fifth (21 per cent) disagreed with the statement that "a man gets ahead better by keeping out of trouble than always demanding his rights" when facing a white interviewer; almost twice as many (39 per cent) disagreed when faced by a Negro interviewer.[70]

If Negro parents succeed in teaching the techniques they consider essential for getting along in the white world, their children will learn how to live behind their masks with at least a modicum of comfort. But more than a mask is involved in being a Negro.

TEACHING CHILDREN HOW TO BE NEGROES

Richard Wright wrote of his "first lesson in how to live as a Negro." He had become involved in a fight with white boys who threw broken bottles at him and his friends; he was badly cut.

> I sat brooding on my front steps, nursing my wound and waiting for my mother to come home from work. . . . When night fell, my mother came from the white folks' kitchen. I raced down the street to meet her. I could just feel in my bones that she would understand. I knew she would tell me exactly what to do next time. I grabbed her hand and babbled out the whole story. She examined my wound, then slapped me.
>
> "How come yuh didn't hide?" she asked me. "How come yuh always fightin'?"
>
> I was outraged, and bawled. Between sobs I told her that I didn't have any trees or hedges to hide behind. . . .

[68] Pettigrew, *op. cit.*, p. 50.
[69] *Ibid.*, p. 50.
[70] *Ibid.*, p. 51.

She grabbed a barrel stave, dragged me home, stripped me naked, and beat me till I had a fever of one hundred and two. She would smack my rump with the stave, and, while the skin was still smarting, impart to me gems of Jim Crow wisdom. I was never to throw cinders any more. I was never to fight any more wars. I was never, never, under any conditions, to fight *white* folks again. And they were absolutely right in clouting me with the broken milk bottle. Didn't I know she was working hard every day in the hot kitchens of the white folks to make money to take care of me? When was I ever going to learn to be a good boy? She couldn't be bothered with my fights. She finished by telling me that I ought to be thankful to God as long as I lived that they didn't kill me.[71]

This happened a long time ago, but a researcher discovered that Negro schoolchildren in the South in the early 1960s reported the same lessons imparted by parents in the same way.

"I just know I can't go there," a girl told me, and how she *came* to know her city's local ordinance involved spankings and threats—not from her city or its police or judges, but from her mother, and especially from her father. "I had to drive it into her," he explained to me, "so I just did what you have to do and licked her until she knew." . . .

The outside world enforces its truths . . . through the sanctions of parents upon children. Or, put more bluntly by a Negro mother: "You have to let them know before they get out of their own backyard." At his peril the Negro child leaves his home for school if he has not learned where he can sit, or what he cannot do when he gets hungry or thirsty. At five, just as surely as at fifteen or twenty-five, he must know his "place." In fact, at five, his awareness of this "place" is freshest. At fifteen these early perceptions have become reflexes, no longer even noticed.[72]

He has, in brief, become a Negro.

The child learns that if he sits down in the front part of the bus, his parents will drag him to the back. To the child, the parents' action may seem cruel; to the parents, it is an essential lesson in survival. The most heart-rending task Negro parents in a segregated society have to face is that of inducting their children into the world of Jim Crow: the prohibitions and restrictions, the snubs, slights, insults, derision—not to mention physical violence—which is to be their lot as adults. They have to look at their trusting infants, as dear to them as infants to parents anywhere, and know that sooner or later the happy innocence in the child's eyes will be turned to hurt, even suffering. They know that nothing they can do—and upper-class families can do a great deal—will protect their children from this fate.

---

[71] Richard Wright, "The Ethics of Living Jim Crow," *American Stuff* (New York: Harper & Row, Publishers, 1937). Present citation from Brown, Davis, and Lee (eds.), *The Negro Caravan* (New York: The Dryden Press, 1941).

[72] Robert Coles, "Racial Identity in School Children," *Saturday Review* (October 19, 1963), 68.

Negro parents, in short, have to teach their children the role of the Negro. They must teach, and the child must learn, that no matter how unjustly he is treated he must control his anger and conceal his hostility. He must be obsequious and subservient even to those he knows to be his inferiors. He must be polite in the face of provocation. He must walk with eyes straight ahead, unmoved by the taunts and jeers on all sides. (Little did the parents of the sit-in generation know in what good stead these lessons would stand.)

Negro parents in segregated areas have had to socialize their children into a world in which danger lurks everywhere. A boy might be killed if he looked at a white woman, as Emmet Till was. The best protection, many parents feel, is the early inculcation of fear; they must punish the child or the hostile environment will punish him even more severely. They hope to protect him by early implantation of inhibitions. Even if they must themselves use violence in the process, it is better, they argue, that the child learn from them rather than from others what lies in store for him. Just as the skin develops pigment to protect itself against the destructive environment of sun rays, so the Negro child must develop protection against his hostile environment. His family sees to it that he does.

Negro parents have to teach their children not only how to act the Negro role but also how to think and feel it. Frazier describes the way this was done a generation ago in Washington, D.C., and Louisville, Kentucky. In the lower-class family—then usually of Southern background—children were cautioned by their parents to avoid getting into conflicts, to ignore insults, to use such techniques as "acting like a monkey," flattery, and plain lying in order to get by. Recognizing that this would not be easy without supporting self-conceptions, they inculcated the belief that the Negro was inferior and his subordination to the white man inevitable.[73]

Of special interest, in view of later developments, was the situation in middle-class families: because they did not believe in the inherent superiority of the white man, they were therefore less successful in inculcating the Negro role in their children. By the 1930s, the children, disgusted with their parents' instruction, refused to accept it; they believed that Negroes should prepare themselves to seek power and money, achieve education, and match wits with the white man.[74] Their behavior was conventionally correct and proper not only because they wanted to dissociate themselves from the externally adapted Negroes but also because they wanted to win approval and respect from the white society. The seeds of self-emancipation were beginning to germinate in these

[73] E. Franklin Frazier, *Negro Youth at the Crossroads* (Washington, D.C.: American Council on Education, 1940), p. 263.
[74] *Ibid.*, p. 264.

middle-class children, who were later to become the parents of the sit-in generation.

Upper-class families never tried to inculcate subordination to whites in their children. When they told their children to avoid fights or brawls with whites it was not because this behavior was dangerous but because it was beneath their dignity, unbecoming to their social status.[75] The leadership in self-emancipation a generation later did not come in large measure from the children of this class, for they had been socialized by parents who shielded them from the world of discrimination—for some parents, middle-class and upper-class, dreaded exposing their children to the dangers of the white world. Rather than protect the child by preparing him for the anticipated blows, they tried to isolate him from them as much as possible. Instead of "innoculating" him or allowing his "protective coloring" to develop, they kept him as ignorant as possible of the lot of Negroes in the outside world. These parents out-segregated the white segregationists. Sometimes they forbade the very words *Negro* or *colored* to be uttered in the presence of the child. They tried to hide from the child the fact that they could not enter restaurants, parks, or other public places, or that their schools were segregated. There was always a reasonable explanation why they could not go to the show the child preferred or eat at the restaurant the child selected.[76]

Another way parents tried to protect a child from the destructive effects of his role in a hostile environment was, in effect, to deny the hostile environment. The rejection by the outer world, such parents taught their children, was rejection only of lower-class Negroes. The outside world was not laughing at *them;* its insults were not directed at *them;* it was not denying *them* entry into the hotels and restaurants. It was barring only the lower-class, poorly behaved, uncouth Negroes— Negroes they themselves also rejected. For some families this position might have been successful; it might, in fact, have been valid. But for most, it was not, and the child learned soon enough that at some time or place he was as much an outsider as was the lowest boor. The results for the child were not always auspicious: he often developed ambivalent attitudes toward himself as a Negro and toward Negroes in general.[77]

---

[75] E. Franklin Frazier, *Black Bourgeoisie* (New York: The Crowell-Collier Publishing Co., 1962), p. 176.

[76] *Ibid.*, p. 176.

[77] A generation later some of these children were repeating the same drama with their own children. A young scientist awarded a doctorate at a Northern university turned down several offers of positions in Northern colleges and accepted a lower-paying one at a Negro college because he wanted to protect his children from the trauma of life in the outside world. They would be safe and secure in the Negro academic world. The intergenerational chain is hard to sever. Again: ". . . often the subject of 'race' is never mentioned within Negro families; parents wait breathlessly for the time when their offspring 'will find out.' So where and when does the soul of the Negro become

But if the family felt obliged to inculcate survival patterns into its children, brutally if necessary, it also served as emotional support for the child in assuming the Negro role.

The family and Negro community function early to develop awareness and cushion shock through providing ready rationalizations. . . . Family and school seem to act as "race shelters" for the child and teen-ager. To some extent, the mere fact of being a dependent youth in the family and in school imparts some sense of security, worth, and optimism that counteracts the direct impact of race at that stage.[78]

Families are still protecting their children against the punishment of the outside world a generation later:

Of course, no child can ignore the cries of persistently mean people or continual tension at home or school. However, so long as their parents and teachers survive these trials, the children will usually be no less sturdy. The threats and abuse become part of the many problems which would normally confront them as they develop emotionally. . . . [Ruby's] mother reassured her, taking her to school, telling her daily of her family's support. She never denied Ruby's observations that "They don't like me," but told her that her family, all of them, loved her. Most important, her mother and father are strong and affectionate people, and it is this intimacy between basically sound parents and children which disperses the natural fears in the young. Under such family protection, hard words and scowls are ineffective.[79]

INTERGENERATIONAL CHANGES

The second emancipation has introduced new complexities into parent-child relationships. The old, ingrained patterns of anticipatory socialization, withdrawal, denial are hard to surrender even when they are no longer essential for survival. New patterns of child-rearing, designed not to inculcate the role of Negro but to prepare the child for full participation in the outside world, have to be worked out.[80] Some parents are torn between their wish to protect their children by isolating them from the barbs of the outside world and their desire to break down the barriers between that world and their own. Their children, for example, are eager to go to desegregated schools, but the parents are afraid for them. In one city, for example:

---

corroded? When he leaves the confines of home to circulate in the only world he knows —White America" (E. J. Johnson, letter to *The New York Times Magazine*, December 13, 1964, p. 29).

[78] Lewis, *op. cit.*, p. 110.

[79] Robert Coles, "In the South These Children Prophesy," *Atlantic Monthly* (March 1963), 111-12.

[80] Dr. Benjamin Spock recognized this new problem in his column in *Redbook Magazine* (October 1964).

For a month before the desegregation of the Atlanta schools, these nine families were subjected to incredible threats and abuse. In several homes even the parents, knowing fully the penalties and fearing job loss, opposed the children's wish to attend the white schools. Though these midnight callers, spewing desperate warnings, are only a small number, for the Negro families those few are a thousand, and the memory of accumulated suffering prevents calm detachment.[81]

The parents of many of the early college sit-in leaders and participants were torn between fear for their children and pride in them. They would have wanted to protect them against police brutality, against derision, humiliation, insults. But these young people did not want parental protection. Some of them had concluded that if they were going to be made to suffer by the outside world in any event, their suffering ought to have significance. Some of them reminded one researcher that:

. . . [W]e're always being insulted and treated badly. . . . This is a chance to do something even though you may get the same treatment as you get downtown in a store or in the park. . . . I'd rather go through it now, because I know it's got some meaning to it. . . . I'm doing something about it by going through with it this time.[82]

Thus it is often the child himself who determines the outcome of the parental dilemma: he does not want to be protected by them; he wants to try. And sometimes he succeeds.

Many older Negro children have fought not only reluctant school boards and brooding white classmates for their new recognition, but their own parents' fears and prohibitions as well. Many younger Negro children have been sent to white schools by parents who were determined and angry, but far from hopeful that their child would have an easy time of it. . . . An Atlanta mother whose adolescent boy had defied her wishes said: "His daddy and I both opposed his going through this, because we know what it's like to be a Negro, and the one thing we hoped for was to spare him the worst of it. But he's getting through it, and I suppose it's his life." [83]

These pioneering "third-generation" Negroes know how to be Negroes in a new and different way. Flushed with victory over the restraints which have held them back, and secure in their own status as first-class Americans, they may be able to do something their own parents were incapable of doing. They might be willing to go to the lower classes of the externally adapted with love, rather than with loathing. This alone would have enormous therapeutic effect on the most rejected people in our society. And even if they found the parents unable to respond, there would be all those children, ready and willing to follow these triumphant pipers.

---

[81] Robert Coles, *loc. cit.*, pp. 112-13.
[82] *Ibid.*, p. 113.
[83] Coles, "Racial Identity in School Children," *loc. cit.*, p. 69.

INDEX

INDEX

A

Abortion, attitude toward, 139
Absent father, living arrangements of, 114-115
Acculturated families, *passim*.
attitude of, toward out-of-wedlock births, 50-55
fathers in, 110-111, 118-124
mothers in, 118-124
rapprochement with externally adapted families, 65, 150
relative prevalence of, 57-58
Acculturation, 41 ff.
examples of, on plantation, 44
mass media in, 46
personal influence in, 43-46
process of, 43 ff.
structural impediments to, 45
versus institutionalization, 27, 42
Age at marriage, effect of, on marriage, 82-83
preferred, for children, 139
trends in, 82-83
Aid to Families of Dependent Children, and out-of-wedlock births, 20, 106
and role performance of mother, 106, 107
Anderson, Charles S., 79-80, 84
Aspirations of parents for children, in education, 107, 135-136
in occupation, 107, 136-137

B

Baldwin, James, 118, 128
Bales, Robert W., 118
Barron, Milton L., 85

Bell, Robert, 19, 40, 53, 83, 93, 94, 95, 104, 105, 107, 126, 139
Beresford, John C., 14, 15, 16, 130
Berg, Renée, 106
Bernard, Jessie, 24, 39, 112, 132, 142
Bernard, Sydney E., 107
Bigman, Stanley, 53
Black bourgeoisie, as convergence of two cultures, 46-49
as cultural anomaly, 92
and reverse socialization, 48
Black Muslims, as acculturators, 46
as convergence of two cultures, 46
Blake, Judith, 31
Blau, Zena Smith, 45
Blood, Robert O., Jr., 89, 91, 92, 97, 98, 99
Bogue, Donald J., 88
Botkin, Benjamin A., 9, 10, 36, 68, 70, 72, 73, 77, 90, 96, 104, 109
Braithwaite, Lloyd, 31
Broderick, Carlfred, 80-81, 84
Brody, Eugene B., 76, 90, 91, 97, 114, 129
Broom, Leonard, 36, 134
Buerckle, Jack, 35
Burchinal, Lee, 82, 83
Burgess, E. W., 9
Burton, R. V., 125
Butler, George O., 105

C

Cambria, Sophie T., 52
Carney, Morgan D., 61, 65
Cayton, Horace, 28, 29, 30, 48, 89, 93, 110, 111
Childers, A. T., 51

153

Children, family status of, 119
Chilman, Catherine, 108
Christenson, Harold, 101
Clark, Kenneth B., 30, 32, 34, 56, 58, 62, 100, 138
Class, criteria of, 41, 47 ff.
    color, 49
    education, 47-48
    family behavior, 41-42, 47, 49
    income, 47
    money, 47, 48
    occupation, 47, 48
    cultural complications of, 62-63
    versus culture, 28-30, 41-42
Clausen, J. A., 129
Cleanliness as value, 141-142
Coles, Robert, 141, 146, 149
Color, and dating, 84, 85
    and mate selection, 78, 84, 85, 87
Conformity to norms of monogamic marriage, as external adaptation, 27, 33
    as internalized acculturation, 27, 33, 42
    as measure of institutionalization, 2
    different levels of, 12, 27, 33
Consumption as value, 33, 140
Contraception, attitude toward, 139
Courtship, among acculturated, 82
    among freedman's generation, 78
    in Puerto Rico, 79
    in Southern mill town in 1940's, 79
    today, 79-80
    under slavery, 77
Crowding, 129-133
    effects of, on personality, 131-133
    extent of, 130
Cultural bifurcation among Negroes, 35 ff., 58 ff.
    after emancipation, 36-38
    under slavery, 35-36
Culture, concept of, 30-32
    acculturated, characteristics of, 33
        prevalence of, 57-58
    externally adapted, 33-34
        and "culture of poverty," 40-41
        characteristics of, 33-34
        creativity in, 65-66
        in upper income levels, 92, 93
        prevalence of, 57-58

Culture (Cont.)
    versus class, 28-30, 41-42
Culture conflict, 58 ff.
    between income classes, 59-62
    implications of, for community, 63
    within income classes, 58-59
"Culture of poverty," 23
    and female-headed family, 23
    not same as externally adapted culture, 40-41

D

Dating, 79-81
    on college campus, 79-80
        qualities valued in, 80
    in Pennsylvania town, 80-81
        sex differences in, 81
Davie, Maurice R., 69, 87
Davis, Allison, 59
Derbyshire, Robert L., 76, 90, 91, 97, 114, 129
Divorce, 101-102
Dizard, Jan E., 88
Dollard, John, 59, 75, 99
Donald, Henderson, 1, 2, 10, 11, 12, 39, 103, 104, 110
Drake, St. Clair, 28, 29, 30, 48, 89, 93, 110, 111
Dubois, W. E. B., 42, 55

E

Ebony Magazine, 30
Edmonson, Munro, 24
Edwards, G. Franklin, 125
Elkins, Stanley M., 71-72, 109
Ellis, Albert, 137
Ellison, Ralph, 46
Emancipation, self, effects of
    on Negro male's masculinity, 77
    on "third generation," 149-150
Externally adapted families, 35 ff.
    attitude of, toward out-of-wedlock births, 50-55
        toward work, 55-57
    fathers in, 111-113
    rapprochement with acculturated families, 65, 149-150

Externally adapted families (Cont.)
  rejection of acculturated families, 58 ff.
  relative prevalence of, 57-58
Extralegal unions, monogamous while they last, 39

F

Families, acculturated, see acculturated families
  externally adapted, see externally adapted families
  fatherless, effect of, on socialization, 124-126
  female-headed, see female-headed families
  husband-wife, *passim.*
  nonverbal, 143-144
  one-parent, 19, 40, 53, 83, 104, 105, 107, 124, 126
  patrifocal, 86
  rural, see plantation families
  urban, as adaptation to new conditions, 39-40
Family, as companionship, 9
  as institution, 9
  changes in, *passim.*
  plantation, 36-38
  proletarian, 92
  versus household, 13
Fathers, absent, 13, 113-116
  denigrated, 128-129
  effect of too many, on child, 127-128
  in acculturated families, 110-111, 118, 124
  in externally adapted families, 111-113
  temporary, 127
Female-headed family, 13 ff.
  and concept of social generation, 23-25
  and "culture of poverty," 23
  as adaptation to new conditions, 39-40
  distribution of, 14
  increase of, in third phase of trajectory, 14, 19 ff.
  alleged reasons for, 19 ff.

Female-headed family (Cont.)
  alleged reasons for (Cont.)
    cultural regression, 20-21
    poverty, 23
    public assistance policies, 20
    unemployment, 21-22
    urbanization, 20
  maternal role performance in, 104
  not same as plantation family, 20-21
  proportion of, as index of institutionalization of marriage, 1, 13 ff.
Female heads of families, 14 ff.
  changes in frequency of, 1940-1960, 14
  by age, 14
  changes in marital status of, 1950-1960, 15
  with children under 18, by age, 1960, 16, 17, 18
  marital status of, 17
  changes in, 1940-1960, 17, 18
Fischer, John, 106
Folk culture among slaves, 36
Frazier, E. Franklin, 2, 12, 20, 21, 28, 29, 32, 40, 41, 42, 43, 47, 48, 49, 58, 60, 61, 63, 64, 65, 76, 84, 88, 91, 92, 93, 96, 101, 108, 122, 123, 147, 148
Freedmen, courtship among, 78
  marriage among, 10-13

G

Gebhard, P. H., 50, 137, 139
Generation, social, 23-25
  institutionalizing, 24
  self-emancipating, 24
  "third," 24, 63, 150
  transitional, 24
  urbanizing, 24
"Genteel tradition," 49
Glenn, Norval, 134
Glick, Paul C., 101, 102, 114
Goode, W. J., 31
Gordon, Joan, 63, 108, 131
"Granny," 40
  as matriarch, 108-109
  contribution of, to family, 108-109
Gross, L., 20

H

"Hawthorne Effect," 144-145
Heberle, Rudolf, 24
Heer, David M., 86-87, 89
Height, Dorothy, 129
Hellpach, Willy, 24
Henriquez, F. M., 31
Herberg, Will, 63
Hertz, Hilda, 51
Herzog, Elizabeth, 50, 63, 105
Himes, Joseph S., 54, 79-80, 85
Hoffman, Lois, 90
Household, versus family, 13
Hughes, Langston, 104
Husbands, absent, 13
    role performance of, as evaluated by
        wives, 97-99
"Hustling," 56

I

Inimical environment, 73 ff.
Institutional norms, 1
    implications of, that conformity is
        possible, 38-39
Institutionalization of marriage, 2, 9-13
    and welfare programs, 12
    by church, 12
    by Freedmen's Bureau, 11
    by military authorities, 11
    by school, 12
    diffusion of, 5
    female-headed families as index of,
        1, 13 ff.
    first phase of, 9-13
    in cities, 20
    indexes of, relationship between, 18-
        19
    legislative approaches to, 10-11
Institutionalization versus accultura-
    tion, 27, 42
Institutionalizing generation, 24
Intergenerational changes, 149-150
Interracial marriage, 85 ff.
    attitudes toward, 88-89
        among Negroes, 88
        among whites, 87
    changing nature of, 88-89

Interracial marriage (Cont.)
    sanctions against, 85-86, 88
        legal, 85-86
        nonlegal, 88
        religious, 85
    sex differentials in, 87
    reasons for, 87
    social status of brides and grooms,
        88-89
    trends in, 86-87
In-wedlock births, as index of institu-
    tionalization of marriage, 1-2
Irish, Donald P., 39

J

Jacobson, Paul, 86
James, Rita M., 46
Johnson, C. S., 20, 33, 37, 38, 39, 44,
    60, 78, 105
Johnson, E. J., 149
Johnson, James Weldon, 29

K

Kardiner, Abram, 59, 61, 62, 63, 100,
    138
Kephart, William, 101
King, Martin Luther, 143
Kinsey, Alfred C., 50
Knapp, Patricia, 52
Kohn, M. L., 129

L

Lewis, Hylan, 28, 29, 32, 35, 52, 59, 60,
    63, 69, 79, 111, 112, 113, 119,
    120, 123, 131, 133, 137, 139,
    141, 142, 143, 144, 149
Liebow, Elliott, 112, 113, 114, 115, 116,
    126
Lincoln, C. Eric, 46
Little, Sue Warren, 51
Locke, Harvey J., Jr., 9
Lott, Albert J., 46, 49
Lott, Bernice E., 46, 49
Love, importance of, 36, 39, 98
Lynn, D. B., 125

M

McCarthy, 6, 7, 8
Mannheim, Karl, 24
Marital status,
of female head of family,
changes in, 1940-1960, 15, 17
by community background, 1950-1960, 14
of men, 19
by employment status, 1960, 23
Marriage, age at, 82-83
among freedmen, 10
among slaves, 9-10
as status symbol, 11
evaluation of, by wives, 93-95
institutionalization of, see institutionalization of marriage
interracial, see interracial marriage
Marriage instability, 102
Marriage trajectory, Chapter 1
as measure of institutionalization of marriage, 1-9
first phase of, 2-5
in-wedlock births as measure of, 1, 13
overview, 1-2
second phase of, 5-6
third phase of, 6-9, 13 ff.
three trends of, 1-2
Mass media and acculturation, 46, 47
Mate selection,
among acculturated, qualities sought in, 80
among freedmen, 78
and color, 84-85
under slavery, 77-78
Maternal role,
performance of, 103 ff.
preferred to conjugal role, 37, 104
"Matriarch,"
"granny" as, 92
fallacy of, 95
Matza, David, 31
Mentre, François, 24
Miller, Herman P., 23
Miller, Walter B., 23, 125
Monogamic marriage,
imperatives of, 38-39
norms of, 1, 6, 117

Monogamic marriage (Cont.)
norms of (Cont.)
conformity to, as measure of institutionalization of marriage, 1, 6
demand lifelong commitment, 1
differing levels of conformity to, 12-13
forbid births outside of marriage, 1
Montagu, Ashley, 68
Multiparous mothers, 8
Murray, Pauli, 84, 87, 90, 104, 141

N

Negro, *passim.*
Negro husband, evaluation of, by wives, 97-99
in expressive role, 98-99
in role of companion, 98
in role of provider, 97-98
in understanding role, 98
Negro men,
as fathers, 109 ff., 118-124
as husbands, 95-99
after emancipation, 95-96
evaluation of role performance of, by wives, 97-99
today, 97-99
as mates under slavery, 95
environment of, more inimical than environment of Negro women, 73 ff.
marital status of, 19
relations of, to women subverted by slavery, 70 ff.
sexuality of, 99-101
under slavery, 70-73
strategies of, vis-à-vis master, 72-73
Negro women,
as heads of families, see female heads of families
as mates under slavery, 89-90
as mothers, 103 ff.
as slaves, 68
as wives, 90 ff.
as contributors to support of family, 91
as interpreters of outside world to family, 90

Negro women (Cont.)
  as wives (Cont.)
    evaluation of marriage by, 93-95
    in black bourgeoisie, 92-93
    in decision-making role, 92
    impact of slavery on, 67, 68
    sexuality of, 100-101
    "unnatural superiority" of, 68-70
    effect of, on marriage, 90
    in acculturation, 69
    in class, 69-70
    in education, 69
    in occupational level, 69
Neighborhood, as site of conflict be-
    tween cultures, 133-134
New England missionaries,
  and acculturation, 43
  and institutionalization of marriage,
    12
Newman, Dorothy K., 21, 91
Noble, Jeanne, 61
"Non-respectables" versus "respecta-
    bles," 27
Nonverbal families, 143-144
Non-white, distinguished from Negro,
    13
Norms of monogamic marriage, see
    monogamic marriage, norms of
Norton, Dolores Griffin, 16
Nye, Ivan, 92

O

Order, lack of, in life of slum child,
    132-133
Osili, A'Leila Josephine, 53
Out-of-wedlock births,
  customs and mores dealing with, 50-
    55
    among acculturated, 50-55
    among externally adapted, 50-55
  increases in, 6-9, 13 ff.
  reasons for, 14, 19 ff.
Ovesey, Lionel, 59, 61, 62, 63, 100, 138

P

Parity, 6-8
  as index of nonconformity, 9
  trends in, of out-of-wedlock births, 8

Pakter, Jean, 106
Parker, Frieda Alice, 53
Parsons, Talcott, 118
"Passing,"
  by men, 69
  by women, 87
Paternal role, see fathers
Pavela, Todd H., 89
Personal influence in acculturation,
  by already acculturated, 44-46
  by Black Muslims, 46
  by employers, 43
  by masters, 42-43
  by New England missionaries, 43-44
  by "talented tenth," 44
  by teachers, 44
Peterson, William, 31
Pettigrew, Thomas F., 124, 125, 129,
    142, 144, 145
Plant, James, 131-132
Plantation family,
  characteristics of, 36-38
  norms of, 39-40
  not female-headed, 21
Podell, Lawrence, 63, 108, 131
Pope, Hallowell, 39
Powdermaker, Hortense, 142
Powledge, Fred, 65
Primary group,
  family under slavery as, 12
  plantation family as, 36, 109
Primiparous mothers, 6
Property, as value, 140
Protestant ethic, 140
  and acculturated, 49, 50 ff.
  and externally adapted, 50 ff.
  sex and work as touchstones of, 50 ff.
Putnam, Peter, 128

R

Race relations and sex relations, 67
Raff, Morton S., 21
Reiss, Ira L., 39, 138, 139, 140
"Respectables," 27 ff., 49
  and "nonrespectables," 27 ff.
Reynolds, Josephine, 51
Riese, Hertha, 39, 128, 131, 132
Rivlin, Alice, 14, 15, 16, 130

Rodman, Hyman, 31, 32
Rohrer, John H., 24
Role,
   conjugal, see Negro women as wives,
      Negro men as husbands
   maternal, see Negro women as
      mothers
   of Negro, socialization into, 145-149
   parental, see socialization
   paternal, see Negro men as fathers
Rosen, Bernard C., 134
Rural-urban migration,
   culture shock and, 25
   peak now passed, 25
   rates of, 20

S

Sachar, A. L., 77
"Sambo,"
   as creation of slave-owner, 72
   legacy of, on marital relations, 77
Sawrey, W. L., 125
Schachter, Joseph, 6, 7, 8
Schelling, Thomas C., 73
Schleifer, Carl, 90, 91, 97, 98, 99, 114,
   129
Schorr, Alvin L., 127, 133
Self-emancipating generation, 24
Separation, 101-102
Serial polygamy, 83
Sewell, William M., 117
Sex,
   attitudes toward, 137
   parental teachings on, 137
   permissiveness toward, 137-139
Sex ratio,
   low among Negroes, 68-69
      and competition for mates, 70, 83-
      84
      effect of, on marriage and family,
      83
      reasons for, 69
Sexes, relations between and race rela-
   tions, 67
Sexuality of Negroes, 99-101
Shapiro, Sam, 6
Shipman, Gordon, 103
Slavery,
   courtship and mating under, 77

Slavery (Cont.)
   effects of, compared with effects of
      concentration camps, 71-72
   marriage under, 9
   men under, 71
      as fathers, 109
      as husbands, 95
   women under, 68
      as mothers, 103
Social mobility, 30
Socialization, Chapter 4
   circumstantial, 118 ff.
   conjugal relations and, 123-124
   definition of, 117
   family structure and, 118-124
   into role of Negro, 144-149
   manners and morals, 137-140
   verbal, 135
Spock, Benjamin, 149
Stanton, Hazel, 79
Straus, Murray, 119, 120, 121, 123

T

Taeuber, Irene, 25
Taeuber, Karl, 130
"Talented tenth," 44, 65
"Third generation effect," 63, 150
Thrift as value, 140
"Token" Negro, 34
Transitional generation, 24
Tuthill, Dorothy D., 6

U

Urban adaptation, female-headed family as, 39
Urbanization,
   and institutionalization of marriage,
      20
   inadequate as explanation of increase
      in female-headed families, 20
Urbanizing generation, 25

V

Value pre-emption, 35
Values, 134 ff.
   cleanliness, 141-142
   consumption, 140-141
   education, 135-136

Values (Cont.)
  non-violence, 143
  occupation, 136-137
  property, 140-141
  sex, 137-140
  thrift, 140-141
  violence, 142-143
Vernon, Elizabeth Ann, 16
Violence as value, 142-143

W

Washington, Booker T., 44, 55, 140
Watts, Louis G., 45, 75, 133

Whiting, J. W. M., 125
Wilkins, Roy, 65
Williamson, Henry, 56
Wolfe, Donald M., 91, 92, 97, 98, 99
Women, Negro, see Negro women
Work, ethos of, 55-56
Wright, Richard, 145-146

Z

Zelditch, Morris, Jr., 118
Zuckerman, S., 70